Nikolai Gogol
and the
Baroque Cultural Heritage

Nikolai Gogol

—— *and the* ——

Baroque Cultural Heritage

Gavriel Shapiro

The Pennsylvania State University Press
University Park, Pennsylvania

Library of Congress Cataloging-in-Publication Data

Shapiro, Gavriel.
    Nikolai Gogol and the baroque cultural heritage / Gavriel Shapiro.
        p.   cm.
    Includes bibliographical references (p.   ) and index.
    ISBN 0-271-00861-X
    1. Gogol', Nikolaĭ Vasil'evich, 1809–1852—Style.
2. Civilization, Baroque.   3. Russian literature—19th century
—History and criticism.   4. Baroque literature—History and
criticism.   I. Title.
PG3335.Z8S52 1992
891.78'309—dc20   91–47505
                                                              CIP

Published by The Pennsylvania State University Press,
Suite C, Barbara Building, University Park, PA 16802-1003

It is the policy of The Pennsylvania State University Press to use acid-free paper for
the first printing of all clothbound books. Publications on uncoated stock satisfy the
minimum requirements of American National Standard for Information Sciences—
Permanence of Paper for Printed Library Materials, ANSI Z39.48–1984.

Frontispiece: Karolina Pavlova, *Portrait of Nikolai Gogol,* early 1840s

*To the memory of my father, Dr. Yaakov Shapiro,
and to my mother, Dr. Ella Leizerovsky*

Contents

Preface and Acknowledgments   ix

List of Illustrations   xi

List of Abbreviations   xv

Introduction   1

1   Gogol and the "Baroque Milieu"   11

2   Forms   25

    Facetia   27

    Vertep   40

    Lubok   58

    Emblem   106

3   *Topoi*   129

    Theatrum mundi   130

    Life Is a Dream   139

    Brevitas vitae   144

    Carpe diem   150

    Vanitas   155

    Memento mori   162

    The End of the World   170

    The Last Judgment   174

4   Figurative Language   183

    Anaphora and Epiphora   184

    Asyndeton   194

    Antithesis   199

    Chiaroscuro   205

    Oxymoron   214

    Conceit   218

    Wordplay   224

Afterword   233

Bibliography   237

Index   255

Preface and Acknowledgments

Nikolai Gogol and the Baroque Cultural Heritage began life in 1984 as a doctoral dissertation at the University of Illinois at Urbana-Champaign. I wish to thank Clayton Dawson, Ralph T. Fisher, Jr., Maurice Friedberg, and Temira Pachmuss for the help they gave it at that earlier stage. I would also like to thank my former Northern Illinois University colleagues, George J. Gutsche, W. Bruce Lincoln, and Jack Weiner, and my present Cornell University colleagues, Patricia J. Carden, George Gibian, William J. Kennedy, Nancy Pollak, Michael Scammell, and Marena and Savely Senderovich, for their warm support and friendly counsel as this project grew, and Diane Williams for piloting me, with great skill, through turbulent administrative waters at the time of my writing this book and thereafter. At its final phase, my book has especially benefitted from invaluable comments by John M. Kopper, Lauren G. Leighton, Richard A. Peace, Harold B. Segel, and James B. Woodward.

In carrying out this study, I was greatly assisted by the reference and interlibrary-loan staffs of the University of Illinois and of Cornell University Libraries. I thank my editors, Dafna Allon and Rachel Davis, for saving me from many stylistic pitfalls, and Adria Moskowitz, for computer-formatting my manuscript and for patiently enduring my last-minute corrections, and Kate Capps, Janet Dietz, Cherene Holland, Andrew Lewis, and especially Philip Winsor, of Penn State Press, for showing me that book production can be a pleasant experience. Last but not least, I thank my sister, Luba Freedman, for her unflagging encouragement and advice.

Chapter 1 appeared in somewhat different form in *Slavic Review* (1986). Portions of Chapter 2 on *facetia, vertep,* and emblem appeared in earlier versions in, respectively, *Transactions of the Association of Russian-American Scholars in the U.S.A.* (1984), *Harvard*

Ukrainian Studies (1985), and *Comparative Literature* (1990). The system of transliteration I have used throughout the book is a modification of that used by the Library of Congress.

Unless otherwise stated, all references to the works of Gogol are to his *Polnoe sobranie sochinenii,* 14 vols. (Moscow and Leningrad: Akademiia Nauk SSSR, 1937–52); in both the text and the notes, they are given in arabic numerals by volume and page numbers. And, unless otherwise indicated, all translations are mine.

I am grateful to the following institutions for permission to reproduce illustrations: Sovetskaia Rossiia (jacket illustration and frontispiece); Slavic and Baltic Division, The New York Public Library, Astor, Lenox and Tilden Foundations (Figs. 2, 7, and 27); Slavonic Library, Helsinki University Library (Figs. 8 and 9); Vsesoiuznoe Agentstvo po Avtorskim Pravam (Figs. 21, 29, 38, 39, and 46); Librairie Gründ, Paris (Fig. 28); Verlag Peter Lang AG (Fig. 40); Garland Publishers (Fig. 41); Klinkhardt & Biermann (Fig. 42); J. B. Metzler Verlag (Fig. 43); Almqvist & Wiksell (Fig. 44).

List of Illustrations

Frontispiece: Karolina Pavlova, *Portrait of Nikolai Gogol,* early 1840s. (R. V. Duganov, comp. *Risunki russkikh pisatelei XVII–nachala XX veka* [Moscow: Sovetskaia Rossiia, 1988], ill. 124)

1. *A Cossack Bandura-Player* (M. P. Bazhan, ed., *Istoriia ukraïns'-koho mystetstva,* 6 vols. [Kiev: Akademiia Nauk URSR, 1966–70], 3:233, fig. 174)

2. *The Ladder of the Venerable John Climacus* (Rov. 1881, *Atlas,* 3, fig. 774)

3. *St. Nikita* (Bazhan, *Istoriia ukraïns'koho mystetstva,* 2:252, fig. 171)

4. *Miliktrisa* (Iurii Ovsiannikov, *The Lubok* [Moscow: Sovetskii khudozhnik, 1968], fig. 59)

5. *Eruslan* (Ovsiannikov, *The Lubok,* fig. 57)

6. *Foma and Erema, Two Brothers* (Rov. 1900, fig. 297)

7. *His Highness the Crown Prince of Persia* (*Narodnye kartinki, preimushchestvenno istoricheskogo i religioznogo soderzha-niia. Tridtsat' vosem' graviur i litografii, 1831–1879.* Mounted and bound by the New York Public Library, 1937, fig. 27. The New York Public Library, The Slavonic Collection)

8. *The Subjugation of the City of Adrianople by Count Dibich-Zabalkanskii on August 8, 1829* (Helsinki University, The Slavonic Library, Sl. K. 171)

9. *The Commander-in-Chief of Russian Troops, the Prince of War-saw, Count I. F. Paskevich-Erivanskii* (Helsinki University, The Slavonic Library, Sl. K. 171)

10. *Suvorov and Bagration* (Rov. 1900, fig. 163)

11. *Bobelina* (Vladimir Bakhtin and Dmitrii Moldavskii, comps., *Russkii lubok XVII–XIX vv.* [Moscow and Leningrad: IZOGIZ, 1962], fig. 50)

12. *Glutton and Imbiber* (Rov. 1900, fig. 70)

13. *Tolerant Father* (Rov. 1900, fig. 233)

14. *A Lesson to Foolish Husbands and Their Foppish Wives* (Bakhtin and Moldavskii, *Russkii lubok,* fig. 58)

15. *A Dandy of Shuia and an Overdressed Fortune-Hunting Woman* (Rov. 1900, fig. 115)

16. *Pan Tryk and Khersonia* (Rov. 1900, fig. 313)

17. *A Miser* (E. P. Ivanov, *Russkii narodnyi lubok* [n.p.: IZOGIZ, 1937], fig. 39)

18. *The Nose Grinder* (Rov. 1900, fig. 76)

19. *Pinch Your Own Nose* (Rov. 1900, fig. 210)

20. *The Escapades of the Nose and of the Severe Frost* (Rov. 1900, fig. 323)

21. *A Bachelor's Arguments on Marriage* (Alla Sytova, ed., *The Lubok* [Leningrad: Aurora Art Publishers, 1984], fig. 107)

22. *A Conversation Between the Foolish Bridegroom and the Stupid Matchmaker* (Rov. 1900, fig. 122)

23. *The Bridegroom and the Matchmaker in Buffoon Costumes* (Rov. 1900, fig. 121)

24. *The Register of the Ladies and Beautiful Maidens* (Bakhtin and Moldavskii, *Russkii lubok,* fig. 26)

25. *The Dowry Inventory* (Rov. 1900, fig. 124)

26. *Reprimand to Boastful People* (Rov. 1900, fig. 213)

27. *Transforming Heads* (Rov. 1881, *Atlas,* 1, fig. 284)

28. *Everything Is Healthy for a Russian* (Pierre-Louis Duchartre, *L'imagerie populaire russe et les livrets gravés, 1629–1885* [Paris: Gründ, 1961], fig. 117)

29. *The Aerial Journeys of Madame Garnerin with a Russian Lady in Moscow, May 8 and 15, 1804* (Sytova, *The Lubok,* fig. 71)

30. *A Crinoline or the Means of Occasionally Substituting It for a Balloon* (Ivanov, *Russkii narodnyi lubok,* fig. 53)

31. *The Ship Cast into Safety by a Storm* (Nestor Maksimovich-Ambodik, *Emvlemy i simvoly izbrannye* [St. Petersburg, 1788], fig. 103)

32. *A Broken Sword* (Maksimovich-Ambodik, *Emvlemy i simvoly izbrannye,* fig. 229)

33. *A Beehive* (Maksimovich-Ambodik, *Emvlemy i simvoly izbrannye,* fig. 466)

34. *A Beehive* (Maksimovich-Ambodik, *Emvlemy i simvoly iz-brannye,* fig. 346)

35. *A Beehive* (Maksimovich-Ambodik, *Emvlemy i simvoly iz-brannye,* fig. 816)

36. *Flies Flying near a Burning Candle* (Maksimovich-Ambodik, *Emvlemy i simvoly izbrannye,* fig. 310)

37. *Avarice* (Joseph Stöber, *Ikonologiia* [Moscow, 1803], fig. 113)

38. Nikolai Gogol's own cover design for *Dead Souls* (Igor' Zolotusskii, *Gogol'* [Moscow: Molodaia gvardiia, 1979], following 224)

39. Nikolai Gogol. A drawing on one of the dying writer's notes (Zolotusskii, *Gogol',* following 384)

40. *The Letters with Which the Book of the World Was Set.* From Johann Arndt, *Sämtliche geistreiche Bücher vom wahren Christenthum* (Frankfurt am Main, 1700) (Michael Schilling, *Imagines Mundi* [Frankfurt am Main: Peter Lang, 1979], fig. 3)

41. *Theatrum Vitae Humanae.* From Jean Jacques Boissard, *Theatrum Vitae Humanae* (Metz, 1596) (Lynda G. Christian, *Theatrum Mundi* [New York: Garland, 1987], fig. 1)

42. Antonio de Pereda, *The Knight's Dream.* Madrid, Academia de San Fernando (August L. Mayer, *Geschichte der spanischen Malerei* [Leipzig: Klinkhardt & Biermann, 1922], fig. 312)

43. *Vita Brevis.* From Juan de Borja, *Empresas morales* (Prague, 1581) (Artur Henkel and Albrecht Schöne, *Emblemata, Handbuch zur Sinnbildkunst des XVI. und XVII. Jahrhunderts* [Stuttgart: J. B. Metzlersche Verlagsbuchhandlung, 1967], 1008)

44. Crispin van de Passe, the Elder (inv. Marten de Vos), *Adolescentia Amori* (1596) (Allan Ellenius, "Reminder to a Young Gentleman. Notes on a Dutch Seventeenth-Century *Vanitas,*" in *Idea and Form,* ed. Nils Gösta Sandblad [Stockholm: Almqvist & Wiksell, 1959], 109)

45. *Vanitas* (Ivanov, *Russkii narodnyi lubok,* fig. 86)

46. "Look Closely, Mortal . . . " (Sytova, *The Lubok,* fig. 119)

47. *Memento mori.* From 1702 *Sinodik* (Rov. 1900, fig. 243)

48. *An Apocalypse Scene: Death on the Pale Horse* (Rov. 1900, fig. 7)

49. *The Last Judgment* (Ivanov, *Russkii narodnyi lubok,* fig. 75)

50. *The Last Judgment* (Rov. 1900, fig. 238)

List of Abbreviations

Ehre
: *The Theater of Nikolay Gogol: Plays and Selected Writings,* ed. Milton Ehre (Chicago: University of Chicago Press, 1980).

Gibian
: Nikolai Gogol, *Dead Souls,* ed. George Gibian (New York: W. W. Norton, 1985).

Hill
: John Peter Hill and Enrique Caracciolo-Trejo, eds. and trans., *Baroque Poetry* (London: Dent, 1975).

Kent
: Nikolai Gogol, *The Complete Tales,* 2 vols., ed. Leonard J. Kent (Chicago: University of Chicago Press, 1985).

Proffer
: Nikolai Gogol, *Letters,* ed. and trans. Carl R. Proffer (Ann Arbor: University of Michigan Press, 1967).

Rov. 1881
: D. A. Rovinskii, *Russkie narodnye kartinki,* 5 vols., and *Atlas,* 3 vols. (St. Petersburg, 1881–93).

Rov. 1900
: D. A. Rovinskii, *Russkie narodnye kartinki,* 2 vols. (St. Petersburg: Golike, 1900).

Segel
: Harold B. Segel, ed., *The Baroque Poem* (New York: Dutton, 1974).

Tulloch
: Nikolai Gogol, *Arabesques,* trans. Alexander Tulloch (Ann Arbor: Ardis, 1982).

Zeldin
: Nikolai Gogol, *Selected Passages from Correspondence with Friends,* trans. Jesse Zeldin (Nashville: Vanderbilt University Press, 1969).

Introduction

The creative work of Nikolai Gogol (1809–52) has deep roots in the cultural heritage of the Baroque. Gogol's interest in the Baroque, having taken shape in his native Ukraine, grew during his Russian period and especially during his prolonged stay in the West, primarily in Rome. I shall explore here Gogol's creative adaptation of the cultural heritage of the Baroque—the epoch to which he felt a strong affinity. I shall also examine the diverse and ingenious ways in which Gogol accommodated this heritage in his verbal art.

One of the primary questions scholars and critics have addressed concerning Gogol has been the genesis of his oeuvre. Already in Gogol's lifetime his contemporaries associated his works with other cultures and other epochs. Naturally enough, they first drew attention to Gogol's literary connections with the Romantics.[1] But some of them aspired to establish his more distant literary ancestry, tracing it to antiquity and the Middle Ages.[2] In Gogol's day, there were also

1. For example, Pushkin likened Gogol to Sir Walter Scott and Belinskii compared him to E.T.A. Hoffmann. See, respectively, A. S. Pushkin, *Polnoe sobranie sochinenii,* 17 vols. (Moscow and Leningrad: Akademiia Nauk SSSR, 1937–59), 12:27, and V. G. Belinskii, *Polnoe sobranie sochinenii,* 13 vols. (Moscow: Akademiia Nauk SSSR, 1953–59), 1:181. Gogol's literary connections to the Romantics have been studied in depth only in the twentieth century. See, for example, Adolf Stender-Petersen, "Gogol und die deutsche Romantik," *Euphorion* 24 (1922): 628–53; Iu. V. Mann, "Évoliutsiia gogolevskoi fantastiki," in *K istorii russkogo romantizma,* ed. Iu. V. Mann, I. G. Neupokoeva, and U. R. Fokht (Moscow: Nauka, 1973), 219–58; and T. E. Little, "Gogol and Romanticism," in *Problems of Russian Romanticism,* ed. Robert Reid (Brookfield, Vt.: Gower, 1986), 96–126.

2. Thus Konstantin Aksakov drew parallels between *Dead Souls* and *The Iliad,* and Herzen associated it with *The Divine Comedy.* See, respectively, K. S. Aksakov, "Neskol'ko slov o poéme Gogolia 'Pokhozhdeniia Chichikova, ili Mertvye dushi,' " in *Russkaia éstetika i kritika 40–50-kh godov XIX veka,* comp. V. K. Kantor and A. L. Ospovat (Moscow: Iskusstvo, 1982), 42–53, and A. I. Herzen, "Dnevnik 1842–1845," in his *Sobranie sochinenii,* 30 vols. (Moscow: Akademiia Nauk SSSR, 1954–66), 2:220. Gogol's relation to Homer has been examined more substantially only by modern scholarship. See S. I. Radtsig, "Gogol' i Gomer," *Vestnik*

attempts—particularly by Pushkin (according to Gogol himself) and by Stepan Shevyrev—to link him to the writers of the Baroque period, such as Cervantes and Shakespeare, although these attempts did not go beyond mere comparison.[3]

Shevyrev was the first to note Baroque features in Gogol's works. In his article on *Dead Souls*, Shevyrev did not use the term "Baroque" (which was not yet current among scholars), but did point to the highly colorful nature of Gogol's artistic manner, the stylistic embellishments in his language, and the characteristically Baroque lushness and massiveness of his phrasing:

> Gogol's style is a bright brush with all shades of coloring. . . . Gogol's words are broad, plentiful, capacious, and prolific. His speech is as flaky as a fine pastry for which butter was used

---

Moskovskogo Universiteta 4 (1959): 121–38; Carl R. Proffer, "Gogol's *Taras Bulba* and the *Iliad*," *Comparative Literature* 17 (1965): 142–50; and N. V. Vulikh, "Antichnye motivy i obrazy v povesti Gogolia 'Taras Bul'ba,'" *Russkaia literatura* 1 (1984): 143–53. The connection of *Dead Souls* to *The Divine Comedy* was first seriously considered only in the late nineteenth century; see A. N. Veselovskii, "Mertvye dushi," in his *Etiudy i kharakteristiki* (Moscow, 1894), 557–609, especially 593–605. Recently, there have appeared studies investigating the connection between Gogol and Dante in more detail; see E. A. Smirnova, "O mnogosmyslennosti 'Mertvykh dush,'" *Kontekst* (1982): 164–82; T. Baróti, "Traditsiia Dante i povest' Gogolia 'Rim,'" *Studia Slavica* 29 (1983): 171–83; A. A. Asoian, "Dante i 'Mertvye dushi' Gogolia," in his *Dante i russkaia literatura 1820–1850-kh godov* (Sverdlovsk: Sverdlovskii Gosudarstvennyi Pedagogicheskii Institut, 1986), 37–47; and Marianne Shapiro, "Gogol and Dante," *Modern Language Studies* 17, no. 2 (1987): 37–54.

3. See, respectively, 8:439–40 and S. P. Shevyrev, "Pokhozhdeniia Chichikova, ili Mertvye dushi. Poéma N. Gogolia. Stat'ia vtoraia," *Moskvitianin* 8 (1842): 357, 363, and 371. In the rough draft of chapter 11 of *Dead Souls*, Gogol refers to Shakespeare and Cervantes as his literary predecessors; see 6:644.

Again, it was Veselovskii who first discussed the influence of *Don Quixote* on *Dead Souls*; see his "Mertvye dushi," 567–68. Recently, scholars have noted the allusions to *Hamlet* in "Old-Fashioned Landowners" and "Diary of a Madman"; see V. M. Guminskii, "'Taras Bul'ba' v 'Mirgorode' i 'Arabeskakh,'" in *Gogol': Istoriia i sovremennost'*, comp. V. V. Kozhinov, E. I. Osetrov, and P. G. Palamarchuk (Moscow: Sovetskaia Rossiia, 1985), 252–54, and O. G. Dilaktorskaia, *Fantasticheskoe v "Peterburgskikh povestiakh" N. V. Gogolia* (Vladivostok: Izdatel'stvo Dal'nevostochnogo Universiteta, 1986), 61–63. "Diary of a Madman" also contains allusions to *Don Quixote*; see Donald Fanger, *The Creation of Nikolai Gogol* (Cambridge: Belknap Press, 1979), 116–17, and Dilaktorskaia, *Fantasticheskoe*, 64–67.

For a discussion of Baroque elements in the works of Shakespeare and Cervantes, see, respectively, Frances K. Barasch, "Definitions: Renaissance and Baroque, Grotesque Construction and Deconstruction," *Modern Language Studies* 13, no. 2 (1983): 60–67, and Per Nykrog, "The Literary Cousins of the Stock Market: On Mystification and Demystification in the Baroque Age," *Stanford French Review* 7 (1983): 57–71.

abundantly. It pours forth beyond measure like an overflowing glass, filled by the hand of a generous host to whom wine and tablecloth are nothing. That's why his sentence appears as lavishly filled as the pie of an intricate gourmet who bought provisions without calculation and does not spare any filling.[4]

Shevyrev, while appreciatively describing these Baroque elements in Gogol's style, does not attempt to trace their origins or to assess the larger role of the Baroque tradition in Gogol's oeuvre.

Only in the twentieth century were connections between Gogol's work and some specific aspects of Baroque culture established, when Vladimir Peretts, Arsenii Kadlubovskii, Vladimir Rozov, and Vasilii Gippius linked Gogol's writings to the Ukrainian folk theater, comic interludes in school drama, and *vertep*—the Ukrainian puppet theater; however, none of these scholars examined these connections in the broader context of the Baroque cultural heritage.

The first to apply the term "Baroque" to Gogol, Andrei Belyi, compared Gogol's writing to a luxuriant, highly ornate building: "an asymmetrical Baroque structure surrounded with a colonnade of repetitions, calling for phrasing and connected by arches of parenthetical clauses that have exclamations stuck over them like a stucco ornament."[5] As we see, Belyi did not speak of the Baroque as a cultural epoch but rather employed the word merely to emphasize the peculiarities of Gogol's literary style.

It was Dmitrii Chizhevskii who, in his articles devoted to Gogol, repeatedly pointed to Gogol's indebtedness to the Baroque cultural heritage, though only in passing and only in relation to Gogol's native Ukraine.[6] The first scholar to pursue this issue in some detail was Andrei Siniavskii, who suggested that Gogol's works were related not only to the Ukrainian and through it to the Russian, but also to the Italian Baroque. Although Siniavskii fails to substantiate sufficiently many of his statements concerning Gogol's Baroque cultural ties, he

---

4. Shevyrev, "Pokhozhdeniia Chichikova," 375–76.
5. Andrei Belyi, *Masterstvo Gogolia* (Moscow: GIKhL, 1934), 8.
6. Dmitrii Chizhevskii, "Neizvestnyi Gogol', " *Novyi Zhurnal* 27 (1951): 150. See also by the same author: *History of Russian Literature: From the Eleventh Century to the End of the Baroque* (The Hague: Mouton, 1960), 437, and *A History of Ukrainian Literature: From the 11th to the End of the 19th Century* (Littleton, Col.: Ukrainian Academic Press, 1975), 315, 329, and 349.

clearly understood the importance of such connections and their study when he asserted, somewhat exaggeratedly, that it is possible "to deduce Gogol entirely from the concept of the *Baroque,* in which he fits more fully than in incomparably more rigid and less intelligible schemes of 'realism' or 'romanticism.' "[7]

Vladimir Turbin expressed an even more extreme point of view when he dubbed Gogol a Baroque writer, propagating thereby the idea of the recurrent Baroque,[8] a concept flawed mainly by its complete disregard for the unique features of the Baroque as a cultural and historical phenomenon, features particularly manifest in its literature.

Aleksandr Morozov justly criticized this anachronistic concept of a recurrent Baroque, but nevertheless admitted the existence of a bond "worth studying" between Gogol and the historical Baroque. Specifically, Morozov, however, followed Chizhevskii, linking Gogol only to the Ukrainian Baroque.[9] Finally, in her recent study on *Dead Souls,* Elena Smirnova, though also following tradition in tracing Gogol's poetics only to the Ukrainian Baroque, nonetheless made a number of concrete and perceptive remarks on the subject, connecting Gogol's works to the writings of Stefan Iavorskii and Grigorii Skovoroda.[10]

Although these scholars established Gogol's debt to the Baroque cultural heritage, occasionally made concrete observations, and recognized the need for further research into the subject, none of them

    7. Andrei Siniavskii, *V teni Gogolia* (London: Overseas Publications Interchange, 1975), 348; also see 349–53.

    8. See, for example, V. N. Turbin, *Pushkin. Gogol'. Lermontov. Ob izuchenii literaturnykh zhanrov* (Moscow: Prosveshchenie, 1978), 21–32. Turbin shares this attitude with Aleksei Chicherin, who placed Dostoevskii in the same category; see A. V. Chicherin, "Dostoevskii i barokko," in his *Ritm obraza. Stilisticheskie problemy* (Moscow: Sovetskii pisatel', 1973), 181–92.

    The concept of a recurrent Baroque is by no means new in literary scholarship. Friedrich Nietzsche opined more than a century ago (1879) that a "baroque" always occurs when great art decays. Half a century later, Nietzsche's countryman Werner Weisbach expressed a similar opinion, as did the Spanish scholar, Eugenio d'Ors. See Friedrich Nietzsche, *Human, All Too Human,* trans. R. J Hollingdale (Cambridge: Cambridge University Press, 1986), 246; Werner Weisbach, *Die Kunst des Barock in Italien, Frankreich, Deutschland und Spanien* (Berlin: Propyläen, 1924), 9, and Eugenio d'Ors, "La querelle du baroque," in his *Du baroque* (Paris: Gallimard, 1935), 161–73.

    9. A. A. Morozov, "Izvechnaia konstanta ili istoricheskii stil'?" *Russkaia literatura* 3 (1979): 86–87.

    10. See E. A. Smirnova, *Poéma Gogolia "Mertvye dushi"* (Leningrad: Nauka, 1987), 62–64.

dealt with it systematically and at length. It is the modest intention of this book to partially fill this serious lacuna.

A number of authoritative studies on the Baroque—the historical-cultural epoch centered in the seventeenth century but extending to the second half of the eighteenth—have appeared in recent decades, making it unnecessary to engage in elaborate discussion of this phenomenon here.[11] Therefore I shall point only to those features especially relevant to my discussion.

The profound changes that occurred in various realms of life before and during the Baroque strongly affected the European world view. In the atmosphere of religious and political disunity within the Christian world and of the "battle for souls" between different Christian sects, the principle of a synthesis of the arts, designed to appeal to all human senses, grew in importance. And so did the artistic forms based on this principle: first and foremost, theater (particularly, puppet theater and its Ukrainian version—*vertep*), as well as the broadsheet (and its Russian variant—*lubok*), and the emblem. Commonly using these forms, and others such as the *facetia*, for education and propaganda, the literati of the Baroque applied another familiar principle—*docere, movere, delectare*—for they were well aware that their audience would better respond to their instruction if also moved and amused. In their pursuit of these effects, Baroque writers resorted to figures of language based on repetition, cumulation, and wordplay, such as anaph-

---

11. James V. Mirollo, a distinguished expert on the Baroque, wrote almost a decade ago, "Now we have reached a point in time when hardly anyone bothers to argue the meaning of *baroque* anymore, whereas only a short time ago every book that dealt with any aspect of the baroque opened with an obligatory review of the status of the question." See James V. Mirollo, *Mannerism and Renaissance Poetry* (New Haven: Yale University Press, 1984), 3.

My perception of the Baroque was shaped by the following studies, to name only a few: René Wellek, "The Concept of Baroque in Literary Scholarship" and "Postscript 1962," in his *Concepts of Criticism* (New Haven: Yale University Press, 1973), 69–127; Frank J. Warnke, *Versions of Baroque* (New Haven: Yale University Press, 1972); Segel (see Abbreviations); and José Antonio Maravall, *Culture of the Baroque. Analysis of a Historical Structure* (Minneapolis: University of Minnesota Press, 1986).

The Baroque culture established itself in Russia later than in other European countries. It is curious that the belatedness of this process has corresponded to the belated recognition of this phenomenon in that country. By now, the Russian Baroque has been accepted, albeit with some reservations, by Western and Soviet scholars. For the most recent discussion of the Russian Baroque, see I. R. Titunik, "Baroque, the Russian," in *Handbook of Russian Literature,* ed. Victor Terras (New Haven: Yale University Press, 1985), 40–42, and A. N. Robinson, ed., *Razvitie barokko i zarozhdenie klassitsizma v Rossii XVII–nachala XVIII vv.* (Moscow: Nauka, 1989).

ora and epiphora, asyndeton, and antanaclasis and paronomasia. The latter two together with the conceit, or farfetched metaphor, also manifest the emphasis of the Baroque on ingenuity, inventiveness, and acuity of mind—an emphasis characteristic of the aesthetics of an age of great geographic and scientific discoveries, discoveries that inspired the Baroque writer to view author and oeuvre as a creative analogue of God and the Universe.

At the same time, by overturning long-held tenets, these discoveries begot general skepticism and disbelief. The disruptions in the lives of nations and individuals caused by wars, epidemics, and other calamities led to a thematic emphasis in Baroque literature on instability and transience, and inspired extensive meditation on the illusory nature of life and the vanity of earthly pleasures, the swift passage of time and the inevitability of death. Upheavals in society intensified the eschatological mood. During the Baroque people lived in anticipation of the end of the world and the subsequent Last Judgment. This notion of the brevity of human existence also provoked the opposite reaction—to taste earthly pleasures in this short life. This antinomy in human attitudes and an awareness of the dichotomies of reality impelled a Baroque writer to seek a reconciliation by linking extremes through the discovery of similarities—*discordia concors.* These incongruities also drew attention to paradox and contrast and prompted the employment of such figures of language as oxymoron, antithesis, and chiaroscuro. The last of these, chiaroscuro, originated in the fine arts and was adopted by literature to manifest *ut pictura poesis*—an ancient precept that proved especially significant in the Baroque era.

Thus, the Baroque, with its keen interest in classical rhetoric, its fascination with medieval religiosity, and its adaptation of Renaissance humanism, was the summation, as it were, of the two-millennia-old European culture. It is hardly surprising, therefore, that Gogol, by drawing on the Baroque cultural heritage, absorbed not only uniquely Baroque elements, but also the European cultural heritage at large, which he saw primarily through the lens of this nearby epoch.

Gogol's exposure to the Baroque cultural heritage occurred in three main chronological stages (which I discuss in more detail in the following chapter):

1. The Ukrainian period (1809–28). In these formative years, Gogol learned the Baroque heritage of his native land—art and architecture, literature and theater—and through the Ukrainian Baroque its

Western models. Gogol also became directly acquainted with Western and Russian Baroque forms from the sources at his disposal at the
Nezhin Gymnasium and the Troshchinskii library.

2. The Russian, primarily St. Petersburg, period (1829–36). For
seven years Gogol lived in the two capitals of Russia, St. Petersburg
and Moscow, where he acquired firsthand knowledge of the country's folk art, which he had opportunities to observe at public outdoor festivals. No less important was his daily exposure to the cities'
numerous Baroque architectural and sculptural monuments.

3. The overseas, primarily Italian, period (1836–48). During this
time, Gogol had a unique opportunity to familiarize himself closely
with the culture of Italy—that cradle of the Baroque—and most
especially with its splendid art and architecture. Fluent in Italian,
Gogol also became acquainted with Italian Baroque literature.

Searching Gogol's oeuvre for connections to the Baroque, I considered the creative legacy of this writer in all its diversity—his poetry,
prose, and dramaturgy, his drawings, correspondence, and notebooks. I explored materials that Gogol used or to which he was
exposed throughout his life. I sought out the very origins of Gogol's
ties to the Baroque, for the first time scrutinizing the Nezhin Gymnasium textbooks and reexamining the Troshchinskii library collection
for Baroque sources.[12]

With some Baroque materials Gogol's familiarity is well established. For example, Gogol undoubtedly knew Cervantes's *Don Quixote,* for he refers to it directly on a number of occasions in his
works. It is also certain that he knew the *vertep* and the *lubok,* whose
characters he mentions or alludes to in his writings. Gogol's acquaintance with other Baroque materials is not documented, but there are
good reasons to assume that he was familiar with them because of
their popularity in his ambiance. For example, Gogol never refers to
the Ukrainian Late Baroque poet and philosopher Grigorii Skovoroda,
but Skovoroda's popularity in the contemporaneous Ukraine and
some distinct parallels between their world views leave no doubt
that Gogol knew the writings of the Ukrainian Socrates, which he

---

12. G. I. Chudakov was the first scholar to list and examine the West European holdings in
the Troshchinskii library in relation to Gogol's oeuvre, although without considering specifically works of the Baroque period. See G. I. Chudakov, *Otnoshenie tvorchestva N. V. Gogolia k
zapadnoevropeiskim literaturam* (Kiev, 1908).

could have read as early as his adolescence in the library of his maternal relative, Dmitrii Troshchinskii.[13] Similarly, Gogol never mentions Giambattista Marino, but the presence of Marino's work (in Russian translation) in the Troshchinskii library, a reference to him in the Nezhin Gymnasium textbook, and Gogol's interest during his prolonged stay in Rome in Italian Baroque literature, all suggest Gogol's acquaintance with Marino's oeuvre.[14]

Because of the specific focus of this study, several important issues must be slighted. One of the most conspicuous is the issue of the Baroque and Romanticism. The affinity of Romanticism to the Baroque has long been noted, and some concrete separate studies within several national literatures have been done, but so far there is no systematic comprehensive research on the subject.[15] In this book I will deal with the subject when it becomes absolutely essential. Another limitation, somewhat related to this, is that only very seldom do I compare Gogol's relation to the Baroque with that of his contemporaries, par-

13. See E. Ia. Fedorov, *Katalog antikvarnoi biblioteki, priobretennoi posle byvshego ministra D. P. Troshchinskogo* (Kiev, 1874), which on page 36 lists Skovoroda's *Nachal'naia dver' ko khristianskomu dobronraviiu.* On the connection between Gogol and Skovoroda, see Ignatii Zhitetskii, "Gogol'—propovednik i pisatel'," *Zhurnal Ministerstva Narodnogo Prosveshcheniia* 8 (1909): 50–52; and Marianna Bogojavlensky, "Gogol and Skovoroda," in her *Reflections on Nikolai Gogol* (Jordanville, N.Y.: Holy Trinity Monastery, 1969), 33–39. For the most recent works dealing with the subject, see Smirnova, *Poéma Gogolia,* 62–63, and Mikhail Vaiskopf, "Put' palomnika (O masonskikh i teosofskikh istochnikakh Gogolia)," in *Russian Literature and History: In Honour of Professor Ilya Serman,* ed. Wolf Moskovich (Jerusalem: Hebrew University of Jerusalem, 1989), 58.

14. For more details on the possible sources of Gogol's familiarity with Marino, see the following chapter.

15. For a discussion of general kinship between the Baroque and Romanticism, see Julian Krzyżanowski, "Barok na tle prądów romantycznych," in his *Od średniowiecza do baroku* (Warsaw: Rój, 1938), 7–53; D. S. Likhachev, "Barokko i ego russkii variant XVII veka," *Russkaia literatura* 2 (1969): 22; and Dmitrii Chizhevskii, *Comparative History of Slavic Literatures* (Nashville, Tenn.: Vanderbilt University Press, 1971), 16 and 103. For specific studies dealing with this kinship within various national cultures, see Nelly Heusser, *Barock und Romantik* (Leipzig: Huber, 1942). V. L. Britanishskii, "Pol'skie romantiki o pol'skom barokko," *Sovetskoe slavianovedenie* 1 (1972): 78–89; N. I. Balashov and Ia. V. Staniukovich, "Obraz v poézii pol'skogo barokko i romantizma," in *Slavianskie literatury: VII mezhdunarodnyi s"ezd slavistov. Doklady sovetskoi delegatsii,* ed. M. P. Alekseev et al. (Moscow: Nauka, 1973), 338–56; I. A. Terterian, "Barokko i romantizm: k izucheniiu motivnoi struktury," in *Iberica: Kal'deron i mirovaia kul'tura,* ed. G. V. Stepanov (Leningrad: Nauka, 1986), 163–78; and Josef Hanzal, *Od baroka k romantismu: Ke zrození novodobé české kultury* (Prague: Academia, 1987).

ticularly his countrymen.[16] Such comparisons are important for understanding Gogol's uniqueness in dealing with the Baroque and for reaching general conclusions on the role of the Baroque heritage in Russian
literature of the ensuing periods, but can be competently made only
after research that is beyond the space and scope of the present study.

Despite these limitations, however, I hope to shed additional light
on Gogol's literary genesis and contribute to a better understanding
of his poetics. I also hope that my work will be followed by analogous
research that will eventually allow scholars to draw more comprehensive conclusions concerning the importance of the Baroque period in
the history of human culture.

---

16. To the best of my knowledge, only two Russian writers, Narezhnyi and Dostoevskii,
have been considered so far, albeit on a very limited scale, for their connections with the
Baroque. See P. V. Mykhed, "V. T. Narizhnyi i barokko (Do pytannia pro styl' pys'mennyka),"
Radians'ke literaturoznavstvo 11 (1979): 74–83, and V. V. Borisova and S. M. Shaulov,
"Dostoevskii i barokko (Tipologicheskii aspekt problemy mira i cheloveka)," in *Kontseptsiia
cheloveka v russkoi literature,* ed. B. T. Udodov (Voronezh: Izdatel'stvo Voronezhskogo Universiteta, 1982), 77–88.

1

Gogol and the "Baroque Milieu"

Baroque culture, having filtered in from Europe through Poland, flourished in the Ukraine in the seventeenth and eighteenth centuries, influencing all major art forms there, including architecture and painting.[1] A typical example of Baroque architecture in the Ukraine is the Church of the Transfiguration, commissioned by Hetman Daniil Apostol in the village of Sorochintsy in 1732. The luxuriant costumes worn by the biblical figures depicted in the icons, the rich adornment of the iconostasis, the exterior and interior of the church, all are characteristic of the Baroque style. Gogol was baptized in this church and he undoubtedly visited it on more than one occasion.[2] Later, when Gogol studied in Nezhin, he had an opportunity to observe architectural monuments there, such as the St. Nicholas Cathedral (1668) and the Cathedral of the Annunciation Monastery (1702–16). These and other examples of Baroque architecture and art in the Ukraine certainly influenced Gogol's aesthetic taste.[3]

1. See G. G. Pavlutskii, "Barokko Ukrainy," in *Istoriia russkogo iskusstva,* 6 vols., ed. Igor' Grabar' (Moscow: Knebel', 1910–14), 2:339–40.

2. For a detailed description of this church, see D. I. Évarnitskii, "Preobrazhenskaia tserkov' v m. Bol'shikh-Sorochintsakh, Poltavskoi gubernii, gde krestili N. V. Gogolia," *Istoricheskii Vestnik* 2 (1902): 667–78, and Vadym Shcherbakivs'kyi, "Materialy do istorii ukraïns'koho mystetstva (Ikonostas tserkvy het'mana Danyla Apostola v s. Sorochintsiakh)," *Pratsy ukraïns'koho istorychno-filolohichnoho tovarystva v Prazi* 5 (1944): 47–70.

3. See L. A. Pliashko, *Gorod, pisatel', vremia. Nezhinskii period zhizni N. V. Gogolia* (Kiev: Naukova dumka, 1985), 87–93.

Gogol also came under the influence of Baroque traditions in his familial environment. The Baroque historical epoch was particularly important to the Gogol family, who believed that they were descendants of Ostap Gogol, a seventeenth-century colonel. The Golden Age of Ukrainian Cossackdom occurred during the seventeenth and eighteenth centuries, when Baroque culture permeated Ukrainian life, and many of Gogol's ancestors were prominent Cossack figures of that age, among them the hetmans Mikhail and Petr Doroshenko and Ivan Skoropadskii.[4] The young Gogol was fascinated by accounts of his family's past. His keen interest is reflected in "The Lost Letter," in which the narrator exclaims:

> Ah, the old days, the old days! What joy, what gladness it brings to the heart when one hears of what was done in the world so long, long ago, that the year and the month are forgotten! And when some kinsman of one's own is mixed up in it, a grandfather or great-grandfather—then I'm done for: may I choke while praying to St. Varvara if I don't think that I'm doing it all myself, as though I had crept into my great-grandfather's soul, or my great-grandfather's soul were playing tricks in me. (1:181; Kent, 1:77)

Further, Gogol's paternal ancestors—including Dem'ian Ivanovich and Afanasii Dem'ianovich Gogol-Ianovskii, Semen Efimovich and Semen Semenovich Lizogub, and Vasilii Mikhailovich Tanskii—as well as his maternal kin, Dmitrii Prokof'evich Troshchinskii, all graduated from the Kiev Academy.[5] Founded in the 1630s, the Kiev Academy (known until 1701 as the Kiev Collegium), was modeled after Polish Jesuit colleges and universities. As Alexander Sydorenko has pointed out, "The major achievement of the Kievan Academy lay in its profound and decisive impact on the intellectual and spiritual fabric of both Ukraine and Russia. To Ukraine it represented the leading center of the Ukrainian baroque spirituality characteristic of the 17th and

    4. See Oleksander Ohloblyn, "Ancestry of Mykola Gogol (Hohol)," *The Annals of the Ukrainian Academy of Arts and Sciences in the United States* 12, nos. 1–2 (1969–72): 12–16 and 32. Gogol included a letter written in 1711 by the hetman Ivan Skoropadskii, in his *Book of Odds and Ends, or a Manual Encyclopedia;* see 9:504.
    5. Ohloblyn, "Ancestry of Mykola Gogol (Hohol)," 10–40 and passim; V. L. Modzalevskii, *Malorossiiskii rodoslovnik,* 3 vols. (Kiev, 1908–12), 1:292–95 and 3:102–6.

18th centuries."[6] In *Taras Bulba* and "Vii," Gogol demonstrates his familiarity with the Kiev Academy's program of instruction and the living conditions of its students.

Although Gogol's father, Vasilii Afanas'evich, did not study at the Kiev Academy, he did study at the Poltava Seminary, which was modeled after it.[7] That Gogol *père* absorbed much from the Baroque literary tradition is attested to by his comedies, which stemmed in large part from comic interludes in Ukrainian school drama and *vertep*. As Volodymyr Bezushko has remarked, "As a little boy Nicholas was introduced by his father into the Ukrainian theater life, with its comical sketches, puppet shows, and so on, which was permeated with a spirit of the luxurious baroque epoch."[8] And later in Nezhin, Gogol watched such performances of the Ukrainian folk theater at the Nezhin fair and, furthermore, himself acted in comical sketches drawn from everyday Ukrainian life on the Nezhin Gymnasium stage.[9]

Among Gogol's ancestors were other well-known writers of the Ukrainian Baroque, including his above-mentioned great-great grandfather, Vasilii Tanskii, and Georgii Konisskii. Tanskii was remembered in the nineteenth-century Ukraine as the author of comic interludes (none of which have survived), and Konisskii was known as a poet, playwright, and author of sermons.

The Nezhin Gymnasium (since 1833 known as the Nezhin Lyceum), where Gogol studied for seven years (1821–28), also played an important role in the development of his interest in the Baroque. The gymnasium reading list included a great many Baroque writers. Among the books its director Ivan Orlai recommended for the students were works of Western Europeans such as Milton and Fénelon and of such Jesuit preachers as Bossuet, Bourdaloue, Fléchier, and Massillon. Orlai's list also included Ukrainian and Russian writers whose works are either Baroque or possess a strong Baroque flavor,

6. Alexander Sydorenko, *The Kievan Academy in the Seventeenth Century* (Ottawa: University of Ottawa Press, 1977), 1.

7. See Ohloblyn, "Ancestry of Mykola Gogol (Hohol)," 35. Concerning the effect of the Baroque on instruction in the Ukrainian Orthodox educational institutions of the seventeenth and eighteenth centuries, see Paulina Lewin, "Barokko v literaturno-ésteticheskom soznanii prepodavatelei i slushatelei russkikh dukhovnykh uchilishch XVIII veka," *Wiener Slavistisches Jahrbuch* 23 (1977): 180–98.

8. Volodymyr Bezushko, *Mykola Hohol'* (Winnipeg: Kul'tura i osvita, 1956), 93.

9. Pliashko, *Gorod, pisatel', vremia,* 78, and Igor' Zolotusskii, *Gogol'* (Moscow: Molodaia gvardiia, 1979), 58.

such as Iavorskii, Prokopovich, Lomonosov, and Derzhavin.[10] For his literary studies in the gymnasium, Gogol used Aleksandr Nikol'skii's *Osnovaniia rossiiskoi slovesnosti* (The Foundations of Russian Philology; see 10:54), Iakov Tolmachev's *Pravila slovesnosti* (The Rules of Philology), and the two six-volume anthologies, *Sobranie obraztsovykh russkikh sochinenii i perevodov v stikhakh* and *Sobranie obraztsovykh russkikh sochinenii i perevodov v proze* (The Collection of Exemplary Russian and Translated Works in Verse, and The Collection of Exemplary Russian and Translated Works in Prose; see 10:47–49).[11]

All four textbooks discuss important principles that underlie Baroque literature. For example, the preface, entitled "Opyt kratkoi ritoriki" (An Attempt at Concise Rhetoric), to the prose *Collection* discusses the guiding Baroque principle of ingenuity (*ingenio*); Tolmachev's *Rules* mentions the related Baroque concept of acuity of mind (*acutezza*). Both of these textbooks speak of the threefold task that the Baroque inherited from antiquity—*docere, movere,* and *delectare* (to instruct, to move, and to amuse).[12] The authors of the textbooks illustrate their definitions with citations from various writers, primarily French (Bossuet, Massillon, and Fléchier) or Russian (Lomonosov, Petrov, and Derzhavin).

Through his school reading, Gogol also became familiar with forms prominent in the Baroque period, such as the emblem, which was introduced to him in Nikol'skii's textbook. He was also introduced to the *topoi,* which, although they did not originate in the Baroque, figured prominently in the literature of that period. The following example, Vasilii Petrov's "Ode to Count Orlov," taken from Tolmachev's textbook, contains four of the most prevalent *topoi,* "life is a dream," *brevitas vitae, vanitas,* and *memento mori:*

10. For Orlai's list, see M. N. Speranskii, ed., *Gogolevskii sbornik* (Kiev, 1902), 336.

11. A. S. Nikol'skii, *Osnovaniia rossiiskoi slovesnosti,* 2 vols. (St. Petersburg, 1809); Iakov Tolmachev, *Pravila slovesnosti,* 4 vols. (St. Petersburg, 1815–22); *Sobranie obraztsovykh russkikh sochinenii i perevodov v stikhakh,* 6 vols. (St. Petersburg, 1821–24) [hereafter cited in the notes as *Sobranie v stikhakh*]; *Sobranie obraztsovykh russkikh sochinenii i perevodov v proze,* 6 vols. (St. Petersburg, 1822–24) [hereafter cited in the notes as *Sobranie v proze*].

12. Quintilian 3, 5:2–3. See Quintilian, *The Institutio Oratoria,* 4 vols., trans. H. A. Butler (Cambridge: Harvard University Press, 1920–22), 1:396–97; also see *Sobranie v proze,* 6:clix and 3:xcvi–ciii, and Tolmachev, *Pravila,* 2:307 and 3:157.

Wealth, splendor, power—all dies with us,
All passes as a dream, all is swallowed by eternity.
Mortals' birth is the first step towards death.[13]

And Gogol learned of the figures of language that were extensively used in Baroque literature, such as anaphora, epiphora, antithesis, conceit, oxymoron, and wordplay, in all of his textbooks.

In "Opyt rossiiskoi piitiki" (An Attempt at Russian Poetics), his preface to the poetry *Collection,* Iosif Sreznevskii surveys the history of foreign and Russian literatures of the seventeenth and eighteenth centuries. In the section on Italian literature, Sreznevskii mentions Marino, and in the section on Spanish literature, Cervantes, Góngora, Lope de Vega, and Calderón.[14] Among the English Baroque writers, he includes Donne, Crashaw, and Drayton and also mentions Cowley's *Davideis,* Milton's *Paradise Lost,* and Dryden's *Absalom and Achitophel.*[15] In the section on Polish literature, he notes such Baroque poets as Samuel Twardowski and Wespazjan Kochowski. In his discussion of Russian literature, Sreznevskii mentions Polotskii's *Rifmologion, The Comedy-Parable of the Prodigal Son,* and *The Furnace Play;* St. Dmitrii of Rostov's *Nativity Play, Dormition Play,* and *Sinner's Repentance;* and Prokopovich's *De arte poetica, Tragicomedy of St. Vladimir,* "O, Vain Man," and "To Fever in Fever."[16] *The Collection* also contains an essay by Mikhail Kachenovskii that surveys Russian literature prior to Lomonosov. In it, Kachenovskii mentions distinguished Ukrainian-Russian ecclesiastical Baroque writers such as Galiatovskii, Radivilovskii, Baranovich, and Buzhinskii.[17]

Gogol remained profoundly interested in Ukrainian-Russian ecclesi-

---

13. Tolmachev, *Pravila,* 1:165.

14. *Sobranie v stikhakh,* 1:xlviii–xlix and lxxv–lxxviii. Iosif Evseevich Sreznevskii (1780–after 1828) was the uncle of a distinguished philologist, Izmail Ivanovich Sreznevskii (1812–80). Gogol corresponded with Izmail Sreznevskii, whose *Zaporozhskaia starina* (Kharkov, 1833) was for Gogol an important source on the history of the Ukraine.

15. Ibid., 1:lxxxiii–lxxxvii.

16. Ibid., 1:ciii and cxxiv–cxxvii. Sreznevskii does not mention Twardowski's first name, but it is certain that he refers to Samuel, an epic poet, popular among literary scholars in the eighteenth- and early-nineteenth-century Ukraine and Russia proper, and not to his contemporary, Kasper, an author of love and meditative poetry, who was virtually unknown there at that time.

17. M. T. Kachenovskii, "Vzgliad na uspekhi Rossiiskogo vitiistva v pervoi polovine istekshego stoletiia," in *Sobranie v proze,* 1:5–32.

astical Baroque literature throughout his life. During his stay abroad, he repeatedly asked his friends to send him books of an ecclesiastical nature. In a letter on October 5, 1843, for example, he asked Nikolai Iazykov to send him such books as "(1) St. Dmitrii of Rostov's *Search,* (2) *Trumpets of Words* and *The Spiritual Sword* by Lazar' Baranovich, and (3) *Works* by Stefan Iavorskii in three parts, his sermons" (12:219). Corresponding with his friends, Gogol often recommended that they read Ukrainian-Russian ecclesiastical writings of the Baroque epoch. Thus he wrote in a letter on June 4, 1845, to Aleksandra Smirnova: "When things become too hard for you to bear and your grief is great, don't forget to get the *Works* of St. Dmitrii of Rostov (in 5 volumes). After praying to God vigorously, read the conversation between the *comforter* and the *mourner* in the first volume and then reread it more than once" (12:491; italics are Gogol's). In Gogol's notebook of 1846 there is a long list of ecclesiastical works; among them are many written by Ukrainian-Russian Baroque church writers (9:561–62).[18]

Gogol's textbooks also contained many examples from French Jesuit ecclesiastical writers of the Baroque period, including Bossuet.[19] Many years after he had read these textbooks, Gogol, in a letter on March 26, 1844, advised Smirnova to read Bossuet's works:

> Don't forget the old, or to put it better, eternal preachings among Ravignans and all sorts of new preachings. Buy right away, without delay, Bossuet's *Oeuvres philosophiques,* a smallish volume published by Charpentier, and right away read the last two articles at the end of the volume: first, *Élévation à Dieu sur les mystères de la religion Chrétienne* and secondly, *Traité de la concupiscence.* They can help you in your search for God. (12:278; italics are Gogol's)[20]

An instructive example of the influence of the gymnasium education on Gogol's later literary taste can be found in *Selected Passages from Correspondence with Friends,* in the section entitled "On the Essence

---

18. For detailed information on Gogol's interest in ecclesiastical writings, including those of the Baroque period, see N. I. Petrov, "Novye materialy dlia izucheniia religiozno-nravstvennykh vozzrenii N. V. Gogolia," *Trudy Kievskoi Dukhovnoi Akademii* 6 (1902): 270–317.

19. See, for example, *Sobranie v proze,* 1:270–71.

20. Gustave François de Ravignan (1795–1858) was a Jesuit preacher whose writings were quite fashionable in his native France in the first half of the nineteenth century.

of Russian Poetry and on Its Originality." Gogol devoted a great deal of space to an analysis of Lomonosov's and Derzhavin's poetry. He also devoted several lines to the appraisal of the eighteenth-century poet Vasilii Petrov, whose works, like those of his more distinguished contemporaries, contain Baroque elements.[21] He wrote:

> By the hand of Lomonosov, odes became customary among us. Festivals, victories, namedays, even illuminations and fireworks became subjects for odes. The composers of them have expressed only an absolute lack of talent in place of enthusiasm. The only possible exception is Petrov, who is not devoid of some power and a poetic flame: he was really a poet, in spite of the rigidity and staleness of his lines. (8:372; Zeldin, 203)

Gogol's inclusion of Petrov here can perhaps be traced to the gymnasium. In Gogol's textbooks, Petrov is cited next to Lomonosov and Derzhavin. And Iosif Sreznevskii had praised Petrov's odes with some reservations, of which Gogol's are reminiscent:

> Petrov also wrote many odes of this kind, which will always have merit for poetry lovers. Two shortcomings in his odes are noticed by critics: the first is that he frequently tries to be conspicuous by erudition and puns; the second is that his style is sometimes verbose and coarse and that he often makes mistakes in regard to purity of the language. But having weighed all pros and cons, one must do him justice. In all of his odes, one can notice the most fervent imagination and the strongest rapture.[22]

Another important source of Baroque literature for Gogol was Dmitrii Troshchinskii's library, to which Gogol had easy access.[23] The library catalogue lists many translated works of prominent Baroque writers: among them, Marino's *Massacre of Innocents* in two differ-

---

21. See Dmitrii Chizhevskii, "Das Barock in der russischen Literatur," in *Slavische Barock-literatur I*, ed. Dmitrii Chizhevskii (Munich: Fink, 1970), 34–36.

22. *Sobranie v stikhakh*, 2:cxcvi–cxcvii.

23. I. M. Kamanin, "Nauchnye i literaturnye proizvedeniia N. V. Gogolia po istorii Malorossii," in *Pamiati Gogolia*, ed. N. P. Dashkevich (Kiev, 1902), 77.

ent translations, Gracián's *Hero* and *Manual Oracle, or the Art of Prudence,* and Tallemant's *Voyage to the Island of Love.* The catalogue contains works of Ukrainian-Russian Baroque ecclesiastical writers, such as St. Dmitrii of Rostov's *Daily Notes,* Buzhinskii's *Complete Collection of Instructive Words Said in the Presence of Peter the Great,* Prokopovich's *Instructive, Praiseworthy, and Congratulatory Addresses and Speeches,* and Iavorskii's *Omens of Antichrist's Coming and of the End of the Age as They Appear in the Holy Scriptures.*[24] The catalogue also includes some emblematic literature, such as Nestor Maksimovich-Ambodik's *Selected Emblems and Symbols* and Joseph Stöber's *Iconology.*[25]

Gogol's interest in pre-nineteenth-century Russian literature was also kindled by his literature professor at the Nezhin Gymnasium, Parfenii Nikol'skii (not to be confused with the author of the textbook), who like Iosif Sreznevskii was a graduate of the Moscow Theological Academy, which was modeled after the Kiev Academy. A classmate of Gogol's, poet and playwright Nestor Kukol'nik, recalled that Nikol'skii was "a resolute conservative in literature and philosophy.... He argued with us, as they say, until we were in tears. He forced us to admire Lomonosov, Kheraskov, even Sumarokov." Despite some reservations, Kukol'nik admits that he and other students at the gymnasium "owe much to Parfenii Ivanovich. He positively forced us to learn Russian literature before Pushkin."[26]

At the gymnasium, Gogol studied not only the literature of the Baroque period but also its history. Many historical essays concerned with the Baroque appear in the prose *Collection.* Mikhail Kachenovskii contributed an essay, "On the Reasons for the Deposition of Nikon, the Moscow Patriarch," in which he deals with the subject against the historical background of seventeenth-century Russia. Nikolai Karamzin contributed "On the Moscow Rebellion in the Reign of Tsar Alexis." The prose *Collection* also contains Karamzin's "Historical Reminiscences and Remarks on the Way to Trinity Monastery," in which the eminent historian describes episodes from Russian history related to the monastery from the early fifteenth to the late eighteenth centuries, and Mikhail Murav'ev's "Unification of Apanage

24. Fedorov, *Katalog,* 283, 36 and 76, 208, 2, 13, 25, and 24.
25. Ibid., 183 and 42.
26. Nestor Kukol'nik, "P. I. Nikol'skii," in *Gimnaziia vysshikh nauk i Litsei kniazia Bezborodko,* ed. N. V. Gerbel' (St. Petersburg, 1881), 294 and 296.

Principalities into One State," which deals with the period of Russian history from the reign of Ivan III, the grand duke of Muscovy (1462), to the Andrusovo Treaty with Poland in the reign of Tsar Alexis (1667).[27]

Gogol's interest in the history of the Baroque epoch extended beyond the classroom. In 1826, when he was still a student at the Nezhin Gymnasium, Gogol began his *Book of Odds and Ends, or a Manual Encyclopedia.* In this notebook, among other things, he copied extracts from the accounts of foreign travelers who had observed Russian customs in the seventeenth century. One such account was written by a German diplomat, Adam Olearius, who visited Russia from 1636 to 1639 as a member of the embassy of Frederick III, duke of Schleswig-Holstein (9:520–22 and 654).[28] Another was written by Baron Augustin Meierberg, an Austrian diplomat who described the 1661–62 negotiations conducted in Moscow, the purpose of which was to offer Austria's assistance in concluding the peace treaty between Russia and Poland (9:519–20 and 654).

After Gogol completed his education in the Nezhin Gymnasium, he continued studying the Baroque period. In his notes for lectures at the Patriotic Institute in St. Petersburg, where he taught from 1831 to 1835, Gogol wrote at length about the history of the Ukraine in the seventeenth century and the events in Europe that influenced its destiny (9:89). At the end of 1833, Gogol wrote to the minister of education, Sergei Uvarov, to apply for the position of professor of general history at Kiev University. With his application, Gogol included an outline for a proposed course of study. In this outline, he discussed events and trends significant in determining the character of the Baroque epoch, including geographic discoveries, the Reformation and the Counter-Reformation, the rise of nationalism in Europe, and the devastating wars of that period:

> The Europeans greedily headed for America and brought back piles of gold; the Atlantic and Eastern oceans were in their power; and at that time papal missions penetrated northeastern Asia and Africa—and the world was suddenly opened up in all

27. *Sobranie v proze,* 4:22–54, 3–22, 232–74, and 154–98.
28. For a modern English translation of this travel account, see Adam Olearius, *The Travels of Olearius in Seventeenth-Century Russia,* trans. and ed. Samuel H. Baron (Stanford: Stanford University Press, 1967).

its vast expanse. Meanwhile in Europe people were gradually
beginning to doubt the justice of papal power and, as previously the commerce of Venice had been killed off by a poor
Genoese, so the Pope's power was curtailed by the Augustinian
monk Luther. How this thought was formed in the peaceful
monk's mind and how stubbornly he defended his position!
How, after his fall, the Pope became even more terrifying and
resourceful: he introduced the awful Inquisition and the Jesuit
Order with its terrible unseen power, which suddenly spread
out over the whole world, penetrating into everything and in
secret communication with its own factions from one end of
the world to the other. But the more fearsome the Pope became, the greater was the resistance shown by the typographi-
cal presses. All Europe was divided into two groups, and these
groups finally took up arms, and a long, cruel war, both inside
and outside the states, gripped the whole of Europe. . . . Spiritual power waned. Sovereigns increased their power. I must
now illustrate how Europe changed after these wars. States and
nations became fused together in indivisible masses. There was
no longer that division of power which there had been in the
Middle Ages. Europe concentrated more on the individual.
(8:34; Tulloch, 50)

Gogol's interest in the history of the Baroque epoch continued long
after his teaching career ended. In a letter on July 27, 1842, Gogol
asked Sergei Aksakov to send him Grigorii Kotoshikhin's *On Russia
in the Reign of Tsar Alexis,* published in 1840 (12:83 and 606). Later,
in 1844, he recommended that Nikolai Iazykov read Pavel Stroev's
*Appearances of Sovereigns, Tsars and Grand Princes Michael, Alexis
and Theodore.* He wrote:

Recently, a book has fallen into my hands. . . . One would think
it dull, but it has words and names of imperial decorations, of
rich fabrics and precious stones—a real treasure for a poet;
each word should be enshrined in your verse. You will marvel
at the jewels in our language: its sonority is already a gift;
everything is grained and hard as pearls, and, really, the name
is still more jewel-like than the thing itself. Yes, if you only
ornament your verse with words of this kind you will lead the

reader wholly into the past. As for me, after having read three pages of this book, it was as though I saw everywhere a Tsar of olden times reverently going to evening services in all his antique imperial attire. (8:279 and 793; Zeldin, 86–87)

While living in Russia proper, primarily in St. Petersburg and occasionally in Moscow, Gogol was constantly exposed to Baroque art and architecture. In St. Petersburg, he saw Late Baroque architectural and sculptural monuments, particularly the works of Rastrelli and the monument to Peter the Great by Falconet. And in Moscow, he saw Baroque architecture manifested in the Churches of the Trinity of the Georgian Virgin (1628–53) and of the Intercession of the Virgin in Fili (1690–93), both mentioned in his notebooks (see 9:546 and 548). In both cities he could also see examples of *lubok* in art shops, like the one described in the opening passage of "The Portrait" (see 3:79–80; Kent, 2:252–53), or at outdoor festivals, like the one mentioned in *Marriage* (5:51; Ehre, 41).[29]

Also contributing to the development of Gogol's interest in the Baroque period was the time he spent in Rome. Gogol stayed abroad for almost eleven years and spent six of them in Rome. As Victor Erlich has noted, "Gogol responded powerfully . . . to the lushness of the Roman baroque."[30] Andrei Siniavskii contends that the main outcome of the writer's stay in Italy was his finding there "the homeland of the Baroque, which Gogol had apprehended solely in this wonderful country, foreseen with his heart, and responded to in his multifigured roulades."[31]

Gogol was fascinated first and foremost with Italian Baroque architecture and art. His fondness for Baroque architecture has been noted by Sigrid Richter: "Clearly Gogol knew how to derive great pleasure from the Baroque in all its manifestations, especially from the churches in which splendor and opulence are most markedly developed."[32]

---

29. For a detailed discussion of outdoor festivals in Moscow and St. Petersburg, see A. F. Nekrylova, *Russkie narodnye gorodskie prazdniki, uveseleniia i zrelishcha. Konets XVIII–nachalo XX veka* (Leningrad: Iskusstvo, 1988).

30. Victor Erlich, *Gogol* (New Haven: Yale University Press, 1969), 161.

31. Siniavskii, *V teni Gogolia,* 349.

32. Sigrid Richter, "Rom und Gogol'; Gogol's Romerlebnis und sein Fragment 'Rim' " (Ph.D. diss., University of Hamburg, 1964), 66.

It should be emphasized, however, that Gogol's interest in Baroque architecture, which he had many opportunities to see in both the Ukraine and the two Russian capitals, developed before his arrival in Rome. Thus, Gogol's article "On Present-Day Architecture" (1835) contains an architectural project amazing in its grandeur, disproportion, and abundance of embellishment (8:74–75; Tulloch, 133–34). Of the proclivity towards the Baroque, which Gogol reveals in this article, Siniavskii has remarked, "No matter how fantastic Gogol's architectural hyperboles are, one can clearly see in them the *Baroque* style which pervades his aesthetic speculations and creative practices."[33]

Gogol's experience in Rome intensified his interest in Baroque architecture. In his fragment "Rome" (1842), he writes of Italian architects such as Vignola, della Porta, Bernini, and Borromini (3:235). When Smirnova visited Rome, Gogol showed her a variety of Roman sites. Among them were the Church of San Giovanni di Laterano, for which Borromini had created a Baroque interior; the Church of Santa Maria in Campitelli, built by Rainaldi (1663–67); and the Church of Santa Andrea della Valle (1591–1663), designed by della Porta and built by Maderno, and with later work by Rainaldi. His itinerary for Smirnova also included palaces such as the Palazzo Madama (1642), built by Marucelli, and the Palazzi Rospigliosi (1603) and Sciarra-Colonna (1610), both built by Ponzio (9:490 and 650).

Gogol was interested not only in the Baroque architecture of Italy but also in its painting. In "Rome" he mentions the Carracci and Guercino (3:219); in the 1842 edition of "The Portrait" he refers to Reni (3:85; Kent, 2:258). In his itinerary for Smirnova, Gogol also included Reni's ceiling fresco *Aurora* (1613–14) in the Palazzo Rospigliosi, as well as Domenichino's *The Four Cardinal Virtues* (1628–30) in the Church of San Carlo in Catinari.

Gogol also exhibited an interest in Baroque artists from other countries. For example, in the 1842 edition of *Taras Bulba* Gogol mentions the Dutch artist van Honthorst, and in his letter of February 17 the same year to Mariia Balabina he speaks of the French artist Lorrain, and advised Balabina's brother, Viktor, an amateur painter, to develop his talent by copying the works of this Baroque master of the decorative-mythological landscape (12:37–38).

33. Siniavskii, *V teni Gogolia,* 347; italics are Siniavskii's.

During his years in Rome, Gogol, who was fluent in Italian, also became well acquainted with Italian literature.[34] In his letter of April 1838 to Mariia Balabina, he revealed his great interest in Italian literature of the seventeenth and eighteenth centuries and specifically mentioned having read a collection entitled *Autori burleschi italiani* (see 11:143; Proffer, 74).[35]

Thus it is clear that Gogol possessed a thorough knowledge of Baroque cultural traditions, literary, historical, and artistic. He grew up in an environment that included Baroque architecture and art, and later as an adult he sought out and admired Baroque art forms in Rome. He had studied the history of the Baroque epoch at home and at school and continued to learn and to collect information about it throughout his life. Long after his graduation from the gymnasium Gogol was still asking his friends to send him copies of Baroque writings; significantly, he considered them to be so valuable that he would frequently recommend them to his friends.

34. Gogol could already read Italian during his teaching career in St. Petersburg; see Daria Borghese, *Gogol a Roma* (Florence: Sansoni, 1957), 129.

35. A recent study has linked Gogol's works, such as "Rome" and *Dead Souls,* to poems by Marino, Tassoni, Casti, and Parini. See E. Iu. Saprykina, "Gogol' i traditsii ital'ianskoi satiry," in *Gogol' i mirovaia literatura,* ed. Iu. V. Mann (Moscow: Nauka, 1988), 62–83, and esp. 78–80.

2

Forms

    The forms I shall consider in this chapter were all immensely popular in the Baroque period. Two of them, the *facetia* and the emblem, originated in Renaissance Italy and underwent considerable change, reaching their zenith of popularity in the Baroque period. The others, *vertep* and *lubok,* took shape in the Baroque period itself, in the Ukraine and Russia proper, but not without influence from their Western counterparts.

    The *facetia* (a Latin word for "drollery" or "joke") manifested the characteristic Baroque principle of *docere, movere, delectare:* it tended toward didacticism and was witty and funny. Poggio Bracciolini, the acknowledged inventor of this form, intended these witty anecdotes about human folly, primarily in the less genteel strata of society, for a highly select circle of his friends. But later, in the seventeenth and eighteenth centuries, this distinction blurred as both written and oral *facetiae* spread widely among all layers of society.

    The Baroque character of *vertep,* the Ukrainian puppet theater, manifested itself especially in the *discordia concors* of highly serious religious and low comical secular scenes, a dichotomy reflected in the two-story structure of its house-shaped stage. Combining in itself elements of literature, fine arts, music, and dance, *vertep* also, like some other forms of theater, exemplified the Baroque predilection for synthesis. Further, during the Baroque period, the formation of nations and states with their diverse ethnic composition, on the one hand, and close contacts of various countries in times of peace or warfare, on the other, drew attention to different ethnic and religious groups, whose portrayal, albeit distinctly stereotypical, was character-istic of *vertep.*

Lubok, a broadsheet with illustration and text, was, like *facetia,* typically a combination of the didactic, amazing, and funny. It was intended by its more educated authors for a semiliterate audience— an interaction, also characteristically Baroque, of the high-cultural and the popular. The turnover device, by which flipping over a pic-ture turns the image into its opposite, employed in *lubok* was a manifestation of the *discordia concors.* And Baroque tendencies are also manifest in *lubok*'s predilection for theatricality, with its fre-quently dialogue-like captions and the attention-catching postures of its characters.

Like *lubok,* emblem involved a sententious and witty interaction of verbal and pictorial elements, but on a more sophisticated level. Baroque predilections are evident in the *ingenio* and *acutezza* exhib-ited by the author and expected from the reader. Initially a highly elitist artistic-literary form, which its creator, Andrea Alciati, in-tended for the chosen few, the emblem degenerated into platitude and became more widely spread in the course of time.

What is the connection between these four forms? The *facetia,* with its dialogues and depictions of crude characters in funny situa-tions, undoubtedly exerted considerable influence on *vertep,* with its coarse humor and stock personages. In its turn, *vertep* can be viewed as a source for the theatrical orientation of *lubok*—the dialogue-like captions and the stage-like postures, aimed at the reader-spectator, of its characters. The didactic quality of *lubok* captions are also rem-iniscent of the *facetia.* The emblem, like *lubok,* is based on the in-teraction of verbal and pictorial elements, but unlike in *lubok,* the interaction of the verbal and the pictorial in emblem tends to be not straightforward and illustrative but rather intricate and metaphorical. And finally, like the *facetia,* the emblem was guided by the threefold task of *docere, movere, delectare.*[1] It too was initially intended for a select audience, but in the course of time degenerated into cliché,

---

1. Cf. Barbara C. Bowen, "Two Literary Genres: The Emblem and the Joke," *The Journal of Medieval and Renaissance Studies* 15 (1985): 29–35.

thereby becoming a form with wider appeal, even though not quite the mass appeal of the *facetia*.

Facetia

Facetiae are short, humorous, and witty narratives. They explored various contrarieties of everyday life and ridiculed the vices of various groups of society. This ridicule often turned into satire.[2] *Facetiae* usually had so-called nomad plots: as they migrated from country to country, they would accumulate details that made them specific to their new homeland.

Parables, another form well-known before and during the Baroque, tended, like *facetiae,* to be concise and didactic; however, unlike the *facetiae,* parables were devoid of humor; they were also allegorical and therefore could not be understood out of context. These two forms also differed in purpose: if the principal aim of the *facetia* was to amuse and ridicule, the main aspiration of the parable was to clarify, illustrate, or prove a point.[3]

Gogol departed considerably from established tradition when he endowed the *facetia* with a parabolic function.[4] We shall see this by examining his employment of two previously existing *facetiae* and then by looking at two *facetiae* of Gogol's own composition.

2. For more information about the *facetia,* see N. K. Gudzii, "Fatsetsiia," in *Literaturnaia éntsiklopediia,* 11 vols. (Moscow: GIKhL, 1929–39), 11:672–73; Julian Krzyżanowski and Kazimiera Żukowska-Billip, "Facecja staropolska," in *Dawna facecja polska,* ed. J. Krzyżanowski and K. Żukowska-Billip (Warsaw: Państwowy Instytut Wydawniczy, 1960), 5–22; O. A. Derzhavina, *Fatsetsii. Perevodnaia novella v russkoi literature XVII veka* (Moscow: Akademiia Nauk SSSR, 1962); Joanna Bridzle Lipking, "Traditions of the *Facetiae* and Their Influence in Tudor England" (Ph.D. diss., Columbia University, 1970); and Sante Graciotti, "Il ruolo della letteratura faceta umanistica italiana nelle 'facezie' polacche e russe," in *Mondo slavo e cultura italiana: Contributi italiani al IX Congresso Internazionale degli Slavisti. Kiev 1983,* ed. Jitka Kresalkova (Rome: Il Veltro Editrice, 1983), 162–87.

3. For discussion of the parable, see Eta Linnemann, *Parables of Jesus* (London: S.P.C.K., 1966); John Dominic Crossan, *Cliffs of Fall* (New York: Seabury Press, 1980); S. S. Averintsev, "Pritcha," in *Kratkaia literaturnaia éntsiklopediia,* 9 vols. (Moscow: Sovetskaia éntsiklopediia, 1962–78), 6:20–21; and Iu. I. Levin, "Logicheskaia struktura pritchi," *Trudy po znakovym sistemam* 15 (1982): 49–56.

4. For a discussion of Gogol's use of the *facetia* that does not consider its function as a parable, see Gavriel Shapiro, "The Role of *Facetiae* in Gogol's Early Works," *Transactions of the Association of Russian-American Scholars in the U.S.A.* 17 (1984): 69–74.

Among the best-known *facetiae* are some involving the inappropriate use of Latin. One such already appears in the *Facetiarum* of Poggio Bracciolini (1380–1459). In this collection there is a story about a foolish physician who volunteered to accompany a fowler to a forest. When the physician saw some birds, he scared them away by shouting in Italian; the fowler rebuked him and asked him to keep quiet. But when the birds came back, the physician yelled in Latin, which also scared the birds away. Thereupon the physician concluded that the birds understood not only Italian, which seemed to him natural enough, but, to his surprise, Latin as well (*facetia CLXXIX*).[5]

A variation on this *facetia* by Bracciolini is one about a student-"Latinizer" who indiscriminately mixes Latin and his native tongue. This story was especially popular in the sixteenth and seventeenth centuries and often appeared in collections not unlike Bracciolini's. With the development of the novel of the Late Renaissance and the Baroque, the story could at times be found as a digression. A striking example before Gogol's day of this use of the *facetia* within a larger piece of fiction is found in Rabelais (ca. 1495–1553).[6] This *facetia* portrays a student who emulates contemporary Parisian fashionable manners and latinizes his French beyond comprehension. Annoyed by the student's gibberish, Pantagruel takes him by the throat and threatens to flay him. The frightened student undergoes an immediate "transformation" and starts speaking intelligible French (*Gargantua and Pantagruel*, bk. II, chap. 6).

This *facetia* was equally popular in neighboring Germany. As Aleksander Brückner states, a story about a student-"Latinizer" can be found in every collection of German *facetiae*,[7] for example, in

5. All references to Bracciolini's *facetiae* are to the following edition: Poggio Bracciolini, *Facezie* (Milan: Rizzoli, 1983).

6. This is an additional illustration, albeit an indirect one, of Gogol's literary ties to Rabelais, first pointed out by Mikhail Bakhtin. See Bakhtin's article, "Rable i Gogol' (Iskusstvo slova i narodnaia smekhovaia kul'tura)," in his *Voprosy literatury i éstetiki* (Moscow: Khudozhestvennaia literatura, 1975), 484–95. For the influence of Bracciolini on Rabelais, see Richard Cooper, "Les 'contes' de Rabelais et l'Italie: Une mise au point," in *La nouvelle française à la Renaissance,* ed. Lionello Sozzi (Geneva and Paris: Slatkine, 1981), 183–207.

7. As cited in Iaroslav Hordyns'kyi, *Z ukraïns'koï dramatychnoï literatury XVII–XVIII st.* (Lvov: Naukove tovarystvo imeni Shevchenka, 1930), 205 n. 1.

Thomas Murner's *Schelmenzunft* (1512) and in Martin Montanus's *Gartengesellschaft* (1556).[8]

In Poland, always receptive to Western influences, and in other Slavic countries as well, this *facetia* appears both in collections and as a digression in novels. Indeed, in *Peregrynacyja Maćkowa*, modeled on Till Eulenspiegel's adventures, the protagonist Maciek, upon his return from his journey, vows that he will never again leave home and that he will work, "taking the rake-atus in his hands and raking dung-atus from the cow-shed to the cart-atus."[9] The anonymous Polish author does not even tell the *facetia* in its entirety. It was so popular a tale in that country that he expected his readers to recognize it from the "Latin" words of that one sentence.

A Ukrainian version of this *facetia* can be found in an eighteenth-century school anthology. In this version, the hero of the story, a peasant's son, Hryts'ko, delivers a speech to the pigs, using such pseudo-Latin words as *sviniantus, zhryzantus,* and *travantus* ("pig-antus," "nibble-antus," and "grass-antus"). As a result, he gets a beating from his father because his "Latin" speech frightens the animals.[10]

A somewhat similar motif is present in another *facetia* adapted from Polish into Russian by an anonymous writer at the end of the seventeenth century:

> A certain peasant sent his son to study at one of the schools in Cracow. The son, being lazy, did not want to speak Latin but preferred to frequent places where wine-glasses clinked. After squandering all his allowance, he returned to his father to get more money from him. Though a simpleton, the father thought, "He got a lot and he's asking for more. Oh vanity! What good will come of my son?" He wanted to ask his son what the Latin

8. See Thomas Murner, *Schelmenzunft* (Hamburg: Hauswedell, 1968), 8; and Martin Montanus, *Schwankbücher* (*1557–1566*) (Tubingen: Literarischer Verein in Stuttgart, 1899), 272–74.

9. See Stanisław Grzeszczuk, ed., *Antologia literatury Sowiźrzalskiej XVI i XVII wieku* (Wrocław: Zakład Narodowy imienia Ossolińskich, 1966), 559–60.

10. See Hordyns'kyi, *Z ukraïns'koï dramatychnoï literatury,* 205. Concerning the popularity of the genre of *facetia* in the Ukraine throughout the mid-nineteenth century and the migration of Bracciolini's plots to the Ukraine via Poland, see M. Ie. Syvachenko, "Pro humoresku S. Rudans'koho 'Hospod' dav' ta ïï nimets'ku i italiis'ku literaturni paraleli," *Radians'ke literaturoznavstvo* 1 (1984): 44–55.

was for one thing or another but did not know how. It so happened that the father was shoveling dung, while the son stood and watched him work. The father asked, "Son, how do you say rake, dung, and cart in Latin?" The son replied, "Father, rake in Latin is rake-atus, dung is dung-atus, and cart is cart-atus." Ignorant though he was, the father immediately realized that his son was not studying at school but rather outside of it. He hit him over the head with the rake, handed it over to him and said, "From now on, study in the pig-sty instead of the school. Take the rake-atus in your hand-atus and put dung-atus in the cart-atus, and the rake-atus will also be your *peratus.*"[11]

These examples illustrate the nature of the *facetiae,* how the basic idea of a *facetia* will remain unchanged—in this instance, the indiscriminate use of Latin, or the use of pseudo-Latin that reveals such human foibles as folly, pretentiousness, and laziness—no matter how far the story has traveled. As we see, the targets for derision in *facetiae* are different strata in society, such as doctors, students, and peasants. These *facetiae* often close with a didactic-sounding moral, which can seem "tacked on." The Russian adaptation of the Polish *facetia* cited above is followed by a short didactic motto, contemptuous of the peasantry, "It will be a long time before the one whose heart is attached to a plough becomes a philosopher." As Ol'ga Derzhavina remarks, this conclusion in no way follows from the story itself.[12]

The *facetia* I am concerned with here belongs in all its variants to the "school" type, its subject learning or rather pretense at learning, its protagonists current or former students. Our examples of this "school" *facetia* demonstrate its great popularity all over Europe in the course of several centuries.[13] Gogol continued the tradition of employing this popular *facetia,* or as Vasilii Gippius called it, this

11. Derzhavina, *Fatsetsii,* 122. The last word in the quoted text is apparently made up. See *Oxford Latin Dictionary* (Oxford: Oxford University Press, 1968), 1329. It is possible, however, that it conveys in metaphorical form the idea that the son's working with a rake, that is, his peasant labor, should become his way of breadwinning, since *pera* in Latin means "a bag for carrying a daily provision" (ibid., 1327).

12. See Derzhavina, *Fatsetsii,* 68.

13. This *facetia* can be found in Italian, French, German, Swedish, Lithuanian, Latvian, Slovenian, Serbo-Croatian, Russian, Ukrainian, and Belorussian. See A. N. Afanas'ev, *Narodnye russkie skazki,* 3 vols. (Moscow: Nauka, 1984–85), 3:414–15.

"wandering anecdote."[14] In the preface to part 1 of the *Evenings on a Farm near Dikanka,* Gogol exploited this *facetia* about a student-"Latinizer":

> And one of the visitors. . . . Well, he is such a fine young gentle-man that you might any minute take him for an assessor or a high officer of the court. Sometimes he will hold up his finger, and looking at the tip of it, begin telling a story—as choicely and cleverly as though it were printed in a book! Sometimes you listen and listen and begin to be puzzled. You can't make head or tail of it, not if you were to hang for it. Where did he pick up such words? Foma Grigorievich once told him a funny story satirizing this. He told him how a student who had been getting lessons from a deacon came back to his father such a Latin scholar that he had forgotten our language: he put *us* on the end of all the words; a spade was *spadus,* a female was *femalus.* It happened one day that he went with his father in the fields. The Latin scholar saw a rake and asked his father: "What do you call that, Father?" And, without looking at what he was doing, he stepped on the teeth of the rake. Before the father had time to answer, the handle flew up and hit the boy on the head. "The damned rake!" he cried, putting his hand to his forehead and jumping half a yard into the air, "may the devil shove its father off a bridge, how it can hit!" So he remembered the name, you see, poor fellow! (1:105; Kent, 1:5–6)

This *facetia* about the student-"Latinizer" combines the traits of the *facetia* and the parable. Like the *facetia,* it is funny and edifying; like the parable, it is allegorical (and therefore cannot be understood out of context) and designed to illustrate a point. The story functions in Gogol's text on two allegorical planes, contextual and metatextual. On the contextual plane, the deacon Foma Grigor'evich, to illustrate his point, tells this story to the fancifully speaking *panich* ("young gentleman"), whom he wishes both to ridicule and to instruct. On the metatextual plane, Gogol is aiming this story at his many contem-poraries who showed a predilection for everything foreign. It should

---

14. Vasilii Gippius, *Gogol'* (Leningrad: Mysl', 1924), 31.

not be forgotten that the cycle was written at a time when Russian literature was flooded with imitations of English, French, and German writers, and when polemics on *narodnost'* ("national character") were quite common.[15]

Another "school" *facetia* appears in what is believed to be a fragment of Gogol's early novel, *The Hetman.* The *facetia* belongs to a series of stories about a lazy student and his unresourceful teacher, who accompanies his instruction with beatings, perhaps in the belief that they will help arouse the student's interest in learning. The student's response to such "pedagogy," however, does not meet the teacher's expectations. In one of the stories, the student, disillusioned with this kind of schooling, decides that he would rather learn the art of stealing.[16] Gogol had most probably come across this *facetia* while a student himself in his native Ukraine; in his version a lazy schoolboy, constantly beaten, unwisely decides to chop up the big stick with which the teacher tries to encourage his progress in his studies:

> A schoolboy studied with a deacon, but God's word did not come to him. Perhaps he was stupid or perhaps it was his laziness that prevented it. The deacon beat him with a club once, then a second time, and then a third. "That damned club hits hard," said the schoolboy, who fetched an axe and chopped the club to pieces. "You just wait!" said the deacon, who cut himself a stick as thick as a carriage-shaft, and tickled the boy's ribs with it so that they still hurt. Who is to blame, then? The club? "No, no," shouted the crowd. "It's the king— the king is to blame." (3:284)[17]

The crowd's response, unexpected and seemingly irrational, is clear in context. The story is told by a character called Ostranitsa to a mob

15. For a detailed discussion of the issue in regard to the *Evenings* cycle, see David B. Saunders, "Contemporary Critics of Gogol's *Vechera* and the Debate about Russian *narodnost'* (1831–1832)," *Harvard Ukrainian Studies* 5 (1981): 66–82.

16. See "Skazanie o krest'ianskom syne," in *Russkaia demokraticheskaia satira XVII veka,* ed. V. P. Adrianova-Peretts (Moscow: Nauka, 1977), 87–90, 215–16, 231, and 237–38.

17. According to Aleksei Karpenko, Gogol's *facetia* is based on a Ukrainian folk anecdote. See A. I. Karpenko, *O narodnosti N. V. Gogolia* (Kiev: Izdatel'stvo Kievskogo Universiteta, 1973), 89.

that is about to lynch the Polish king's official representative, the head of the uhlans, who has ill-treated the local Ukrainian population. As we see from the close of the *facetia,* its allegorical nature is well understood by the crowd. This *facetia* functioning as a parable, then, presents the relationship between the Polish king and his Ukrainian subjects allegorically, in what is believed to be Gogol's first attempt at writing a historical novel. The title of the fragment, *The Hetman,* the date of the events in the chapter that contains the *facetia* (1645), and the protagonist's name, Ostranitsa, all indicate that the novel may have dealt with the struggle of the Ukrainian Cossacks against the Rzeczpospolita, which was conducted in a manner different from the schoolboy's shortsighted response to the teacher's clubbing.[18]

Thus in his early writings Gogol already employed *facetia* and parable in a unique manner. Prior to Gogol, these were two separate forms. Gogol's innovation lies in his "fusing" the two to create a *facetia* that functions as a parable, an amusing narrative of didactic but also allegorical nature. Furthermore, this new form constitutes an integral part of his fiction, playing an important role in its composition. In his *Evenings,* the *facetia* that appears in the preface to part 1 sets the tone for the whole cycle. Foma Grigor'evich, who represents the national and folk tradition in the cycle, recounts the *facetia* about the student-"Latinizer" to the *panich,* who has shown a predilection for the bookish and foreign. It is quite obvious that the narrator of the preface, Rudyi Panko, sides with Foma Grigor'evich in this controversy and apparently so does Gogol himself, hiding behind the beekeeper and his name.[19] This *facetia,* set in Gogol's native Ukrainian

---

18. Cf. ibid., 89–90. For a discussion of the relationship of the various chapters of *The Hetman* to one another, see 3:711–716. Concerning the problematic nature of this work, see Paul A. Karpuk, "N. V. Gogol's Unfinished Historical Novel 'The Hetman' " (Ph.D. diss., University of California, Berkeley, 1987), and his most recent "Gogol's Unfinished Novel 'The Hetman,' " *Slavic and East European Journal* 35 (1991): 36–55. As far as the historical setting of *The Hetman* is concerned, the name of the protagonist, Taras Ostranitsa, recalls the historical figure, Stepan Ostranitsa (or, more properly, Iatsko Ostrianin, d.1641) who led the uprising of the Ukrainian Cossacks against Polish rule in the 1630s. For more information about the historical prototype of Gogol's Ostranitsa, see Mikhail Grushevskii, "Ostrianin," in *Éntsiklopedicheskii slovar' Russkogo Bibliograficheskogo Instituta Granat,* 30:709–11.

19. About Rudyi Panko as Gogol's own encoded name, see Gavriel Shapiro, "Nikolai Gogol' i gordyi gogol': pisatel' i ego imia," *Russian Language Journal* 43 (1989): 146–48. The *panich's* detachment from his native roots and his preference for things foreign are underlined by his use of a snuffbox with the face of a Moslem general on its lid. It should be noted that in the world of Gogol's fiction fascination with things foreign, be it on a linguistic, material, or any

countryside, functions as a parable to ridicule the literary affectations of all those who blindly and slavishly imitate everything foreign and neglect their own national roots.[20]

The *facetia* plays a no less significant role in *The Hetman*. Clearly allegorical, the *facetia* was in all likelihood intended to foreshadow the main event in the novel—the Ukrainian uprising against Polish rule. By using a *facetia* that functioned as a parable and therefore represented two popular forms of the Baroque era, Gogol also added considerably to the reader's feeling of the Zeitgeist in the work, set as it was in the mid-seventeenth-century Ukraine.

If in his early works Gogol used already-existing *facetiae,* as we have seen, in his later writings he employed some that he composed himself. An example is found in his letter to Sergei Aksakov of March 6, 1847:

> What if I tell you the following tale? A cook volunteered to serve a fine and even extraordinary dinner as a treat for people who were never in the kitchen themselves, although they ate quite delicious dinners. The cook volunteered—nobody ordered him to cook this dinner. He only said in advance that his dinner would be cooked differently and he would therefore need more time. What should those to whom the dinner was promised have done? They should have kept quiet and waited patiently. Instead, they began to shout, "Serve the dinner!" The cook said, "It's physically impossible, because my dinner is not prepared at all like other dinners. For this, one has to go to a lot more trouble than you can even think of." They said in reply, "You're lying!" The cook, realizing that

---

other level, speaks poorly of a character. Consider, for example, the sorcerer in "A Terrible Vengeance" and Colonel Koshkarev in the second volume of *Dead Souls.* That the *panich*'s snuffbox, by now dented, was inherited a decade later by the tailor Petrovich in "The Overcoat," believed by some scholars to be the devil's agent, further corroborates this. See Dmitrii Chizhevskii, "About Gogol's 'Overcoat,'" in *Gogol from the Twentieth Century,* ed. Robert A. Maguire (Princeton: Princeton University Press, 1974), 295–322, especially 319–21, and Toby W. Clyman, "The Hidden Demons in Gogol''s *Overcoat,"* *Russian Literature* 7 (1979): 601–10.

20. For the literary polemics in the *Evenings* cycle, see A. V. Samyshkina, "K probleme gogolevskogo fol'klorizma (dva tipa skaza i literaturnaia polemika v 'Vecherakh na khutore bliz Dikan'ki')," *Russkaia literatura* 3 (1979): 61–80.

nothing could be done, finally decided to bring the guests themselves into the kitchen. He tried to arrange the pots and the kitchen utensils as best as he could in such a way that they could reach a conclusion about the dinner. The guests saw so great a quantity of strange and unusual pots and utensils, such as one could not even imagine would be required for preparing the dinner, that their heads were spinning. Well, what if there is an element of truth in this tale? (13:241–42)

There are similarities in the circumstances under which Gogol tells this tale in his letter to Aksakov and those under which Ostranitsa tells his to the crowd. Both storytellers wish to restrain their listeners and put a stop to their headstrong actions by making fun of their shortsightedness: Ostranitsa wants to prevent his listeners from lynching the commander of the Polish uhlans by explaining to them allegorically that such an act would not end their sufferings; Gogol wishes to dissuade Sergei Aksakov and other admirers of his literary talent from rebuking him for the "slowness" of his work on the second volume of *Dead Souls* by showing them that he, Gogol, and he alone is master in his literary "kitchen," and that no one should interfere with his work. This *facetia* functioning as a parable, illustrating Gogol's point to his impatient well-wishers in allegorical fashion, shows to what an extent this "hybrid" of the two popular forms had become an integral part of his literary arsenal—he employed it even in his correspondence.

Still another *facetia* functioning as a parable is the well-known story, Gogol's own composition, about Kifa Mokievich and Mokii Kifovich which appears toward the end of the first volume of *Dead Souls:*

> In a remote corner of Russia there lived two men. One of them was the father of a family, by name Kifa Mokievich, a mild-tempered man, who shuffled through life in a dressing-gown and slippers. He neglected his family; his existence was taken up more with cerebration and preoccupied with the following, as he called them, philosophical questions: "Now take any beastie for example," he used to say as he stalked

about his room, "a beastie is born naked. And why should he be born naked? Why does he not hatch out of an egg, like a bird? Very, very strange; the more one delves into it the less one understands of nature!" Such were the meditations of Kifa Mokievich. But that is not the main point. The other man, Mokyi Kifovich, was his son. And he was what they call in Russian *bogatyr* or doughty champion; and while his father was all engrossed in the birth of the beastie, his own twenty-year-old, broad-shouldered nature was bursting to unfold itself. His was not a light touch: either someone's hand would crack in his grip or a lump would spring up on someone's nose. At home and in the neighbourhood everyone from the domestics to the dogs took to their heels at the sight of him; he even reduced his own bed to splinters. Such was Mokyi Kifovich, but he was a good-natured chap withal. But that is not the main point either. The main point is this: "If you please, father and master Kifa Mokievich," his own servants and those of the neighbourhood would say to the father, "what's this for a Mokyi Kifovich you've got? There is no peace from him, he is a regular pest!" "Yes, he's frolicsome, frolicsome," the father would usually answer. "But what are we to do? It's too late to beat him, and if I did so, I would be accused of cruelty; and he is a man of some ambition—and if I were to reproach him in front of someone or other, he'd come to heel, but the rumour of it, that's the trouble! The townsfolk would get to know about it and look on him as on a dog. And can't they imagine how painful it would be for me? Am I not a father? And if I am engrossed in philosophy and have little time to spare for other things, am I less of a father? But no, I am a father, a father, the devil take them, a father! Mokyi Kifovich is right here in my heart!" Hereupon Kifa Mokievich would pound his chest strongly and grow quite passionate. "If he is to be treated like a dog, then it is not for me to tell them that, it is not for me to betray him." And having displayed his paternal feelings, he would leave Mokyi Kifovich to continue indulging in his strong-man antics, and turn his own attention to his favourite theme, setting himself of a sudden some problem of this kind: "Well, if an elephant were hatched from an egg, the shell of it would have to be so thick that you couldn't pierce it with a cannon-ball; one would have to invent a new form of gun." (6:243–44; Gibian, 266–67)[21]

Like the *facetia* about the student-"Latinizer," this one also has a father and son as the two main characters and it too mocks pretentiousness. The pseudo-Latinizing student of the early *facetia* feigns knowledge of the classical language in order to impress his uneducated father; he pretends to be so deeply immersed in it that he has forgotten his native tongue. In reality, however, he forms his "Latin" words by simply adding the ending "-us" to their Russian counterparts. Kifa Mokievich in *Dead Souls* pretends to be a thinker occupied with universal issues, but his "scholarly" contemplations are, it seems, merely an escape from dealing with the real problems of life, in his case bringing up his son, Mokii Kifovich. To judge by his physical prowess, the son appears to be a potential hero; without proper upbringing, however, he causes only pain and suffering to all around him. When approached by complaining servants, Kifa Mokievich admits his son's shortcomings, but he is primarily worried about *glasnost'*. (The word does not really require translation now that Gorbachev has introduced it into the international vocabulary; as can be seen, it was employed by Gogol in the same sense almost one hundred and fifty years before the Soviet leader.) The immediate purpose in incorporating this story is quite clear: the narrator, whose voice sounds especially like Gogol's, unequivocally declares in the section immediately preceding the story that with it he is responding in an allegorical manner to the accusations he anticipated from so-called patriots (accusations which, incidentally, were not long in coming) about his washing Russia's "dirty linen" in front of foreigners. In addition to unmasking and ridiculing his opponents, Gogol undoubtedly included this story to guide readers who might be influenced by this kind of "patriotism."[22]

---

21. In the most recent studies on Gogol, the parabolic nature of this story has been noted by James B. Woodward, Susanne G. Fusso, and Vladislav Krivonos. See, respectively, James B. Woodward, *Gogol's "Dead Souls"* (Princeton: Princeton University Press, 1978), 232–35; Susanne Grace Fusso, "Čičikov on Gogol: The Structure of Oppositions in *Dead Souls*" (Ph.D. diss., Yale University, 1984), 121; and V. Sh. Krivonos, *"Mertvye dushi" Gogolia i stanovlenie novoi russkoi prozy* (Voronezh: Izdatel'stvo Voronezhskogo Universiteta, 1985), 108–20.

22. Those interested in more detail concerning the allegorical planes in this short story should consult the studies mentioned in the preceding note. Of these, Vladislav Krivonos, in his reference to the "comic plane of a parable" (110), comes closest to my idea of the *facetia*.

In considering Gogol's employment of *facetiae* functioning as parables, we have so far looked only at relatively short examples that are incorporated within the texts. If, however, we step back and take a wider look at some of Gogol's separate works, we shall see that each of them can be perceived in its entirety as a *facetia* functioning as a parable.[23] As Vasilii Gippius has already observed, "At the base of *Dead Souls* as well as of *The Government Inspector* lies a wandering anecdote" or, in other words, a *facetia*.[24] Other works such as "The Nose" and "The Overcoat" could be added here, but if we consider only the two works mentioned by Gippius, we realize that each of them as a whole does indeed constitute a *facetia* functioning as a parable.

The Government Inspector is based on an amusing anecdote about mistaken identity, and yet it is definitely didactic, as its silent closing scene clearly demonstrates. At the same time, the play contains allegorical elements characteristic of the parable: in "The Denouement of *The Government Inspector*," written ten years later, Gogol unraveled an important allegorical thread, suggesting that the city is our soul, the bureaucrats are our passions, and the real government inspector is our conscience (see 4:130–33; Ehre, 188–90).

Dead Souls itself, at once amusing and moralizing, is about a swindler who in order to enrich himself purchases rosters of serfs, officially alive but actually deceased. To his readers Gogol addresses moralizing appeals such as the one near the end of the first volume: "And if any one of you is full of Christian humility in the solitude of his heart rather than for all the world to hear, in moments of communion with himself he will ponder this weighty question in the depths of his soul: 'Is there not a chip of Chichikov in me too?' he will ask." (6:245; Gibian, 268). And as for the parabolic nature of the work, it is alluded to by the writer himself. When the town fathers ask themselves: "What sort of a parable was this? What sort of a parable were these dead souls?" (6:189; Gibian, 203), it is Gogol who encourages his reader to contemplate, "What sort of a parable is this *Dead Souls*?"

Before leaving the topic of *facetiae*, let us look briefly at some

23. A comprehensive presentation of *Dead Souls* solely as a parable was made by Fusso; see her "Čičikov on Gogol," 118–21, and most recently her "*Mertvye Dushi:* Fragment, Parable, Promise," *Slavic Review* 49 (1990): 42–45.

24. Gippius, *Gogol'*, 137.

other types of *facetia* that also appear in Gogol's work. Some *facetiae* poked fun at unfaithful, resourceful wives and their simpleton-husbands, and others at hypocritical and lustful clerics. In Bracciolini's collection, one can find *facetiae* of both these sorts, tales in which wives cuckold their husbands and manage to emerge from these situations unscathed (X, LXXXIV, CXXII) and tales that ridicule sanctimonious lechers (CXLI, CXLII, CCX). In Heinrich Bebel's anthology, which dates from the early sixteenth century, these two themes are among the most popular (see, for example, bk. II, 4, 62, and 92; bk. II, 53 and 59; and bk. III, 63, respectively).[25] In Gogol's works, these two themes appear combined in "The Fair at Sorochintsy": Khivria is unfaithful to her simpleton-husband, Solopii Cherevik, with Afanasii, a priest's son. Although a combination like this is to be found in Bracciolini's collection (CCXXXVII), the immediate source that influenced Gogol, according to Gippius, was the comedy written by his own father, Vasilii Gogol, characteristically entitled "A Simpleton."[26] It is quite possible, however, that this plot utilized by Gogol *père* originated in some collections modeled after Bracciolini's, and found its intricate way to Vasilii Gogol's play, perhaps through *vertep,* which I shall discuss in the next section.

In another episode of "The Fair at Sorochintsy," Solopii Cherevik's horse is stolen by the Gypsy, who nonetheless accuses our wretched simpleton of stealing it. This episode can be traced to the *facetia* entitled "About a Dutch Thief Who Stole a Cow," the Russian adaptation of which (from the Polish version) is included in Derzhavina's collection. Derzhavina maintains that an anonymous Polish author had previously borrowed it from Johann Pauli's 1535 anthology, *Schimpf und Ernst.*[27] As with the preceding episode, however, a much closer and more plausible source is "The Dog-Sheep," another play by Gogol *père,* who, according to Nikolai Petrov, adopted this

---

25. See Heinrich Bebel, *Facetien* (Leipzig: Hiersemann, 1931).
26. Gippius, *Gogol',* 30.
27. See Derzhavina, *Fatsetsii,* 127–29 and 35. Cf. also the seventeenth-century Dutch farce *Klucht vande Koe,* on the same subject; see Johan P. Snapper, "The Seventeenth-Century Dutch Farce: Social Refractions of a Guilded Age," in *Barocker Lust-Spiegel. Studien zur Literatur des Barock. Festschrift für Blake Lee Spahr,* ed. Martin Bircher, Jörg-Ulrich Fechner, and Gerd Hillen (Amsterdam: Rodopi, 1984), 63.

motif of roguery and mistaken identity from an anecdote popular in his time in the Ukraine.[28]

In sum, Gogol exploited the *facetia* functioning as a parable throughout his writing. We have seen examples of this in the two preexisting *facetiae* that he used in his early works, the preface to the *Evenings* cycle and *The Hetman,* and the two *facetiae* of his own composition, the one in his correspondence and the other in *Dead Souls.* In addition, separate works of Gogol's such as *The Government Inspector* and *Dead Souls* can be perceived as *facetiae* endowed with a parabolic function. And, finally, Gogol also used thematic situations, such as these in "The Fair at Sorochintsy," popular in *facetiae.* Since these situations are very similar to those in his father's plays, we may infer that that is where he borrowed them from; at the same time, it should be borne in mind that Gogol *père* previously appropriated these situations either directly from *facetiae* or indirectly through *vertep,* that had been, undoubtedly, influenced by *facetia.*

Vertep

The Ukrainian puppet theater, *vertep,* has fared better in Gogol scholarship than any other Baroque form. Early in this century, Vladimir Peretts and Arsenii Kadlubovskii already pointed to the connection between Gogol's works and *vertep.*[29] Soon after, Vladimir Rozov published a detailed analysis of various *vertep* characters as the prototypes for Gogol's own.[30] Vasilii Gippius has since, in his monograph on Gogol, discussed the writer's organic closeness to the Ukrainian puppet theater, and Vsevolod Setchkarev in his study of Gogol's life and works has noted in passing some elements of *vertep.*[31] However,

28. See N. I. Petrov, *Ocherki istorii ukrainskoi literatury XIX stoletiia* (Kiev, 1884), 78–79.

29. See V. N. Peretts, "Gogol' i malorusskaia literaturnaia traditsiia," in *N. V. Gogol'. Rechi, posviashchennye ego pamiati* (St. Petersburg, 1902), 47–55, and A. P. Kadlubovskii, *Gogol' v ego otnosheniiakh k starinnoi malorusskoi literature* (Nezhin, 1911). The latter is an offprint of the speech delivered by Kadlubovskii on the occasion of the Gogol centennial celebration at Kharkov University in 1909.

30. See V. A. Rozov, "Traditsionnye tipy malorusskogo teatra XVII–XVIII vv. i iunosheskie povesti N. V. Gogolia," in *Pamiati Gogolia* (Kiev, 1911), 99–169.

31. Gippius, *Gogol',* 95; Vsevolod Setchkarev, *Gogol: His Life and Works* (New York: New York University Press, 1965), 95.

all these scholars have linked only Gogol's early writings to *vertep*. To the best of my knowledge, the connection of Gogol's later works with *vertep* was first discussed, albeit on a limited scale, in my article on the *vertep* image of the Hussar.[32] I should like here to extend my scrutiny and to examine the connection between Gogol's characters and the characters of *vertep* throughout his entire oeuvre.

The *vertep* that influenced Gogol's work was a highly popular form during the Baroque period in the Ukraine. This marionette theater originated as a dramatization of scenes from the Nativity.[33] *Vertep* performances were usually staged in a largish box built in the shape of a house, divided into two levels. The floor on both levels had slits so that a puppeteer could move the figures across either stage on wires. A *vertep* performance usually consisted of both serious and comic parts. As a rule, the serious scenes would appear on the upper level, whereas the comic episodes, which at times had no connection with the serious scenes, would appear on the lower.[34] Parallel to the *vertep,* there were also live theatrical performances of school drama on biblical subjects, which contained comic interludes that likewise might or might not be connected with the main action.[35] *Vertep,* with its serious and comic episodes, and the school drama, with its solemn

---

32. Gavriel Shapiro, "The Hussar: A Few Observations on Gogol's Characters and Their *Vertep* Prototype," *Harvard Ukrainian Studies* 9 (1985): 133–38.

33. *Vertep* is an Old Slavic word meaning a "cave" and refers in this usage to the cave near Bethlehem where, according to some apocryphal Christian sources, such as the Book of James, Jesus was born. See James Hall, *Dictionary of Subjects & Symbols in Art* (New York: Harper & Row, 1979), 219–220; also cf. "Vertep," in *Ukraïns'kyi dramatychnyi teatr,* 2 vols., ed. M. T. Ryl's'kyi (Kiev: Naukova dumka, 1967), 1:472. This word is also frequently applied to the Russian puppet theater of the same kind. Cf. Nikolai Vinogradov, "Velikorusskii vertep," *Izvestiia otdeleniia russkogo iazyka i slovesnosti Imperatorskoi Akademii Nauk* 10 (1905): 360–82. In Poland, a similar marionette theater, also based on the Nativity story, was called *szopka* (meaning a "little shed" and deriving from the German equivalent, *der Schuppen*), and in Belorussia, *betleika* (stemming from Bethlehem).

34. For detailed information on the Ukrainian and Russian *vertep,* see G. P. Galagan, "Malorusskii vertep," *Kievskaia Starina* 10 (1882): 1–38; Ievhen Markovs'kyi, *Ukraïns'kyi vertep* (Kiev: Vseukraïns'ka Akademiia Nauk, 1929); V. N. Peretts, "Kukol'nyi teatr na Rusi," in *Ezhegodnik Imperatorskikh teatrov 1894–1895 gg.,* supplement, book 1 (St. Petersburg, 1895), 85–185; Elizabeth A. Warner, *The Russian Folk Theatre* (The Hague: Mouton, 1977); and Catriona Kelly, *Petrushka. The Russian Carnival Puppet Theatre* (Cambridge: Cambridge University Press, 1990).

35. For the most recent and detailed discussion of the school theater in Poland, the Ukraine, and Russia, see L. A. Sofronova, *Poétika slavianskogo teatra* (Moscow: Nauka, 1981).

action and amusing interludes, were related through their subject matter, characters, dialogues, and costumes.[36]

Gogol was well acquainted with the *vertep*. In "Vii," for example, he refers to it directly when he describes the seminarists of the Kiev Academy who used to stage puppet-shows on the Orthodox holy days: "On holidays and ceremonial occasions the bursars and the seminarists went from house to house as mummers. Sometimes they acted a play, and then the most distinguished figure was always some theologian, almost as tall as the belfry of Kiev, who took the part of Herodias or Potiphar's wife" (2:179; Kent, 2:134). Gogol was well aware, as we see here, that *vertep* performances were based on biblical motifs from both the Old and the New Testaments; the mention of Potiphar's wife recalls the story of Joseph, while the mention of Herodias, the wife of Herod, evokes the Nativity story, from which the *vertep* itself originated. In fact, in his 1846–51 notebook, Gogol mentions "*Vertep* and the Nativity sacred puppet performances" explicitly (7:362).

Another direct reference to *vertep* appears in "The Tale of How Ivan Ivanovich Quarreled with Ivan Nikiforovich":

> All this taken together made up a very interesting spectacle for Ivan Ivanovich, while the sunbeams, catching here and there a blue or a green sleeve, a red cuff or a bit of gold brocade, or playing on the sword that looked like a spire, turned it into something extraordinary, like the show played in the villages by strolling vagrants, when a crowd of people closely packed looks at King Herod in his golden crown or at Anton leading the goat. (2:229; Kent, 2:175)

The comic episode about Anton and his she-goat to which Gogol alludes here went as follows, according to Ievhen Markovs'kyi's record of the text of Baturin *vertep*: Anton appears on stage with his she-goat, and the choir sings: "Anton is leading a goat, / Anton's goat won't go. / He beats her with the reins, / And she responds with her horns." Then a wolf suddenly emerges and seizes the goat. A Cossack in the costume of a hunter appears and kills the wolf, and Anton

---

36. On the school drama in the Ukraine and its integral part, the comic interludes, see N. I. Petrov, *Ocherki iz istorii ukrainskoi literatury XVII i XVIII vekov* (Kiev, 1911); on the relationship between the school drama and *vertep*, see 469–73.

finally walks offstage, his goat saved.[37] We see from these passages that Gogol was intimately familiar with the *vertep*, its performance techniques and its repertory.

Let us turn now to the *vertep* characters that Gogol utilized in his fiction. A scrutiny of Gogol's *vertep*-related characters reveals that it was the comic *vertep*, especially the lower level, which intricately reflected and at times travestied everyday Ukrainian life, that interested Gogol. These comic *vertep* characters can be divided into three groups: (1) military-ethnic types, for example, the Cossack, the Hussar, and the Pole; (2) nonmilitary ethnic types, such as the Jew, the Gypsy, and, to some extent, the Doctor; and (3) nonethnic types, such as the *diak* (seminarist), the shrewish and crafty woman, the simpleton— and the Devil. Despite their differences, all these *vertep* characters have in common a crude and stilted nature: each of them is identified by one or two main features. Thus, the Gypsy is primarily known as a swindler and the Hussar as a blasphemer. Sometimes *vertep* personages share certain traits that in effect serve as foils to contrast them with each other: for example, both the Cossack and the Pole are portrayed in the *vertep* as boasters, but the Cossack later demonstrates courage—so his boasting deserves credence—whereas the Pole exhibits cowardice that earns him disgrace and ridicule.

The genesis of these *vertep* characters differs from case to case. It is likely that the ethnic types specific to *vertep* in this Eastern Slavic region either originated in the Ukrainian puppet theater itself or were adopted and adapted by it from the neighboring Polish *szopka* and Belorussian *betleika*. A character such as the Doctor, on the other hand, was influenced by his colleague from the *commedia dell'arte*. And even though the nonethnic *vertep* characters, such as the seminarist, acquired many specifically Ukrainian features in their process of taking root in that country, they can be traced to their ancestors in *facetiae*, as I have shown in the preceding section.

The Cossack was the most popular of all the *vertep* characters. He was physically the largest and wore baggy red trousers and a blue jacket.[38] When Gogol described his Cossack characters, he undoubt-

---

37. Markovs'kyi, *Ukraïns'kyi vertep*, 180.
38. See ibid., 19 and table vi–9μ, and Galagan, "Malorusskii vertep," 22. We may observe that *vertep*, among other artistic forms, was indeed where Gogol would have seen Cossacks, since the actual historical Cossacks no longer existed in his day—the Zaporozhian Host had been abolished in 1775, in the reign of Catherine the Great.

edly took these exterior features of the *vertep* Cossack into account. Thus Taras Bulba, the protagonist of the tale of the same name, is portrayed as big and heavy, weighing 700 [!] pounds (see 2:52; Kent, 2:31). The attire of Gogol's Cossacks also corresponds to that of their *vertep* prototypes. In *Taras Bulba,* Gogol depicts a drunken Cossack dressed in "trousers of expensive crimson cloth" (2:62; Kent, 2:40). And a Cossack in "The Lost Letter" bears a striking resemblance to the *vertep* model: "Trousers red as fire, a full-skirted blue coat and bright-flowered girdle, a saber at his side and a pipe with a fine brass chain right down to his heels—a regular Dnieper Cossack, that's all you can say!" (1:183; Kent, 1:79).

The *vertep* Cossack devoted his life to fighting the enemies of the Orthodox faith, the Tartars, Turks, and Poles. In addition to his military pursuits, the Cossack enjoyed heavy drinking. These excerpts from a monologue of his, in which he speaks of himself in both first and third person, are full of nostalgia for his bygone brave and reckless life:

> Heigh, heigh! When I was young,
> What strength I had!
> I used to fight Poles, and my hand never got tired.
> . . . .
> The Cossack Ivan Vinogura—
> He is good-natured:
> He robs those Poles in Poland
> And squanders the money on drinks in taverns.[39]

These sentiments are echoed in Gogol's "Terrible Vengeance," where Danilo, reminiscing about his glorious military past, concludes his recollections with a lament: "Oh, those days, those days! Those days that are past! Whither have you fled, my years? Go to the cellar, boy, bring me a jug of mead! I will drink to the life of the past and to the years that have gone!" (1:266; Kent, 1:158).

The *vertep* Cossack was also fond of eating.[40] His colossal appetite is illustrated in *Taras Bulba,* in the episode when Andrii goes looking

---

39. P. O. Morozov, *Istoriia russkogo teatra do poloviny XVIII stoletiia* (St. Petersburg, 1889), 82.

40. Warner, *The Russian Folk Theatre,* 118.

in the Cossack camp for food to take with him to the besieged Polish city in order to save his beloved. He searches for buckwheat porridge in the cauldrons of his own unit and, to his astonishment, finds them empty, which leads the narrator to remark: "Superhuman powers were needed to eat all they had contained, especially as there were fewer men in their unit than in the others" (2:92; Kent, 2:65).

These features of the *vertep* Cossack—his heroic belligerence and his taste for earthly pleasures—are to be found in a number of Gogol's works set in everyday Cossack life. Yet in the same *Mirgorod* cycle, which includes the Cossack military epic *Taras Bulba,* we can already observe considerable deviation from the *vertep* Cossack figure. In "The Tale of How Ivan Ivanovich Quarreled with Ivan Nikiforovich," Ivan Nikiforovich reminds us of his *vertep* prototype only by still possessing the Cossack outfit he had prepared some twenty years earlier when he intended to join the military, by still wearing a nankeen Cossack coat on Sundays, and by his colossal "Cossack" appetite, which accounts for his obesity. Ivan Ivanovich, in his turn, demonstrates his "Cossack" nature by attacking the enemy's "fortress," the goose-pen, and by asking beggars bothersome questions, which remotely resemble the dialogue of his *vertep* prototype with a Gypsy woman.[41] Thus, in the two Ivans and the characters surrounding them, the bravery and magnanimity of the Cossack, reflected in his *vertep* image, degenerates into cowardice, egoism, and pettiness, thereby pointing to the corruption of the human soul—the *leitmotif* of Gogol's creation.[42] In Gogol's later works, Petr Petrovich Petukh (literally, the Rooster), a fleeting figure in the second volume of *Dead Souls,* is perhaps a downgraded image of the *vertep* Cossack. Although Gogol placed him in a conventionally Russian milieu, the sound of his last name suggests instead that he is a Ukrainian.[43] As in the tale of the two

41. For the latter, see Gippius, *Gogol',* 80.

42. For a discussion of this metamorphosis, see G. A. Gukovskii, *Realizm Gogolia* (Moscow and Leningrad: GIKhL, 1959), 161–64, and Jesse Zeldin, *Nikolai Gogol's Quest for Beauty* (Lawrence: Regents Press of Kansas, 1978), 28–32.

43. Compare Kurochka (literally, the Little Hen), the surname of the narrator in Gogol's early tale, "Ivan Fedorovich Shponka and His Aunt," remarked on by Nina Kaukhchishvili in her article "O khudozhestvennykh priemakh u Gogolia," *Transactions of the Association of Russian-American Scholars in the U.S.A.* 17 (1984): 66. Some scholars have linked Petukh to Storchenko, a petty Ukrainian squire from that same tale (see 1:549). Incidentally, Ukrainian proper names in the Russian environment of *Dead Souls* are not uncommon. For example, among the neighbors of Korobochka, whose name also sounds quite Ukrainian, there is a

Ivans just cited, Gogol demonstrates how far Petukh has departed from his *vertep* prototype, sharing only his gluttony.

Another *vertep* character in the group I have labeled "military-ethnic" was the Hussar, who resembled the Cossack in his weakness for boasting, in his merrymaking, and in sporting a large moustache. The *vertep* Hussar, whose ethnic origin was obscure, characteristically peppered his speech with phrases (often obscene) in various languages, such as Serbian, Polish, and Hungarian. In a typical swaggering monologue mixing these languages, the Hussar bragged that everything in sight belonged to him, including a field, a marsh, water, and gold.[44]

A character in Gogol's *The Hetman* is related to the *vertep* Hussar—he is a blasphemer and a boaster and wears a large moustache.[45] The head of the Polish uhlans, he uses a mixture of languages in his opening speech, which is full of swear-words from all of them, and then, in his dialogue with Ostranitsa, boasts about his huge moustache (see 3:279–81). Another character related to the Hussar figure appears in the fragment entitled "A Bloody Bandura Player," which some scholars believe to be a part of *The Hetman*.[46] In portraying this character, the head of the Polish Detachment, Gogol not only notes his enormous moustache but also emphasizes his linguistic heterogeneity: "Swear-words in various dialects were pouring down from under the huge moustache of the head of the Detachment" (3:302); "the chief thundered in a language to which no one could ascribe a name, from such heterogeneous elements was it composed" (3:303). Later in the story, Gogol further suggests a kinship with the *vertep* Hussar by pointing to a similar ethnic hodgepodge in his character: "It was some sort of mixture of the frontier nations. A Serbian by

certain Kharpakin (see 6:46; Gibian, 44); the name stems from the Ukrainian word *kharpak* (a "wretch").

44. See Markovs'kyi, *Ukrains'kyi vertep,* 66. For more details about this *vertep* character, see Shapiro, "The Hussar."

45. The *vertep* Hussar, as well as the characters related to him in Gogol's writings, may be linked to the Captain in the *commedia dell'arte,* who is rude to the Italian audiences and peppers his speech with his native Spanish. See A. K. Dzhivelegov, *Ital'ianskaia narodnaia komediia* (Moscow: Akademiia Nauk SSSR, 1954), 142–46, and K. M. Lea, *Italian Popular Comedy,* 2 vols. (New York: Russell & Russell, 1934), 1:41–53.

46. See 3:713. For a detailed analysis of the relationship between the different sections of *The Hetman,* see Karpuk, "N. V. Gogol's Unfinished Historical Novel 'The Hetman.' "

birth, who tempestuously uprooted everything human in himself in Hungarian drinking-bouts and robberies, a Pole by his costume and somewhat by his language" (3:304).

A certain similarity to these two early personages can be discerned in a character in *Taras Bulba*—the head of the prison guard, already present in the 1835 version of the tale. That character's most notable trait is his extraordinary ability to curse, greater than anyone else's (see 2:158; Kent, 2:120). But another feature, the huge moustache, is shared by his subordinate—the *gaiduk* (see 2:159; Kent, 2:121; see also 3:716).[47]

Some traits of the *vertep* Hussar emerge in Gogol's later characters. In his play *The Gamblers,* Gogol puts the Hussar's Hungarian curse *teremtete*—Damn it!—in the mouths of Uteshitel'nyi and Shvokhnev (cf. 3:716) and the corresponding Russian curse *chort poberi* (literally, the Devil take it!) in the mouths of Glov, Jr., and Ikharev:

Glov, Jr., reassured. Do you think I don't have the guts to spit on it all as far as that goes? Damn it, long live the hussars!
Uteshitel'nyi. Bravo! Long live the hussars! Teremtete! Champagne!
(*The Waiter brings in several bottles.*)
Glov, Jr., glass raised. Long live the hussars!
Ikharev. Long live the hussars, damn it!
Shvokhnev. Teremtete! Long live the hussars!

(5:91; Ehre, 155)[48]

That Gogol's heroes in this play use this Hungarian curse and its Russian equivalent interchangeably when speaking about hussars au-

47. By calling this character *gaiduk,* Gogol may have been referring to his Hungarian origin. The word derives from the Hungarian *hajdúk* (sing. *hajdú*). *Hajdú* originated in the early sixteenth century as a variant of *hajtó,* which meant "armed cattle drovers." Later, the word was used to refer to freebooters on the Turkish frontier who were in the service of Habsburg, Transylvanian, or Polish monarchs. See *A magyar nyelv történeti-etimológiai szótára,* 3 vols. (Budapest: Akadémiai Kiadó, 1976), s.v. "hajdú."

In Polish, the word *hajduk* historically has meant a soldier of the Hungarian infantry in the Polish army. See, for example, Witold Doroszewski, ed., *Słownik jezyka polskiego,* 11 vols. (Warsaw: Wiedza Powszechna, 1958–69), 3:8. In Ukrainian, Gogol's native language, however, *haiduk* simply means "a soldier of a court guard." See I. K. Bilodid, ed., *Slovnyk ukraïns'koï movy,* 11 vols. (Kiev: Naukova dumka, 1970–80), 2:16. For more on *gaiduk* in Gogol's oeuvre, see James B. Woodward, "The Symbolic Logic of Gogol's *The Nose,*" *Russian Literature* 7 (1979): 544–45.

48. The translation of this passage is mine, albeit based on that of Ehre.

thentically evokes the presence and speech of the Hussar in the
vertep performance. Then, too, both Uteshitel'nyi and Shvokhnev
have military backgrounds, like the *vertep* Hussar and Gogol's early
characters in *The Hetman* and *Taras Bulba.* Uteshitel'nyi says:
"Shvokhnev, I have an idea. Why not toss him in the air—the way we
used to back in the regiment?" (5:91; Ehre, 156).[49]

Another of Gogol's later characters that can be linked to the *vertep*
Hussar is Nozdrev in *Dead Souls.* The Hussar's moustache is transformed into Nozdrev's muttonchop whiskers. Just like his *vertep* prototype, Nozdrev has an inborn inclination for cursing. He uses expressions such as "the devil's horns" (literally, "bald devil"; 6:82; Gibian,
84) and "the devil take you" (6:76; Gibian, 78), and his rude language
makes Chichikov comment: " 'If you want to show off in this way, then
do it in a barracks' " (ibid.). Although not a military man, Nozdrev has
"military" connections that also link him to the *vertep* Hussar.[50] For
example, he enjoys the company of the dragoon officers (dragoons,
like hussars and uhlans, were cavalrymen) and he considers himself
one of them, referring to himself and to them by the collective "we":
"Just imagine, there was a dragoon regiment quartered three miles out
of town. Would you believe it, how many officers there were, forty no
less. . . . And when we started drinking, brother . . ." (6:65; Gibian, 65).
Moreover, to strengthen this military association, Gogol, when describing a heated argument between Chichikov and Nozdrev, likens him to
a "desperately brave lieutenant":

> "Give it to him!" Nozdrev bellowed, dashing forward with his
> cherrywood chibouk, all flushed and perspiring as if he were
> storming an unassailable fortress. "Give it to him!" he shouted
> in a voice that might have been used by some desperately
> brave lieutenant as he yelled, "Forward, lads!" when leading a
> detachment of soldiers to the assault—a lieutenant already so
> well known for his recklessness that orders had to be given to
> hold him back from the fray. (6:86; Gibian, 89)

---

49. Aleksandr Matskin, although unaware of the *vertep* connection, remarks the blatant
parody of the Hussar romance in the play. See Matskin, *Teatr moikh sovremennikov* (Moscow:
Iskusstvo, 1987), 365.

50. Cf. Woodward, *Gogol's "Dead Souls,"* 42–50.

But Nozdrev most resembles the *vertep* Hussar when he boasts about his mythical possessions: " 'Here is the boundary!' Nozdrev announced. 'Everything on this side of it is mine, and on that side too. That forest over there and everything beyond it, are all mine' " (6:74; Gibian, 76). The connection between Nozdrev and his *vertep* prototype is emphasized in this episode by such words as "field" and "water," and by the implication of a marsh (see 6:74; Gibian, 75), all of which appear in the *vertep* Hussar's monologue, described above.

Chichikov's image is also related to that of the Hussar. As James B. Woodward observes, the "counterfeit" Chichikov, that is, Chichikov as he emerges from the rumors, can be likened to the "hussar"—a schoolboy prank that bewilders its victim just as Chichikov's behavior bewilders the fathers of the town (see 6:189; Gibian, 202). When meeting the governor's daughter earlier on, at the ball, Chichikov is said to have felt himself a bit of a hussar (see 6:169; Gibian, 181). Not long after, however, any resemblance between the cautious, calculating Chichikov and a reckless hussar is dismissed (see 6:192; Gibian, 206).[51]

Still another military-ethnic *vertep* character was the Pole, who appeared on stage either in his national costume, *kontusz* ("a Polish noble's robe") and *konfederatka* ("a square-topped cap"), or in military uniform.[52] According to Rozov, the Pole originated in the Polish puppet theater, *szopka,* and underwent considerable transformation in *vertep,* taking on such unfavorable traits as vanity, boastfulness, and ostentatiousness.[53] The Pole of the *vertep* is also portrayed as cruel and cowardly. He plans to beat a peasant boy with a bunch of rods and boasts that he will defeat thirty Cossacks single-handedly, but as soon as he hears a Cossack singing offstage, he runs away.[54]

Some features of the *vertep* Pole are evident in Gogol's characterizations. For example, Gogol demonstrates the vanity and ostentatiousness of Poles when describing a spectator at Ostap Bulba's execution, "a young gentleman, or youth who looked like a gentleman in military uniform, who had put on absolutely everything he had, so that nothing was left in his lodging but a tattered shirt and an old pair of

51. See ibid., 205 and 272 n. 10.
52. Markovs'kyi, *Ukraïns'kyi vertep,* 19.
53. Rozov, "Traditsionnye tipy," 138.
54. Morozov, *Istoriia russkogo teatra,* 81–82.

boots" (2:162; Kent, 2:123). In "A Terrible Vengeance," in accordance with this *vertep* tradition, Gogol paints the Poles in unattractive colors, portraying them as debauched and boastful:

> On the frontier road the Poles had gathered at a tavern and feasted there for two days. There were not a few of the rabble. They had doubtless met for some raid: some had muskets; there was jingling of spurs and clanking of swords. The nobles made merry and boasted; they talked of their marvelous deeds; they mocked at the Orthodox Christians, calling the Ukrainian people their serfs, and insolently twirled their moustaches and sprawled on the benches. (1:264; Kent, 1:156)

In contrast to the one-sided, unfavorable portrayal of the Pole in the *vertep,* Gogol does however bestow positive features on his Polish characters in *Taras Bulba.* He shows his Poles as courageous in the battle with the Cossacks, deviating in this from the *vertep* tradition. The image of the Pole does not appear in Gogol's later works set outside of the Ukraine. The ostentatiousness characteristic of the *vertep* Pole can, however, be found in some of Gogol's later characters, such as the Person of Consequence in "The Overcoat" or Chichikov in *Dead Souls.* It is quite possible that this trait passed over to Gogol's characters from the *lubok* Pole, whose image took shape under the influence of his *vertep* counterpart.

Treatment similar to that of the *vertep* Pole awaits the *vertep* Jew in Gogol's works. The Jew, commonly portrayed as a merchant or a tavernkeeper, was presented in the *vertep* as cowardly, cunning, and greedy.[55] The Jewish religion too was ridiculed and mocked on the *vertep* stage. In some performances, the Jew was supposed to "pray," that is, to pronounce comical gibberish to amuse the audience.[56]

By and large, Gogol followed this *vertep* tradition in his portrayal of the Jew: the most striking example is the image of Iankel in *Taras Bulba.* In the drowning scene, Gogol ridicules his cowardice: "His voice failed and shook with terror" (2:79; Kent, 2:54). He describes how Iankel and other frightened Jews "hid in empty vodka barrels, in ovens, and even crept under the skirts of their wives" (2:78; Kent,

---

55. Rozov, "Traditsionnye tipy," 133.
56. Warner, *The Russian Folk Theatre,* 98.

2:54).[57] Iankel, a tavernkeeper like his *vertep* prototype, is portrayed
as a moneygrubber, and his religion is sneered at: Gogol depicts him
praying, "covered with his rather dirty blanket, and in accordance
with the rites of his religion turned to spit for the last time" (2:150;
Kent, 2:113).

As in the case of the Pole, however, Gogol deviates from the *vertep*
tradition and endows Jews with some attractive traits. He describes
Iankel overcoming his greed when he sees Taras, on whose head the
Polish authorities had placed a reward of two thousand gold pieces;
Iankel also proves himself a faithful and compassionate companion in
Taras's attempts to see his son Ostap for the last time before his
execution.[58] As Rozov maintains, some descriptions of Jewish suffering in Gogol's works were designed to arouse the reader's sympathy
for them, and this constituted an absolute departure from the *vertep*
tradition. The Russian scholar illustrates his point by quoting the
episode from *Taras Bulba* in which Gogol depicts famine victims in
the besieged Polish city—a dead young Jewish woman and her dying
baby.[59]

In *Dead Souls* Gogol reverts to the traditional *vertep* portrayal of
Jews as cunning and greedy. The Polish Jews are depicted as resource-
ful smugglers (see 6:235–36; Gibian, 257–58). This is reminiscent of
Taras Bulba saying to Iankel: "I am not good at strategy, while you
Jews have been created for it. You can cheat the very devil; you know
every dodge" (2:151; Kent, 2:114).

Another ethnic type that appeared on the *vertep* stage was the
Gypsy. As Rozov says, the Gypsy in the *szopka* was simply a juggler
and bear trainer. In *vertep,* however, the character was endowed
with distinctly unfavorable traits, appearing as a fortune-teller, swindler, and thief. He was presented as impertinent, reckless, and tem-
pestuous.[60]

57. According to Rozov, before being ridiculed in the *vertep,* the Jew was already the object
of humiliation and mockery in the old Jesuit theater and later in the Polish *szopka;* see Rozov,
"Traditsionnye tipy," 124–25.

58. Rozov, "Traditsionnye tipy," 135.

59. Ibid., 138. For a different approach to Gogol's portrayal of the Jew and the Pole, see
Felix Dreizin, "Nationalities in *Taras Bulba,*" in his *The Russian Soul and the Jew. Essays in
Literary Ethnocriticism* (Lanham, Md.: University Press of America, 1990), 9–59.

60. Rozov, "Traditsionnye tipy," 147.

Some of these stereotypical features of the *vertep* Gypsy are to be found in Gogol's "The Fair at Sorochintsy":

> There was a look spiteful, malicious, ignoble, and at the same time haughty in the gypsy's swarthy face: any man looking at him would have recognized that there were great qualities in that strange soul, though their only reward on earth would be the gallows. The mouth, completely sunken between the nose and the pointed chin and forever curved in a mocking smile, the little eyes that gleamed like fire, and the lightning flashes of intrigue and enterprise forever flitting over his face—all this seemed in keeping with the strange costume he wore. (1:121; Kent, 1:18)

In this story, the Gypsy is portrayed as a rascal who employs cunning tricks to help Gritsko outwit Solopii Cherevik. The Gypsy does not of course forgo his own profit in this enterprise. For helping Gritsko to marry Cherevik's daughter, Paraska, he obtains oxen at a very advantageous price. The tribe of Gypsies is associated with the Evil Spirit in "The Lost Letter" (see 1:185–86; Kent, 1:82); Gypsies are also mentioned as allegedly having stolen a little boy, Ivas, in "St. John's Eve" (see 1:147; Kent, 1:43). The image of the Gypsy appears only in Gogol's early stories set in the Ukraine, and is always treated along the lines of the *vertep* tradition.

Although strictly speaking not ethnic types, the Doctor and the other characters endowed with healing functions were frequently ethnically defined. Thus, in the *vertep,* a Gypsy woman is summoned to cure a Cossack of a snake bite; she tries to cast a spell on him but he recovers nonetheless. And in the Russian folk theater, we find a Frenchman who advertises his "miraculous" medical treatment as follows: "Not in vain did I acquire fame for curing not a few people. Four or five dozen are in the earth. They come to me on their own feet and leave on a wood sledge."[61]

61. See Markovs'kyi, *Ukraïns'kyi vertep,* 83–84, and V. D. Kuz'mina, *Russkii demokraticheskii teatr XVIII veka* (Moscow: Akademiia Nauk SSSR, 1958), 117. As Kuz'mina remarks, this image of the incompetent doctor can be traced to the *commedia dell'arte;* see Kuz'mina, *Russkii demokraticheskii teatr,* 90, and Dzhivelegov, *Ital'ianskaia narodnaia komediia,* 107–12. In all likelihood, Gogol acquired his firsthand familiarity with the *Dottore* of the *commedia dell'arte* at the Roman carnivals; recall his fragment "Rome," in which, during

The incompetent doctor as such does not appear in any known records of *vertep* texts, and it is noteworthy that Gogol did not include this personage in his works set in the Ukraine. An incompetent doctor with a very German-sounding name, Gibner, whose meaning no Russian will fail to recognize (*gibnut'* in Russian means "to perish"), appears in Gogol's *The Government Inspector*. The outcome of the doctor's inept treatment is apparent from Zemlianika's response to Khlestakov's inquiry about the number of patients in the hospital: "No more than ten. All the others have recovered. It's the way things are arranged, the system we have here. You may not believe it, but since I've taken over, they've been recovering like flies. A patient no sooner sets foot in the hospital than he's cured. And it's not so much our medicines as honest and efficient administration" (4:45; Ehre, 85–86).[62]

Concomitant with the treatment by an incompetent doctor is a comical medical examination. In the Russian puppet theater, the Doctor examines Petrushka, asking him numerous questions about where it hurts.[63] This episode bears a certain similarity to the doctor's examination of Kovalev in "The Nose":

> The doctor appeared immediately. Asking how long ago the trouble had occurred, he took Major Kovalev by the chin and with his thumb gave him a flip on the spot where the nose had been, making the major jerk back his head so abruptly that he knocked the back of it against the wall. The doctor said that that did not matter, and, advising him to move a little away from the wall, he told him to bend his head around first to the right, and feeling the place where the nose had been, said, "H'm!" Then he told him to turn his head around to the left

---

the carnival festivities, the Prince came across "a physician who gave him a long lecture about the contents of his intestine" (3:247).

62. On the comical effect produced by the doctor's oxymoronic name, Christian Gibner, and on the ironic meaning of the phrase, "recovering like flies," which does not go unappreciated by the Russian reader, evoking in his or her mind the saying, "Dying like flies," that is, in large numbers, see Iu. V. Mann, *Smelost' izobreteniia* (Moscow: Detskaia literatura, 1985), 62.

It is tempting to speculate that Gogol came across the name for his doctor in the Troshchinskii library, which contained several treatises on Christianity by an eighteenth-century German writer Johann Gibner; see Fedorov, *Katalog*, 2.

63. Peretts, "Kukol'nyi teatr na Rusi," 163.

side and again said "H'm!" And in conclusion he gave him
another flip with his thumb, so that Major Kovalev threw up
his head like a horse when his teeth are being looked at. (3:68;
Kent, 2:233)[64]

Unlike the Doctor, which is, as I mentioned, a character of the
commedia dell'arte, the *diak* (seminarist) appeared frequently on
the *vertep* stage. Vladimir Peretts characterizes the *diak* and his
vertep reflection in this way: "Having dropped out of school because
of outgrowing it, he is carried away by matters alien to rigorous
spiritual learning: he courts both market-women and noble ladies,
drinks heavily, sings cantos and Psalms under windows to make a
living, and lets himself in for risky undertakings."[65] Singing religious
songs for reward was indeed customary in the seventeenth- and
eighteenth-century Ukraine. This custom is reflected in the following
vertep scene between the *diak* and the peasant Klim, who rewards
him with a pig for his singing:

Diak	Gebal, Amon, and Amalek,
	And all living in Tyre,
	Let God accept your soul in the Ether.
	Also your doomed sacrifice
	We accept with veneration
	And always embrace your necks.
Klim	Same to you, Mr. Seminarist.
	(The seminarist exits.)
	It is amazing how this damned seminarist
	Performed so well that
	Tears came to my eyes.[66]

The comic effect in this *vertep* scene is achieved by showing this
ignorant peasant's exaggerated admiration for the *diak*'s senseless
pseudoreligious hodgepodge.
    A similar episode appears in Gogol's "Vii," with the seminarists

    64. On the connection of the doctor and medical examination in "The Nose" to those in the
folk theater, see V. Ia. Propp, *Problemy komizma i smekha* (Moscow: Iskusstvo, 1976), 61–62,
and Dilaktorskaia, *Fantasticheskoe,* 95–96.
    65. Peretts, "Gogol' i malorusskaia literaturnaia traditsiia," 50–51.
    66. Markovs'kyi, *Ukraïns'kyi vertep,* 105.

singing songs unfathomable by an uneducated peasant, songs which bring tears to his eyes and a reward to the singers:

> The master of the house, some old Cossack villager, would listen to them for a long time, his head propped on his hands; then he would sob bitterly and say, turning to his wife: "Wife! What the scholars are singing must be very profound. Bring them bacon and anything else that we have." And a whole bowl of dumplings was emptied into the sack; a big piece of bacon, several flat loaves, sometimes a trussed hen, would go into it, too. (2:180; Kent, 2:135)

The *diak* was also known for his amorous escapades, as Peretts observes, but he often hid his lascivious intentions behind bombastic pronouncements full of clerical terms. He generally chased maidens and widows but would not forgo an opportunity for an affair with a married woman.[67] This notorious trait of the *diak* we recognize, for example, in Khoma Brut in "Vii." It is also apparent in the twin-like characters, the priest's son Afanasii Ivanovich in "The Fair at Sorochintsy" and the sexton Osip Nikiforovich in "Christmas Eve."

An echo of the *diak* of the *vertep* can also be heard in *Dead Souls*. As we recall, an early defeat of Chichikov's was caused by his calling a colleague, an amorous rival of his, a priest's son—which he was indeed, but which he nevertheless took as an insult (see 6:236–37; Gibian, 258).

The prototype of Gogol's shrewish woman, the paramour of the *diak* or the characters related to him, can be found in the Belorussian *betleika*. The woman is unfaithful to her husband and sometimes suffers from his beatings, but in the end she always prevails over him. A related personage appears in a Ukrainian interlude: a Gypsy woman, fed up with her lazy husband, is seeking a newer, younger one.[68] An unfaithful and ill-tempered woman like this appears in

---

67. As we saw at the end of the preceding section, the image of the lecherous seminarist or priest can be traced to *facetiae*.

68. See Rozov, "Traditsionnye tipy," 160. The image of a cunning and ill-tempered woman unfaithful to her husband and yet reproaching him can be found in the whole corpus of late medieval literature; the novellas of Boccaccio come to mind first, as well as numerous Renaissance and Baroque *facetiae* modeled after Bracciolini's *Facetiarum,* as discussed in the preceding section.

Gogol's first tale of the *Evenings* cycle, "The Fair at Sorochintsy," in the image of Khivria. In the same cycle, we meet in "Christmas Eve" a somewhat similar character in Solokha, who manages to outmaneuver all her suitors. Likewise, in the tale of the Petersburg cycle, "The Nose," we come across a shrewish woman in the person of the barber's wife, and, finally, in *Dead Souls,* in the episode of amorous rivalry already mentioned, a foxy woman manages to fool both Chichikov and his colleague of priestly paternity with a third admirer, the staff-captain Shamsharev (see 6:237; Gibian, 258).

The third party of this triangle, a simpleton henpecked by his wife, is well known in the Polish *szopka.* He also appears in Ukrainian interludes, such as the second interlude to *The Comic Play* by Mitrofan Dovgalevskii, in which he is cheated by a Gypsy woman. The simpleton's gullible nature is exploited not only by his wife and other cunning females but by male characters as well. For example, in the play *Spiritual Communion of Saints Boris and Gleb,* there is a simpleton whose mare is stolen and, without his noticing, replaced with a horse's skin.[69]

Such simpletons also populate Gogol's works. The best-known example, Solopii Cherevik, appears in "The Fair at Sorochintsy." His wife Khivria cuckolds him with the priest's son; Cherevik is also cheated by the Gypsy and ends up being accused of stealing his own horse. The barber, Ivan Iakovlevich, who is henpecked by his shrewish wife, certainly represents the simpleton type in the Petersburg cycle. In *Dead Souls,* it is Mizhuev, the weak-willed husband, who is bossed around by his brother-in-law, Nozdrev, and who is seriously worried that his delayed report about the fair will anger his wife (see 6:69 and 77; Gibian, 70 and 78–79).

As Kadlubovskii points out, Gogol borrowed all three characters— the *diak,* the unfaithful and shrewish wife, and the simpleton—from his father's comedies, *Dog-Sheep* and *The Simpleton.* Kadlubovskii also maintains that Vasilii Gogol, for his part, drew inspiration for his plays from the *vertep* and the Ukrainian interludes—the form related to *vertep*—and, I may add, from other East European folk theaters, both puppet and live.[70] Gogol *fils,* adopting the three characters and

69. Rozov, "Traditsionnye tipy," 162–63.
70. See Kadlubovskii, *Gogol' v ego otnosheniiakh,* 6.

some situations from his father's plays, drew indirectly from the tradition of the East European folk theater, and in particular from *vertep.*

The Devil is usually portrayed comically in folk theater. In Polish
szopka, a schoolboy and a woman get the upper hand when they are
confronted by the Devil: the boy successfully solves the Devil's rid-
dles, and the woman beats him with a poker. In *vertep,* the Devil also
plays a comic, servile role. He is summoned by the Cossack, carries
out his orders, is mocked and beaten by him and, when he tries to get
the better of the Cossack, he always fails.[71] The Devil emerges in the
same way in Gogol's stories of the Ukrainian cycle. In "Christmas
Eve," the Devil tries to hurt Vakula as a reprisal for the painter's
disdainful depiction of him on icons, but he ends up serving as
Vakula's horse, carrying him to St. Petersburg and back. In return,
Vakula beats him and mocks him.

For all that, early on in the *Evenings* ("Ivan Fedorovich Shponka
and His Aunt") and more clearly in the works written after this cycle,
Gogol's presentation of the Devil is entirely different from the *vertep*
tradition. His Devil is no longer personified and amusing but rather
frightening and ever-present—the embodiment of *poshlost',* which
Dmitrii Merezhkovskii defined as the physiognomy of the crowd, the
aspiration to be like everyone else.[72] The only exceptions to this rule
in Gogol's later works are found in *Dead Souls,* in which images of
the Devil reminiscent of the *vertep* tradition appear in Korobochka's
dream with horns "longer than a bull's" (6:54; Gibian, 54) and in
Pliushkin's threat to his housekeeper, Mavra, that Devils will roast her
on their iron forks (see 6:127; Gibian, 133).[73]

In sum, many of Gogol's characters have features derived from
their *vertep* prototypes. This connection is easily recognizable in the
early works set in the seventeenth- and eighteenth-century Ukraine,
with Gogol by and large preserving the crudity and stiltedness of the
vertep characterizations, at times deviating only slightly from the
vertep scheme. This loyalty to the technique of the *vertep* stems, in
my view, from Gogol's desire to convey the Zeitgeist of the Baroque

71. Rozov, "Traditsionnye tipy," 122–24.

72. See D. S. Merezhkovskii, *Gogol' i chort* (Moscow: Skorpion, 1906), 4ff. On Gogol's
treatment of the Devil in his later works, see also Chizhevskii, "About Gogol's 'Overcoat,' "
319–20, and Clyman, "The Hidden Demons in Gogol' 's *Overcoat,*" 601–10.

73. See Smirnova, *Poéma Gogolia,* 45–46. I discuss this episode from *Dead Souls* further in
the next chapter.

Ukraine as reflected and preserved in the *vertep* tradition. In his later works, in contrast, features peculiar to the *vertep* are far more difficult to discern. Although he continued to draw on his native cultural heritage, Gogol deliberately toned down exaggerations and stereotypes of the *vertep* that he found inappropriate in nineteenth-century Russia. More important, however, Gogol was now striving toward a more psychological portrayal of his characters in depth, and the crude, stereotypical *vertep* images would have been out of place.

Lubok

The *lubok* was a form of primitive folk art: a broadsheet consisting of a crude print illustration, frequently accompanied by a text. The word *lubok* most likely refers to the limewood boards of which the prints were made or to the bast baskets in which the broadsheets were carried, since both were made of *lub,* the inner bark of the linden tree. The *lubok* "took root" in the Ukraine in the early seventeenth century. The Ukrainian engravers of Kiev and Lvov, such as Pamva Berynda, Leontii Zemka, and Il'ia the Monk, were strongly influenced both in style and subject matter by Western models, in particular by the Piscator Bible, the 1541 Wittenberg Bible, and the woodcuts of Albrecht Dürer; to their similar, predominantly religious pictures they added Orthodox iconographical features. A primary purpose of these engravings was to help preserve Orthodoxy and combat Catholicism and other "heresies." In the early nineteenth century when Gogol was growing up in the Ukraine, the *lubok,* like other forms, underwent secularization and was widely used for entertainment and for decorating the home. To maintain the broad appeal of the form, the *lubok* artists drew from everyday Ukrainian life, and the *lubok* therefore came to reflect specifically Ukrainian mores.[74]

Gogol's familiarity with this folk art form and with Ukrainian customs finds expression particularly in his ethnographically accurate

---

74. See P. M. Popov, *Ksylohrafichni doshky lavrs'koho muzeiu* (Kiev: Drukarnia polihrafichnoho fakul'tetu khudozhn'ioho instytutu, 1927), and V. I. Svientsits'ka, "Ukraïns'ka narodna hraviura XVII–XVIII st.," *Narodna tvorchist' ta etnohrafiia* 5 (1965): 47–50, and "Ukraïns'ka hraviura XVII st.," *Narodna tvorchist' ta etnohrafiia* 4 (1970): 37–40.

descriptions, in works set in his native land, of the interiors of Ukrainian houses, frequently decorated with *lubok*.[75] Among the most popular pictures of this kind was one of a brave, carefree Cossack. These pictures and their captions can be often traced to well-known literary works, in this case the early seventeenth-century Polish book entitled *The Life of the Cossacks. And Also Their Successful Skirmishes.* The book's title page portrays a Cossack sitting on a barrel with a mug in his hand; the verse caption, written by the Polish poet Bartłomiej Zimorowic (1597–1677), reads: "And here, noble lads, you have a sworn brother / He is sitting on a barrel as a throne."[76] The very same picture, albeit with another caption, appears in "Vii" on the wall of a cellar belonging to a *sotnik* (the leader of a detachment one-hundred strong):

> Each triangular wall was painted in various designs and had a little door in it. On one of them was depicted a Cossack sitting on a barrel, holding a mug above his head with the inscription: "I'll drink it all!" On the other, there was a bottle, flagons, and at the sides, by way of ornament, a horse upside down, a pipe, a tambourine, and the inscription: "Wine is the Cossack's comfort!" (2:194; Kent, 2:147)

I have not come across a picture that meets the description of the second painting here, but Gogol in all likelihood saw something of the kind in a Ukrainian house.

75. Gogol's links with the *lubok* have not yet been thoroughly scrutinized. A number of separate studies have appeared in the last fifteen years on Gogol's works and on *lubok*, and some place has been devoted to discussion of the relationship between them. See Iu. M. Lotman, "Khudozhestvennaia priroda russkikh narodnykh kartinok," in *Narodnaia graviura i fol'klor v Rossii XVII–XIX vv. (K 150-letiiu so dnia rozhdeniia D. A. Rovinskogo)*, ed. I. E. Danilova (Moscow: Sovetskii khudozhnik, 1976), 262; A. G. Sakovich, "Russkii nastennyi lubochnyi teatr XVIII–XIX vv.," in *Teatral'noe prostranstvo*, ed. I. E. Danilova (Moscow: Sovetskii khudozhnik, 1979), 356–57 and 371–72; and Dilaktorskaia, *Fantasticheskoe*, 101–3.

Gogol's ethnographic accuracy in portraying life in his native land has been noted repeatedly in recent studies. See, for example, V. V. Ivanov, "Ob odnoi paralleli k gogolevskomu Viiu," *Trudy po znakovym sistemam* 5 (1971): 142, and V. N. Turbin, *Geroi Gogolia* (Moscow: Prosveshchenie, 1983), 78–79. On the interior decoration of the Ukrainian house, see K. V. Sherotskii, "Zhivopisnoe ubranstvo ukrainskogo doma v ego proshlom i nastoiashchem," *Iskusstvo v Iuzhnoi Rossii* 6 (1913): 261–70 and 9–10 (1913): 415–25, and M. P. Bazhan, ed., *Istoriia ukrains'koho mystetstva*, 6 vols. (Kiev: Akademiia Nauk URSR, 1966–70), 3:230–37.

76. See Klymentii Zinoviïv, *Virshi. Prypovisti pospolyti* (Kiev: Naukova dumka, 1971), 348.

Another such picture is described in *The Hetman;* it illustrates the recklessness of a Cossack capable of squandering everything he has, down to his shirt, on drink: "Over the doors there was also hanging a small oil painting which portrayed a carefree Cossack with a barrel of vodka, with the inscription 'A Cossack, truthful soul, does not have a shirt,' which even nowadays one can find in the Ukraine" (3:294). The words in the picture are a quotation from a lengthy *vertep* monologue by the Cossack. We also find this *vertep* phrase as a caption in a very popular *lubok* picture of the Cossack Mamai, a paragon of Cossackdom—an instructive example of how the *lubok* was influenced by *vertep* (Fig. 1).[77] In his description of this picture as well as in his reference to its popularity, Gogol again proved a reliable ethnographer. Indeed, this portrayal of a Zaporozhian Cossack with this very caption was extremely popular in the eighteenth-century Ukraine.[78]

Another very popular motif in *lubok* was the heavenly ladder. It originated in the treatise *The Ladder to Paradise* by the theologian and spiritual adviser John Climacus (ca. 569–ca. 649). This influential treatise on monastic spirituality became known in Slavic lands as early as the tenth century, and miniatures with the heavenly ladder appeared in manuscripts there in the fourteenth century. These depictions retained their popularity in icons and in the *lubok* throughout the nineteenth century.[79] It is likely that the illiterate Levko in "A May Night" saw one of these very common depictions (see Fig. 2). When his beloved says: " 'But they do say there is some tree in a distant land the top of which reaches right to heaven and that God descends it on

---

77. See Petrov, *Ocherki iz istorii ukrainskoi literatury XVII i XVIII vekov,* 479 and 512. The *vertep* influence is also apparent in the picture in the unfavorable portrayal of the Pole. Depicted in a servile pose, the Pole is trying to ingratiate himself with the Cossack by offering him a drink.

78. See Mykhailo Vozniak, *Pochatky ukraïns'koï komedii (1619–1819)* (Lvov, 1920), 147, and Ie. P. Kyryliuk, ed., *Istoriia ukraïns'koï literatury,* 8 vols. (Kiev: Naukova dumka, 1967–71), 1:357.

79. See Saint John Climacus, *The Ladder of Divine Ascent,* trans. Colm Luibheid and Norman Russell (New York: Paulist Press, 1982), 68; N. P. Likhachev, *Materialy dlia istorii russkogo ikonopisaniia,* 2 vols. (St. Petersburg, 1906), 2:11 and table cccxxv, no. 628; Ilarion Svientsits'kyi, *Pochatky knyhopechatania na zemliakh Ukraïny* (Lvov: Zhovkva, 1924), table LV, fig. 139; and O. S. Popova, "Russkaia knizhnaia miniatiura XI–XV vv.," in *Drevnerusskoe iskusstvo. Rukopisnaia kniga,* 3 vols., ed., O. I. Podobedova (Moscow: Nauka, 1972–83), 3:9–74, esp. 45–47 and 70–71. The great popularity of the subject throughout the nineteenth century is attested to in Rov. 1881, 3:133–37 and 151–53.

Fig. 1.   *A Cossack Bandura-Player*

the night before Easter when He comes down to the earth,' " Levko
responds to her with great assurance: " 'No, Galya, God has a ladder
reaching from heaven right down to earth. The holy archangels put it
up before Easter Sunday, and soon as God steps on the first rung of it,
all the evil spirits fall headlong and sink in heaps down to hell' "
(1:156; Kent, 1:52).

I also discern an iconographical affinity between a description in
"Christmas Eve" and certain icons and folk pictures that depict a saint
triumphing over the Devil, who is portrayed as ridiculous and pitiful-
looking. One example is an icon of St. Nikita, one hand seizing a petty
demon by the hair and the other raised to strike him (Fig. 3).[80]
Gogol's blacksmith, Vakula, it may be recalled, painted something
similar on the wall of the chapel on the right side of the T——
church: "St. Peter on the Day of Judgment with the keys in his hand

80. For a detailed discussion of the iconography of St. Nikita flogging the Devil, see Natal'ia
Teteriatnikova, "O znachenii izobrazhenii sv. Nikity, b'iushchego besa," *Transactions of the
Association of Russian-American Scholars in the U.S.A.* 15 (1982): 3–33.

Fig. 2. *The Ladder of the Venerable John Climacus*

Fig. 3. *St. Nikita*

driving the Evil Spirit out of hell; the frightened devil was running in all directions, foreseeing his doom, while the sinners, who had been imprisoned before, were chasing him and striking him with whips, blocks of wood, and anything they could get hold of" (1:203; Kent, 1:94). In Gogol's description, as in the icon of St. Nikita, one can detect humorous elements that add a vivid, secular atmosphere; here, as is so often the case in the works of Gogol, it is impossible to draw a clear borderline between the religious and the secular.

Thus in his early works set in the Ukraine, Gogol evoked *lubok* as a reflection of the mores of the country. Such an approach to the *lubok* is not surprising, since Gogol lived in an age when *narodnost'* ("national character") in the Ukraine, Russia, and other countries was being emphasized and studied with care. Gogol showed the folk picture in wide use in the Ukraine of the seventeenth and eighteenth centuries as a source of enlightenment for uneducated people (the heavenly ladder episode from "Christmas Eve") as well as for amusement and decoration. Gogol's fascination with the *lubok* remained with him after his arrival in St. Petersburg.

The *lubok* had appeared in Russia proper in the Muscovy period in the second half of the seventeenth century. It soon became very popular and managed to survive there until the early twentieth century. In the course of its more than two-hundred-year history in Russia, the *lubok* underwent considerable change. As in the Ukraine, in the early stage of its existence it was predominantly religious in nature and was designed to help preserve Orthodoxy and combat Catholicism and other "heresies." From the early eighteenth century on, the *lubok* reflected the changes introduced in the country by Peter the Great. At that time, the Petrine government employed secular *lubok* as propaganda in favor of its reforms. The broad appeal of the *lubok* inevitably led to its "plebeianization" as well as secularization: if at its beginnings the *lubok* decorated the palaces of Russian aristocrats and even of the tsars, in the course of its development the form tended to conform to the tastes of the illiterate and semiliterate. Its mass orientation adversely affected its content and also the quality of the printing, and by Gogol's time the very term *lubok* had become derogatory.[81]

81. See Andrei Somov, "Lubochnye kartinki," in *Éntsiklopedicheskii slovar'* (St. Petersburg: F. A. Brokgauz and I. A. Efron, 1890–1907), 35:57–58; Iurii Ovsiannikov, *The Lubok. 17th–18th*

Gogol's thorough acquaintance with the Russian *lubok,* and with its mass orientation and popularity, is manifest in the well-known example from the opening passage of "The Portrait":

> Nowhere were so many people standing as before the little picture shop in Shchukin Court. The shop did indeed contain the most varied collection of curiosities: the pictures were for the most part painted in oils, covered with dark green varnish, in dark-yellow gilt frames.... To these must be added some engravings: a portrait of Khozrev-Mirza in a sheepskin cap, and portraits of generals with crooked noses in three-cornered hats.
>
> The doors of such shops are usually hung with bundles of pictures which bear witness to the native talent of the Russian. On one of them was Czarina Miliktrisa Kirbityevna, on another the city of Jerusalem, over the houses and churches of which a flood of red color was flung without stint, covering half the earth, and two Russian peasants in big gloves kneeling in prayer.... That the Russian people should gaze at the Eruslan Lazareviches, at the Gluttons and Imbibers, on Foma and Erema, did not strike him [Chartkov] as surprising: the subjects depicted were well within the grasp and comprehension of the people. (3:79–80; Kent, 2:252–53)

In this relatively short passage, Gogol enumerates a great many of the *lubok* images popular with the Russians. Himself an amateur painter, Gogol—like Chartkov—undoubtedly saw many of them in St. Peters-

---

Century Russian Broadsides (Moscow: Sovetskii khudozhnik, 1968), 5–33 (the explanatory text appears both in Russian and in English); William E. Harkins, "Lubok," in *Handbook of Russian Literature,* ed. Victor Terras (New Haven: Yale University Press, 1985), 266–67; and Jeffrey Brooks, "The Popular Lubok Prints," in his *When Russia Learned to Read* (Princeton: Princeton University Press, 1985), 62–67.

The first scholarly reference to the Russian folk picture was made in 1822 by Ivan Snegirev, who perceived it as an expression of Russian national character, worthy of study. The man who did most for the study of the form was Dmitrii Rovinskii. He published a five-volume description of his own collection, which contained over eight thousand Russian prints, supplemented by three volumes of illustrations. For an extensive bibliography on the subject, see P. N. Berkov, "Materialy dlia bibliografii literatury o russkikh narodnykh (lubochnykh) kartinkakh," *Russkii fol'klor* 2 (1957): 353–62.

burg art shops.[82] Let us examine the images listed by Gogol and see which of them are reflected in his other works and in what manner.

Lubok portrayal of Jerusalem was quite common. Indeed, Rovinskii describes numerous such depictions, which reflected the great popularity among nineteenth-century Russians of pilgrimages to the Holy Land.[83] Note how, in his passing depiction of the Jerusalem lubok, Gogol underlines the deterioration of the form, pointing out its crudity and poor artistic quality.

Also reflected in Gogol's account is the adaptation of popular tales by the lubok. He names Miliktrisa, a character from "The Tale of Bova Korolevich," a story of French chivalry especially well known in the lubok version. Miliktrisa's image appears for instance in the second picture of an eight-picture lubok (Fig. 4). Treacherous Miliktrisa, Bova's mother, is portrayed with her lover, Dodon, whom she helped to murder King Gvidon, her husband and Bova's father. Miliktrisa contemplated poisoning Bova, and in the foreground of the picture Bova Korolevich, forewarned, is standing beside the ship on which he is about to escape to the kingdom of Zenzevei.[84]

Another lubok character Gogol mentions is Eruslan Lazarevich, the protagonist of this tale of chivalry that originated in the East. Like "The Tale of Bova Korolevich," "The Tale of Eruslan Lazarevich" had been extremely popular in Russia since the seventeenth century. Rovinskii attests to this, stating in particular that a thirty-two picture lubok was published in Russia between 1810 and 1820 and ran into four editions by 1839. A separate Eruslan picture is also known, which dates from as early as the eighteenth century (Fig. 5).[85]

82. It is quite possible, however, that Gogol familiarized himself with the Russian lubok while still in the Ukraine. See V. M. Fomenko, "Rosiis'ka narodna kartynka na Ukraïni," Narodna tvorchist' ta etnohrafiia 3 (1982): 54–61.

83. See Rov. 1881, 2:315–16 and 319–45. On Russian pilgrimages to Jerusalem in the first half of the nineteenth century, see Stephen Graham, With the Russian Pilgrims in Jerusalem (London: Macmillan, 1916), and Derek Hopwood, The Russian Presence in Syria and Palestine, 1843–1914: Church and Politics in the Near East (Oxford: Clarendon Press, 1969).

84. See Rov. 1900, 192–94. There also existed separate portraits of the characters in the story. Although Rovinskii does not reproduce a separate picture of Miliktrisa, he reproduces pictures of the other characters (see ibid., XI and XII), and there is reason to believe that Miliktrisa pictures existed as well. On the lubok history of this tale, see V. D. Kuz'mina, "Skazka o Bove-koroleviche v russkikh i ukrainskikh lubochnykh izdaniiakh XVIII–nachala XIX veka," in her Rytsarskii roman na Rusi (Moscow: Nauka, 1964), 61–107.

85. See Rov. 1900, 2C3–7. For more details about the Eruslan lubok, see L. N. Pushkarev, "Povest' o Eruslane Lazareviche v russkoi lubochnoi kartinke XIX–nachala XX veka," in Russkaia literatura na rubezhe dvukh épokh (XVII–nachalo XVIII v.), ed. A. N. Robinson (Moscow: Nauka, 1971), 351–70.

Fig. 4. *Miliktrisa*

Gogol also names Foma and Erema, two other extremely popular *lubok* characters (Fig. 6). This *lubok* was based on a *facetia* known in Russia as early as the seventeenth century; there was also a song about these good-for-nothing, clumsy brothers. Gogol's familiarity

Fig. 5. *Eruslan*

Fig. 6.   *Foma and Erema, Two Brothers*

with the song is well established: he knew its Ukrainian version, which he put in the mouth of the blind bandura-player at the close of "A Terrible Vengeance" (see 1:282; Kent, 1:173).[86] Although Gogol did not employ this story about the clumsy brothers directly, we find echoes of it in his works. One example is the pair of uncles, Mitiai and Miniai, who in *Dead Souls* demonstrate great ineptitude in their unsolicited attempts to disentangle the horses of two carriages (see 6:91–92; Gibian, 93). Another example is the pair Bobchinskii and Dobchinskii from *The Government Inspector*. It was their mistaking Khlestakov for the Inspector-General, we recall, that brought disaster

86. See G. P. Georgievskii, "Pesni, sobrannye N. V. Gogolem," in *Pamiati V. A. Zhukovskogo i N. V. Gogolia,* 3 vols., ed. A. N. Veselovskii (St. Petersburg, 1907–9), 2:280–81.

on the town bureaucrats. Like his luckless, awkward folk predecessors, Bobchinskii falls down while eavesdropping so ineptly that the Mayor scolds him: "Couldn't find another place to take a flop! Sprawling out like the devil knows what!" (4:39; Ehre, 80).

Side by side with these fictional characters, the "Portrait" *lubok* list includes a number of popular historical figures, known for their diplomatic or military deeds. Khozrev-Mirza was a Persian prince who visited Russia in 1829 on a conciliatory mission soon after the Russian consulate was attacked by a Teheran mob. A print commemorating this event portrays Khozrev-Mirza and his entourage on horseback, wearing sheepskin caps, as mentioned in "The Portrait," at the gate of a stylized city, most likely St. Petersburg (Fig. 7).[87] As for military portraits, according to Rovinskii, in the first half of the nineteenth century *lubok* abounded in them.[88] From the two final editions of "The Portrait" (1835 and 1842) it is not clear which generals Gogol had in mind. In the variants of the 1835 edition, however, he named two commanders-in-chief, Counts Dibich-Zabalkanskii and Paskevich-Erivanskii (see 3:586). Ivan Dibich distinguished himself in his bold crossing into the Balkans in the Russo-Turkish war of 1828–29. Ivan Paskevich established his military reputation in the campaign of 1826–28, which resulted in the defeat of Persia and Russia's acquisition of part of Armenia, including the city of Erevan. The association of the two commanders in the rough draft of "The Portrait" (cf. 3:662) can be easily understood if we recall that the two campaigns led to the Russian conquest of Adrianople and the subsequent peace treaty there, concluded between Russia and the Ottoman Empire in 1829. A print dedicated to this Russian victory shows Dibich on horseback leading his troops (Fig. 8). The names of these two commanders are also associated with the infamous Polish campaign of 1830–31: Dibich, who headed the Russian troops sent to suppress the Polish uprising, died suddenly of cholera and was succeeded by Paskevich. A print commemorating this campaign portrays

87. Although the print calls Khozrev-Mirza the crown prince, this sixteen-year-old youth, who served as Persia's State Secretary, was in fact a son of Crown Prince Abbas-Mirza. See Ali Asgahr Shamim, *Iran dar dawrah-i saltanat-i Qajar* (Teheran: Ibn Sina, 1964), 77. I am grateful to Svat Soucek of the New York Public Library for this information. For a detailed account of Khozrev-Mirza's mission, see M. G. Rozanov, "Persidskoe posol'stvo v Rossii 1829 goda (Po bumagam grafa P. P. Sukhtelena)," *Russkii Arkhiv* 2 (1889): 209–60.

88. See Rov. 1900, 459.

Fig. 7. *His Highness the Crown Prince of Persia*

Paskevich leading his troops in an attack on the Polish capital (Fig. 9). (This Polish association perhaps prompted Gogol to delete the names of these generals in the final versions of the tale in order to avoid possible trouble with the censors.)

Thus in "The Portrait" Gogol the ethnographer demonstrates the popularity of the historical personages and events depicted in the primitive art of the *lubok*. In *Dead Souls,* Gogol also alludes to *lubok* depictions of military heroes, most notably in his description of the

Fig. 8. *The Subjugation of the City of Adrianople by Count Dibich-Zabalkanskii on August 8, 1829*

house of Sobakevich, where there are portraits of Mavrocordatos, Kolokotronis, Miaoulis, and Kanaris, the Greek leaders of the anti-Turkish revolt, its heroine Bobelina, and that of Prince Bagration as well, the hero of the Russian war against Napoleon (see 6:95; Gibian, 97).[89] The *lubok* portraits of Bagration and Bobelina were well known. Rovinskii states that an enormous number of engraved portraits of Bagration were published between 1808 and 1813 (Fig. 10).[90] *Lubok* portraits of Bobelina were also popular; she is characterized in captions as "the female of fundamental proportions" and as "the famous widow Bobelina who surpasses many men in her courage and

89. George Reavey omitted the name of Kolokotronis from his translation.
90. See Rov. 1900, 156. In this edition, however, Rovinskii reproduces a double portrait of Bagration and his famous commander Suvorov; see 152.

Fig. 9.   *The Commander-in-Chief of Russian Troops, the Prince of Warsaw, Count I. F. Paskevich-Erivanskii*

strength" (Fig. 11).[91] Gogol's emphasis on the physical heft of Bobelina, "one of whose legs seemed to be larger than the whole body of the sort of dandy that crowds our drawing-rooms nowadays" (6:95; Gibian, 97), thus corresponds well with her *lubok* iconography.

These allusions to *lubok*, like those in "The Portrait," recognize historical landmarks of the time, demonstrating the popularity of given historical events and personalities as reflected in this folk art. Here, however, Gogol's goals are more complex. The Greek leaders

91. See Rov. 1900, 159–60.

Fig. 10.   *Suvorov and Bagration*

Fig. 11. *Bobelina*

together with Bagration represent the defenders of Orthodoxy, pro-
tecting their peoples from the adherents of different faiths.[92] Their
military glory and the noble cause they defend only underscore the

92. Smirnova, *Poéma Gogolia,* 31 n. 9.

ridiculousness of Sobakevich's xenophobic, jingoistic pronouncements. The primitive, pre-Petrine attitudes he strikes are, in fact,
Slavophilism reduced *ad absurdum*.[93]

Like the *facetia* and *vertep*, *lubok* was at times satirical, poking fun
at human vices. One more *lubok* character mentioned in the "Portrait" passage, the "Glutton and Imbiber," illustrates this aspect of the
form. Rovinskii maintains that this *lubok* came to Russia from France,
where King Louis XVI was ridiculed in the guise of Rabelais's Gargantua. Rovinskii demonstrates that the Russian picture was copied
from the French original but the title and caption were changed to
avoid political overtones (Fig. 12). The accompanying Russian text
reads: "I take a bull as though a calf, a goat as though a lamb, and
chickens, hens, ducklings, geese, and piglets I consume just for fun."[94]
Gogol's gluttons are akin to their *lubok* prototype, and this is particularly true of Sobakevich, who declaims, "When there's pork, put the
whole pig on the table; when there's mutton, bring along the whole
sheep, when there's goose, the whole goose!" (6:99; Gibian, 102).

"The Portrait" *lubok* list thus reflects Russian mores of the first half
of the nineteenth century: the religiosity of the Russian people, their
fascination with fairy-tale mass literature, their interest in contemporary historical events and prominent personalities, and their apprecia-
tion of satirical views of human foibles and vices.

I should like to explore this satirical aspect of the *lubok* in more
detail, since in my view Gogol's satirizing of human weaknesses and
follies may well spring in part from the *lubok* tradition. Satire is
manifest in the well-known motif of cunning women who easily fool
simpleminded, credulous men, mainly their own husbands, as for
instance in a *lubok* entitled "An Amusing Tale About the Merchant's
Wife and the Shop-Assistant in Eight Pictures." In this tale, the merchant's wife appears as an expert in "women's wiles": whenever her

---

93. The Westernizers did not fare any better with Gogol. He derided their ideas, also in
reductio ad absurdum, in the image of Colonel Koshkarev, in volume 2 of *Dead Souls.* Gogol
mockingly presented the antagonism of these two approaches to Russian history in the characters' last names: Sobakevich derives from the Russian word *sobaka* (a "dog") and Koshkarev
from *koshka* (a "cat"). Cf. Gogol's own use of this expression: "Everyone quarrels: the nobels
among themselves like cats and dogs; the merchants among themselves like cats and dogs; the
petty bourgeoisie among themselves like cats and dogs; the peasants, if they are not forced by
some impelling force to work together, among themselves like cats and dogs" (8:304–5; Zeldin,
117).

94. Rov. 1900, 48–50.

Fig. 12. *Glutton and Imbiber*

husband comes upon her unawares with her lover, she emerges unscathed; on one occasion, she hides her lover in a closet.[95] This maneuver is echoed in Gogol's stories of the *Evenings* cycle, "The Fair at Sorochintsy" and "Christmas Eve," in which Khivria hides her lover in the rafters (1:123; Kent, 1:20) and Solokha hides hers in coalsacks (1:217–19; Kent, 1:108–9).[96]

Another *lubok* dealing with an unfaithful wife and a gullible simpleton-husband is "The Tolerant Father" (Fig. 13). The *lubok*

95. As may be recalled, this motif was popular in *facetia* (see Bracciolini, x, LXXXIV, and CCLXVII, and Bebel, bk. II, 4 and 62, and bk. III, 67; also see my discussion of this motif at the end of the *facetia* section). The *facetia* was undoubtedly one of the sources of this *lubok* motif. For the *lubok*, see Rov. 1900, 95–100.

96. It is more likely, however, that Gogol borrowed this motif directly from his father's play "A Simpleton, or the Tricks of his Wife Outwitted by a Russian Soldier," in which calm and resourceful Paraska hides her lover under the counter. See V. O. Hohol', *Prostak* (Kiev, 1910), 13. See my discussion of the issue in the closing part of the section on the *facetia*.

лоспѣшать скорай домой. неродилсали какой
натура такъ пелитъ. старикъ добръ неленй
рабатакъ носить. свою старушку небросить
и мила мнѣ будеть. рабатакъ прибудеть
і много угодить. какъ двтцать народить

Fig. 13.   *Tolerant Father*

narrative characterizes this father as the one who "was born with horns to everybody's surprise, and who marvels at his multiplying issue."[97] Precisely such a "tolerant father," if Zemlianika in *The Government Inspector* can be trusted, is Dobchinskii the cuckold, all of whose children look like Judge Liapkin-Tiapkin: "The moment this Dobchinskii leaves the house, the judge pops in to while away the time with his wife" (4:64; Ehre, 101). The image of a "tolerant father" like this can be traced to the *facetia,* whence it apparently made its way to the *lubok.*[98]

The motif of a simple-minded man who is easy prey to a variety of swindlers is found in the *lubok* "The Tale About the Thief and the Brown Cow," which can be linked to the *facetia* on the same subject and to a similar *vertep* scene (these are described in the two previous sections). In this tale, a peasant-simpleton, without knowing what he is doing, sells his cow and gives the profit to the thief.[99] This *lubok* tale, along with the *facetia* and the *vertep* scene, is echoed in the episode of "The Fair at Sorochintsy," in which the Gypsy robs Solopii Cherevik of his horse and then succeeds in getting him accused of stealing it (see 1:131–33; Kent, 1:27–30).[100]

A variation on the simpleton theme is a story about a husband who squanders money on his wife's clothes. In Russian folklore there is a comical song about a peasant who to please his foppish wife sells a horse and a cow and buys her a new *sarafan* (a tunic dress worn by Russian peasant women). All summer long the wife has a good time in her new outfit, but in winter, to teach her a lesson, the husband harnesses her to the sleigh. This song inspired a rather didactic folk picture, "A Lesson to Foolish Husbands and Their Foppish Wives" (Fig. 14). The picture succinctly illustrates the caption based on the song. At the bottom right, the picture also portrays another peasant, a

97. See Rov. 1900, 280.

98. Cf. the seventeenth-century Dutch farce *Jan Saly;* see Snapper, "The Seventeenth-Century Dutch Farce," 64. See also Bebel, bk. III, 139.

99. See Rov. 1881, 1:226–29, and Rov. 1900, 214–15. Cf. the seventeenth-century Dutch farce, *Klucht vande Koe,* on the same subject. See Snapper, "The Seventeenth-Century Dutch Farce," 63.

100. It should be recalled that this episode is based on the main situation of Vasilii Gogol's play "The Dog-Sheep," which, in its turn, was derived from the first interlude in Jakub Galiatowicz's drama. See Kadlubovskii, *Gogol' v ego otnosheniiakh,* 6, and L. Ie. Makhnovets', ed., *Davnii ukraïns'kyi humor i satyra* (Kiev: Derzhavne vydavnytstvo khudozhn'oï literatury, 1959), 43–52.

Fig. 14. *A Lesson to Foolish Husbands and Their Foppish Wives*

civil servant, and their wives watching the story unfolding; in this way, its author points to the broad moralizing appeal of this "lesson."

This *lubok* motif with the same didactic tone found expression in Gogol's writings. Chichikov, the protagonist of *Dead Souls,* speaks very disapprovingly about the balls for which bureaucrats' wives buy expensive apparel, while the bureaucrats themselves, who cannot afford such a financial burden, are compelled to take bribes:

> "May the devil take you all whoever invented these balls!" he was saying in his heart. "Why that foolish merriment? . . . They put on all their female finery! To think of it, some of them had a thousand roubles' worth of rags on them! And all squeezed out of the peasants or, worse still, at the expense of their own conscience. We know why they take bribes and play fast and loose with their conscience. To get a wife, a shawl or some frills or whatever they are called. And why do they do it? Oh, simply that some upstart Sidorovna might not say that the postmaster's wife was wearing a better dress! And that's where the thousand roubles goes!" (6:174; Gibian, 186–87)

Gogol himself voiced similar thoughts in his letter to Count Aleksandr Tolstoi, included in *Selected Passages from Correspondence with Friends* under the title "It Is Necessary to Travel through Russia." In this letter Gogol insists that one should point out to all female fashion-lovers "that they do not sin because they indulge in this vanity and waste money, but because they have made this way of life a necessity for others, that for it some woman's husband has extorted bribes from a brother official" (8:307; Zeldin, 119).

Foppishness and vice are frequently depicted in the *lubok* as going hand in hand. Thus, one picture (Fig. 15) portrays an overdressed, fortune-hunting woman with an enormously high coiffure, flirting with "the dandy of Shuia, where he used to wear a goat fur coat" (this caption is obviously making fun of provincial pretentiousness).[101] In "Nevsky Prospekt," a beauty who turns out to be a prostitute is wearing a bright expensive cloak (see 3:16; Kent, 1:213). And the provincial Kovalev from "The Nose," vainglorious and flirtatious, just like the dandy of Shuia, is always very fastidiously dressed, wearing a multitude of cornelian seals on his golden chain (see 3:54 and 56–57; Kent, 2:220 and 223).[102]

---

101. Rov. 1900, 94.

102. In *Selected Passages from Correspondence with Friends,* Gogol also characterized fashion as a "nasty, foul luxury which is the ulcer of Russia, the source of bribery, of injustice, and of all abominations among us" (8:309–10; Zeldin, 123).

Fig. 15. *A Dandy of Shuia and an Overdressed Fortune-Hunting Woman*

Fig. 16. *Pan Tryk and Khersonia*

The *lubok* contains another overdressed couple: Khersonia, who "does not sleep at nights" (an allusion to her ancient profession), and *pan* (Polish gentleman) Tryk, "who has not eaten for three days but picks his teeth" (Fig. 16).[103] This *lubok* image of *pan* Tryk, reminiscent of the *vertep* Pole, is reflected in the description of the young

103. Rov. 1900, 92–93 and 280–81. Incidentally, there is a saying in Ukrainian and Russian about pretentious people like Tryk: "A dandy, his tail in the air: at home soup without groats and outside an expensive hat." See O. I. Bilets'kyi et al., eds., *Materialy do vyvchennia istorii ukrains'koï literatury,* 5 vols. (Kiev: Radians'ka shkola, 1959–66), 1:517. This saying appears in truncated form in Gogol's *Marriage:* a matchmaker, Fekla, in her verbal skirmish with Kochkarev remarks: " 'His hat's expensive, but his purse is empty' " (5:30; Ehre, 22. In this translation, the saying is rendered in idiomatic English, but literally it reads: "A rouble-worth hat and *shchi* ["cabbage soup"] without groats). The image of Tryk reminds us of the hidalgo from *The Life of Lazarillo of Tormes* (1554): he would also be hungry for two or three days and yet "would take a toothpick (and there weren't very many of those in the house either) and go out the door, picking at what didn't have anything between them." See *The Life of Lazarillo of Tormes,* trans. Robert S. Rudder (New York: Ungar, 1973), 68.

Polish nobleman referred to in the previous section, who appears in the scene of Ostap Bulba's execution:

> In the front, close to the whiskered warriors who made up the town guard, was standing a young gentleman, or youth who looked like a gentleman in military uniform, who had put on absolutely everything he had, so that nothing was left in his lodging but a tattered shirt and an old pair of boots. Two chains with some sort of coin on them hung about his neck, one above the other. (2:162; Kent, 2:123–24)[104]

Later in the description of this scene, it is suggested that this young gentleman and others like him (and like Tryk of the *lubok*) may be going hungry much of the time:

> Often a black-eyed roguish girl would seize a cake or fruit in her little white hand and throw it into the crowd. A throng of hungry knights held out their caps to catch it, and a tall one, whose head stood out above the crowd, in a faded red coat with tarnished gold braid on it, was the first to catch one, thanks to his long fingers; he kissed the prize, pressed it to his heart, and then put it in his mouth. (2:163; Kent, 2:124)

So in this episode, too, as in the case of Tryk, poverty hides behind tarnished ostentation.[105] The same theme is present in "Nevsky Prospekt" in the image of a gentleman in a splendidly tailored frock coat; according to the narrator, he is not wealthy at all and "all his wealth lies in his coat" (3:45; Kent, 1:238).[106]

Contrasting with the themes of foppishness and ostentation, we

---

104. The *shliachtich*'s habit of wearing various chains as well as Kovalev's predilection for numerous seals and chains has its origins in *facetia:* in Bracciolini's collection there is a story about a Milanese who came with his city's embassy to Florence and who liked to show off around Florence with various chains hanging around his neck, for which habit he was proclaimed an outstanding fool; see CCLIV.

105. As I remarked in the *vertep* section, ostentatiousness is characteristic of the folk-theater image of the Pole, to which Gogol's images of Poles can be traced.

106. Deceit and pretense are basic themes in Gogol's work. For a detailed discussion of the subject, see Iu. V. Mann, "Khudozhestvennaia simvolika 'Mertvykh dush' Gogolia i mirovaia traditsiia," in his *Dialektika khudozhestvennogo obraza* (Moscow: Sovetskii pisatel', 1987), 249–51.

find the theme of avarice. I shall show later that Gogol created the character Pliushkin, who became a synonym for avarice in Russian literature, under the influence of the age-old allegory of Avarice, to which the image of Pliushkin is akin in many iconographical details. It is quite possible that another source of Gogol's Pliushkin was the image of the miser in the *lubok*. In particular, there is one *lubok* portraying two episodes in the miser's life (Fig. 17): on the right side of the picture, the Devil opens a trunk full of gold and points to it. A miser sitting nearby on a bench tries to reach for the treasure. In his hand he holds a key and a purse; there is another purse at his feet with riches pouring out of it. The left side shows the miser lying dead on the trunk, still hanging onto its lock and clutching the key. Next to him is the Devil, and on the floor a burning candle and a tightly stuffed purse. Ivan Krylov's fable "A Miser" is the text for this picture. Krylov's fable was first published in 1825, but it is not clear whether the picture appeared prior to 1835, when Gogol started working on *Dead Souls,* or later, so we cannot affirm that this picture influenced the portrayal of Pliushkin, but one can certainly speak of a thematic resemblance. Of course, this theme is also to be found in many other sources, ranging in Russian literature before Gogol from proverbs to works by Vasilii Maikov, Aleksandr Sumarokov, Vasilii Kapnist, and Krylov himself,[107] and in Western literature all the way from Phaedrus's fable "The Fox and the Dragon" to Molière's "The Miser." An echo of the *lubok* miser is to be discerned in Chartkov, the protagonist of "The Portrait." In the description of Chartkov's avarice, we also find gold, trunks, and, in a metaphorical sense, a corpse, when the writer likens the miser's heart to a corpse and the miser himself to a stony coffin:

> Gold became his passion, his ideal, his terror, his pleasure, his goal. Piles of notes grew in his boxes and, like everyone on whom this terrible lot is bestowed, he started becoming dull, inaccessible to everything but gold, a pointless miser, a dissi-

107. See, respectively, Vladimir Dal', *Poslovitsy russkogo naroda,* 2 vols. (Moscow: Khudozhestvennaia literatura, 1984), 1:78–81; Vasilii Maikov, *Izbrannye proizvedeniia* (Moscow and Leningrad: Sovetskii pisatel', 1966), 148–50; A. P. Sumarokov, *Polnoe sobranie vsekh sochinenii v stikhakh i proze,* 10 vols. (Moscow, 1781–82), 7:14–15; Vasilii Kapnist, *Izbrannye proizvedeniia* (Leningrad: Sovetskii pisatel', 1973), 271; and I. A. Krylov, *Basni* (Moscow and Leningrad: Akademiia Nauk SSSR, 1956), 203–4 and 224–26.

Fig. 17.   *A Miser*

pated collector. And he was already about to turn into one of
those strange beings, many of whom can be found in our insensi-
tive world, at whom a man full of vitality and passion looks with
horror, seeing them as stony coffins moving around, and instead of a heart a corpse. (3:110; Kent, 2:281)[108]

Connected to some extent with these images of misers is the tin-
smith, Schiller, in "Nevsky Prospekt," who wants his nose cut off so

108. Kent's rendering of this passage, inaccurate and incomplete, is given here with my
modifications.
   The circumstances of Chartkov's sudden enrichment are reminiscent of those described in
Sumarokov's parable "A Miser." In "The Portrait," as we may recall, the thousand golden pieces
fall out of the molding when the policeman holds the frame of the painting too tightly. In
Sumarokov's "Miser," the thousand golden pieces fall out of the wall, when it is cracked by a
desperate, poverty-stricken man who was preparing to hang himself. In his later miserliness and
tragic end, however, Chartkov resembles Sumarokov's other character, the miser.

that he can save the money he spends on snuff (see 3:37−38; Kent, 1:231). This association also draws our attention to the "nosological" theme, whose popularity in Gogol's works was first noted by Viktor Vinogradov.[109] Vinogradov's article discusses only the literary origins of Gogol's "nosology," however. The first scholar to link this motif to folk culture was Mikhail Bakhtin, who connected it with the farcical image of Petrushka, so popular in the Russian puppet theater.[110] Gogol's "nosological" theme can, however, be linked to the *lubok* as well as to the puppet theater, as others have recently noted.[111] The Schiller episode echoes the folk picture entitled "The Nose Grinder": in the center of the picture, an artisan is depicted grinding his client's nose (Fig. 18).[112]

The *lubok* "Pinch Your Own Nose" (Fig. 19) portrays a crane with a mask of a human face attached to its breast, and on it a large nose, which the crane holds pinched in its beak. Here the nose is only one step short of the complete independence enjoyed by the eponymous hero of Gogol's tale.[113] A complete personification of the nose, akin to that in "The Nose," can be found in the picture "The Escapades of the Nose and of the Severe Frost" (Fig. 20). The picture condemns smoking and drinking and pokes fun at the Nose, a character with an exceptionally big nose, who vainly boasts that tobacco smoke and alcohol heat will help him to withstand severe frost, personified by the other character in the picture.[114]

Gogol's play *Marriage* can also be clearly linked to a series of thematically connected *lubok* pictures. Even its subtitle, "A Competely Unlikely Incident in Two Acts" (5:5; Ehre, 1), reflects *lubok* poster style.[115] The *lubok* pictures on marriage are "A Bachelor's Arguments on Marriage," "A Conversation Between the Foolish Bridegroom and the Stupid Matchmaker," "The Bridegroom and the Match-

109. See his "Siuzhet i kompozitsiia povesti Gogolia 'Nos,' " in his *Poétika russkoi literatury* (Moscow: Nauka, 1976), 5−44.

110. See Bakhtin, "Rable i Gogol'," 488.

111. See Sakovich, "Russkii nastennyi lubochnyi teatr," 357 and 371, and Dilaktorskaia, *Fantasticheskoe,* 100−103.

112. For a discussion of this picture, see Rov. 1881, 1:442−44, and Rov. 1900, 53−54.

113. See Sakovich, "Russkii nastennyi lubochnyi teatr," 357. For the *lubok* description, see Rov. 1881, 1:481−82.

114. See Rov. 1900, 461−62, and Sakovich, "Russkii nastennyi lubochnyi teatr," 357.

115. Sakovich, "Russkii nastennyi lubochnyi teatr," 371.

Fig. 18.   *The Nose Grinder*

Fig. 19. *Pinch Your Own Nose*

maker in Buffoon Costumes," "The Register of the Ladies and Beautiful Maidens," and "The Dowry Inventory" (Figs. 21–25).[116]

In the first picture, the *lubok* bridegroom considers brides from
various ranks of society: "Whether to take from peasant stock—to
become detached from company; to take from serf stock—to be-

116. Ibid.; Rov. 1900, 101–3.

Fig. 20.   *The Escapades of the Nose and of the Severe Frost*

come an object of mockery;... to take from noble stock—a lot of
attire to be kept up..."[117] This reasoning is echoed in Gogol's play
when Podkolesin asks the matchmaker whether the suggested bride
is from a staff officer's family (see 5:13; Ehre, 6). In earlier versions,
Podkolesin inquires whether the bride is "from a staff officer's family
or from the low middle class" (5:282), or "from the official's family or
the merchant's" (5:336). An echo of this social class reasoning can
also be heard on the bride's side, in the argument between the matchmaker and the bride's aunt concerning the advantages of a merchant
or a nobleman (see 5:24; Ehre, 16–17).

    Certain features of the *lubok* suitor in the second picture of this
series recur with Podkolesin and some of his rivals: the *lubok* suitor's
remark, "I am already full of years," is pertinent to Podkolesin as well
as to Zhevakin and Iaichnitsa,[118] and like Podkolesin, who ordered a

117. Rov. 1900, 103.
118. See ibid. Thus Fekla says to Podkolesin: "For God's sake, you're already turning gray.
Soon you won't be fit for a husband's business at all" (5:14; Ehre, 7). From Zhevakin's story

Fig. 21. *A Bachelor's Arguments on Marriage*

about his dress coat it appears that he is approximately fifty years old (if we assume that he became a midshipman at the age of twenty; see 5:27; Ehre, 19); Iaichnitsa is also about fifty (see 5:22; Ehre, 15), and Anuchkin, another suitor, takes him for the bride's father (see 5:26; Ehre, 18).

Fig. 22.   *A Conversation Between the Foolish Bridegroom and the Stupid Matchmaker*

new tailcoat and boots, the *lubok* suitor fancies dressing up (see 5:9–11; Ehre, 3–5).[119]

The farcical *lubok* dialogues between the bridegroom and the

119. Rov. 1900, 103.

Fig. 23. *The Bridegroom and the Matchmaker in Buffoon Costumes*

matchmaker are echoed in this play of Gogol's. In the third picture of this series, the matchmaker offers the bridegroom a selection of brides who possess wealth, intelligence, beauty, and so on; the *lubok* bridegroom ultimately responds: "I want to have peace," reminding

Fig. 24. *The Register of the Ladies and Beautiful Maidens*

Fig. 25. *The Dowry Inventory*

us of Podkolesin, that other indecisive suitor.[120] As we may recall, Podkolesin constantly postpones seeing the bride until his enterprising crony, Kochkarev, interferes. In the end, however, Podkolesin, who is about to marry Agaf'ia Tikhonovna, changes his mind and flees the house of the bride by simply jumping out of the window.

In the next *lubok* of this marriage series, "The Register of the Ladies and Beautiful Maidens," the prospective brides are listed and each is briefly characterized. For example, "fat and simple—Afrosin'ia, to sing songs—Dar'ia, a good voice—Domna, to tell bad lies—Agaf'ia ..., white lead make-up—Avdot'ia ..., rouge—Malan'ia ..., fond of dressing up—Praskov'ia."[121] The brides' names employed in various editions of the play are actually as if taken from this register: Agaf'ia (the final version), Avdot'ia (see 5:245 and ff.), and Praskov'ia (see 5:290 and ff.). The only notable exception is Anna (see 5:267 and ff.), a name untypical of merchants, which Gogol reserved for the mayor's wife in *The Government Inspector.* Furthermore, some of the traits attributed to each *lubok* bride appear in various versions as traits of the *Marriage* bride. For example, the chief characteristic of the *lubok* Agaf'ia is lying, and this feature is to be discerned in her namesake, the *Marriage* bride, if we recall that the Russian verb for lying (*vrat'*) can also mean "to utter nonsense suddenly, without thinking,"[122] and that Agaf'ia Tikhonovna does precisely this. Egged on it is true by Kochkarev, she blurts out "Scram!" to all the suitors except Podkolesin (see 5:41; Ehre, 33). This outcry comes as a shock not only to the suitors but also to Agaf'ia Tikhonovna herself, who exclaims immediately after it: "Oh my God! What am I saying?"

The identifying trait of the *lubok* Avdot'ia (the use of white lead make-up) was not assigned to the bride in the version of the play in which she was given that name but appears, perhaps, in the final one, where the matchmaker remarks about the bride: "Sugar candy! All white and pink. Peaches and cream" (5:13; Ehre, 6). This may mean that the bride whitens her face and uses rouge, though it should not be forgotten that all these phrases were also clichés for feminine

120. Ibid., 102.
121. Ibid., 104.
122. See Dal', *Tolkovyi slovar' zhivogo velikorusskogo iazyka,* 4 vols. (St. Petersburg: Vol'f, 1880–82), 4:150. Gogol uses *sovrat'* in precisely this sense in "The Fair at Sorochintsy": " 'A man will cry out [*sovret*] everything in his sleep!' " (1:128; Kent, 1:25).

beauty in Russian folklore.[123] The name of Praskov'ia in the corresponding version of the play suits the main feature of her *lubok* namesake (dressing up): indeed, in this version the bride (mistakenly called in this particular episode Agaf'ia) likes to wear a silken dress on Sundays (5:282).

In *Marriage* there are also echoes of the *lubok* parody of the dowry inventory, the comic effect of which is frequently achieved by a disparity between the expectation based on the conventionality of an item and its unpredictably nonsensical composition or purpose, such as "two towels made of an oak log," "festive attire in which they would climb over a fence to steal hens," "a skirt with sleeves trimmed with fleas," and "a pair of pants made of linden and two sets of oak linen."[124] In the play, this disparity between expectation and reality is reflected in the misgivings of Iaichnitsa, who is afraid of being cheated and checks the actual dowry against the inventory. He suspects a disparity between the listed assets and the real ones, when he reads: " 'Carriage, two-horse sleigh with carvings, large rug, small rug.' Probably the sort that are fit for the scrap heap" (5:25; Ehre, 18).

This *lubok* dowry inventory also describes various virtues of the bride in the same parodical manner, indicating in particular that she is "comely and rosy as a monkey." At the beginning of the play, as noted above, the matchmaker tells Podkolesin about the bride's beauty and the rosiness of her cheeks. Moreover, in the matchmaker's praise of the bride in *Marriage,* as in the *lubok,* there is a certain ambiguity when Fekla shows Podkolesin that he will be happy "up to here." (See 5:13; Fekla's gesture, omitted in Ehre's translation [see Ehre, 6], reminds the Russian reader of the expression *syt po gorlo* [lit., "sated up to the throat"], that is, "fed up.") The *lubok* dowry inventory lists the bride's nose as well, indicating that "ashberry grows" in it, and the *Marriage* suitors for their part note the excessive length of Agaf'ia Tikhonovna's nose (5:34–35; Ehre, 26–27). The *lubok* dowry inventory indicates that the bride "has different eyes like a wild goat," and in Gogol's play, Kochkarev exclaims equivocally about Agaf'ia's eyes: "Dammit, what eyes!" (5:36; Ehre, 27). The bride's knowledge of French is the main concern of suitor Anuchkin;

123. At the beginning of his initial conversation with the matchmaker, Podkolesin mistakenly calls the bride Malan'ia (see 5:12; Ehre, 5); her *lubok* characteristic, as we may recall, is the use of rouge; see Rov. 1900, 104.

124. Rov. 1900, 107.

to put his mind at rest, Fekla responds: "She knows it, my dear. She knows everything, German too, and all the other languages. Whatever manners you like, she has them" (5:44; Ehre, 35). The bride's familiarity with foreign languages and manners is also seen in the parodical *lubok* dowry inventory, according to which the bride "walks in German and converses in Swedish." The abundance of these similarities show that *Marriage* undoubtedly stems from the *lubok*; as Sakovich justly affirms, beneath the realistic features of the play one can discern its *lubok* heritage.[125]

"The Nose" and *Marriage* are not the only works of Gogol's that are strongly linked to the *lubok*. The entire plots of such works as "The Coach" and *Dead Souls* can be traced to a particular *lubok*. The plot of "The Coach" echoes the picture "Reprimand to Boastful People" (Fig. 26), while that of *Dead Souls* relates to the picture "A Fable About the Nowhere Homestead."[126] As we recall, the protagonist of "The Coach," Chertokutskii, at a dinner given by the military stationed in the nearby town, decides to respond in kind and invites the officers to dine next day at his estate. Meanwhile he stays at the dinner until very late and gets drunk, and on arriving home he does not give his wife and servants the necessary instructions to prepare for the officers' visit. He wakes up just in time to realize that the officers are already nearing his estate. He orders his servants to tell them that he is not at home and meanwhile hides in the coach; the officers come and inspect the coach because Chertokutskii boasted about its exceptional qualities, and they promptly find him there. The folk picture deals with the same theme. It portrays two guests at the house gates, one of them lifting his club to drive away the dogs, while the host is closing the gate with a bolt and bar. The full title of the picture reads: "Reprimand to the Boastful People Who Invite Many to Their Houses, but Themselves as a Result Run away from Their Homesteads, or Pretend Not to Be There." The *lubok* legend rebukes a host of this kind in the name of his guests, in the following manner: "Oh, deceitful and boastful man, you kindly invited us over but did not instruct your family about dinner. And when we came over to you, we did not find you at home. We walked around your homestead, and went away. You invited us over and did not tell your people about it."[127]

125. See Sakovich, "Russkii nastennyi lubochnyi teatr," 371.
126. Rov. 1881, 1:419–20 and 417–19, respectively. Cf. Sakovich, "Russkii nastennyi lubochnyi teatr," 372.
127. Rov. 1881, 1:419–20.

Fig. 26. *Reprimand to Boastful People*

The correlation between the plot of *Dead Souls* and the picture "A Fable about the Nowhere Homestead" is equally suggestive.[128]

128. This correlation was suggested by Sakovich; see her "Russkii nastennyi lubochnyi teatr," 371.

The plot of Gogol's *poéma* is based on Chichikov's acquisition of serfs actually dead but still recorded as alive. In the *lubok,* too, trading concerns something nonexistent, fictitious, in this case an entire estate. Homeless, like Chichikov, the merchant in the *lubok* asks the middleman: "Do you know where I can find a homestead, a place to live. It is dull to live in taverns without money and it is stifling to pass nights in merchants' bathhouses."[129] In response, the middleman offers him a nonexistent homestead, directing him to the opposite end of Moscow.[130] We may recall that Chichikov's estate in Kherson province was similarly fictitious (see 6:147–52; Gibian, 156–61). At the same time, the nonexistent homestead in the *lubok* has its own "dead souls"—"Foma Mozgov, Anton Drozdov, Shelkotei Blinnik, Erila Myl'nik."[131]

Gogol's works are related to the *lubok* not only thematically but in other ways as well. Gogol also employed some *lubok* techniques, in particular the device of the turnover, which in the *lubok* was often used to striking effect. For example, in the *lubok* "Transitory Beauty of This World," when a flap in the upper part of the picture is turned down, there appear a lady and gentleman in luxurious clothes; when the flap is turned up, the couple is transformed into skeletons.[132] Another picture, which portrays two human images, is entitled "Transforming Heads." The caption under one image reads: "I am an old man and my beard is shaven; if I am turned over, I will look like a fair young woman." When the picture is turned over, the caption reads: "I look like a maiden. From the other side, however, I will look like a bald old man." The caption under the other image reads: "My face and chin are those of a lady, but I shall appear before you as an old man." When the picture is turned over, the caption reads: "In the clerical appearance, I am an old bearded man—I shall turn over and be a lady before you" (Fig. 27).[133] These examples emphasize the *memento mori* and *vanitas* themes that pervaded all Baroque culture, themes I discuss in the next chapter. The *lubok* turnover de-

129. Rov. 1881, 1:417.
130. Ibid., 1:417–18.
131. Ibid., 1:418.
132. Ibid., 3:110–12.
133. Ibid., 1:494–95. For more details about these turnover pictures in the *lubok,* see Lotman, "Khudozhestvennaia priroda russkikh narodnykh kartinok," 258–60, and Sakovich, "Russkii nastennyi lubochnyi teatr," 357–58.

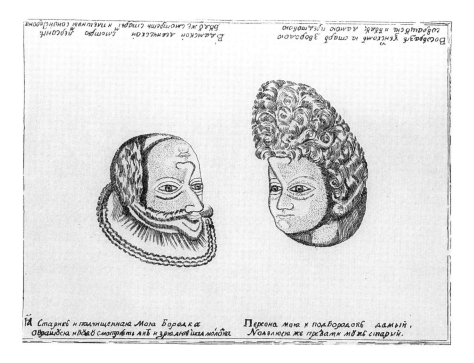

Fig. 27.   *Transforming Heads*

vice, by which flipping over a picture turns it into its opposite and creates incongruity between its images, is also akin to antithesis and oxymoron, figures of language which I discuss in the last chapter. The turnover device is typically Baroque in nature in the way it manifests the principle of *discordia concors,* at one stroke bringing together discordant phenomena such as earthly pleasures and death or the beauty of a young woman and the ugliness of an old man, in order to arrest the attention, to amaze, and to edify morally.

Something similar to this *lubok* turnover device can be discerned in a number of Gogol's works, especially in *Dead Souls,* where the serfs are actually dead but are alive in the census records, and the *poéma*'s protagonist Chichikov is perceived at one moment as a landlord and millionaire and then as a forger of banknotes, at one moment as Napoleon and then as Captain Kopeikin who fought against Napoleon. "The Nose" and *The Government Inspector* also bring to mind this particular *lubok* device: the nose of Major Kovalev either turns up baked in bread, or appears in the live person of a Civil Councilor. or reemerges between the cheeks of its original owner.[134] In Gogol's play, Khlestakov is perceived by the town fathers as a grandee and inspector-general but later turns out to be a good-for-nothing petty clerk. Such "turnovers" achieve in Gogol's works purposes somewhat similar to that of the *lubok* device: they rivet the reader's attention on the complexity and plurality of personalities and phenomena and force the reader to contemplate a different reality under the possibly deceptive surface of things and to strive for deeper understanding.[135]

Not only was Gogol clearly influenced by *lubok* in these diverse ways, but his own works may possibly in turn have influenced *lubok* itself.[136] Sobakevich's tirades in *Dead Souls* (1842) against the French and German doctors who advocate dieting, and his preference for having his fill of food as "the soul dictates" (6:98–99; Gibian, 101–2) are echoed in the 1857 *lubok* entitled "Everything Is Healthy for a Russian" (Fig. 28). The *lubok* portrays a Russian peasant and a foreign doctor at a dining table. The legend records their argument: the doctor recommends moderation in eating; the peasant, just like Sobakevich, retorts, "Our people are sturdy and quite able as far as food is concerned. They possess strength because they know how to have their fill of food."[137]

Another example is the motif of the capacity of fashionable female apparel to float like a balloon. The first balloon ascent in Russia was undertaken in May of 1804 in Moscow and was eternalized in the folk

134. For a more detailed discussion of this subject in "The Nose," see Dilaktorskaia, *Fantasticheskoe*, 101–2.

135. Cf. Gogol's invective directed at the readers of *Dead Souls:* "You are afraid of the deeply probing eye; you are fearful of looking too profoundly into anything yourselves; you prefer to let your unthinking eyes stray over the surface of everything" (6:245; Gibian, 268).

136. If the publication of a Gogol work precedes that of the *lubok,* we may with reasonable certainty assume that it was the source for the *lubok* imitation, though there is always the possibility that the *lubok* on a given topic may have existed in an earlier version overlooked by Rovinskii and his successors. Already E. P. Ivanov supposed that in one of the pictures included in his album, "Necessity Is the Mother of Invention" (1858), the *lubok* types of the dandy and waiter took shape under the influence of Gogol's *The Government Inspector.* See his *Russkii narodnyi lubok* (n.p.: IZOGIZ, 1937), 44 and fig. 54.

137. See Pierre-Louis Duchartre, *L'imagerie populaire russe et les livrets gravés, 1629–1885* (Paris: Gründ, 1961), fig. 117.

РУСКОЮ ВСЕ ЗДАРОВО

Fig. 28.   *Everything Is Healthy for a Russian*

picture (Fig. 29). By comparing female attire to a balloon, Gogol reflected early nineteenth-century fascination with this novelty. In "Nevsky Prospekt" (1835), Gogol's narrator exclaims: "And the ladies' sleeves that you meet on Nevsky Prospekt! Ah, how exquisite! They are like two balloons and the lady might suddenly float up in the air, were she not held down by the gentleman accompanying her" (3:13; Kent, 1:210).[138]

We find a similar portrayal of women's attire in *Dead Souls,* where the narrator says of the women at the ball: "Their light head-pieces just managed to cling to their ears and seemed to say: 'Look out, I

138. In the 1820s and 1830s, a mechanic, Ivan Semenov, frequently entertained people during public festivals by flying in a balloon. See Alla Sytova, *The Lubok* (Leningrad: Aurora Art Publishers, 1984), fig. 71 and the comments on it.

Fig. 29.   *The Aerial Journeys of Madame Garnerin with a Russian Lady in Moscow, May 8 and 15, 1804*

shall fly off. A pity I can't take the beauty with me!' " (6:163; Gibian, 173). An echo of this motif appears in an 1858 *lubok* (Fig. 30). The picture portrays two merchants strolling in the park and observing an unusual sight: the wind has inflated the crinoline of a fashion-loving lady and raised her up in the air, while her dandy-admirer holds onto

ГРИНОЛИНѢ ИЛИ СРЕДСТВО ЗАМѢНИТЬ ИМѢ ПРИ СЛУЧАѢ ВОЗДУШНЫЙ ШАРѢ.

Fig. 30.   *A Crinoline or the Means of Occasionally Substituting It for a Balloon*

her legs in a desperate attempt to bring her down to earth. The mocking inscription sounds very reminiscent of Gogol: "A Crinoline or the Means of Occasionally Substituting It for a Balloon."[139]

139. See Ivanov, *Russkii narodnyi lubok,* 42 and fig. 53.

In sum, we have seen that Gogol, a fairly accurate ethnographer, as far as he goes, evokes the *lubok* as a particular reflection of Ukrainian and Russian mores. He also draws on satirical aspects of the *lubok* to ridicule human weaknesses and follies, adopting and adapting *lubok* situations and incorporating them in his thematically related works, such as "The Nose" and *Marriage.* Further, specific *lubok* pictures appear closely related to the core of the plot in "The Coach" and *Dead Souls.* Gogol appropriates *lubok* techniques, such as the turn-over, to arrest the reader's attention and drive home his edifying messages. Finally, Gogol's oeuvre in the end influenced the *lubok* itself.

Emblem

In Greek, εμβλημα originally meant "insertion" and "grafting." Adopted into Latin, the word stood for "inlay work," particularly "a mosaic." When Andrea Alciati composed his book of epigrams in 1531, he entitled it *Emblemata,* most probably to indicate that the epigrams collected there belonged together as pieces in a mosaic. Initially, *Emblemata* was intended for the learned reader and contained no illustrations. Editors later added illustrations in order to make Alciati's epigrams intelligible to a wider audience. By the mid-sixteenth century, "emblem" had come to mean not a mosaic of epigrams but an individual entry composed of verbal and pictorial elements.[140]

As a rule an emblem consisted of three parts: *inscriptio, pictura,* and *subscriptio.* The *inscriptio,* a short motto to introduce the emblem, was placed above the *pictura,* which depicted objects, persons, or events, real or imaginary. The *subscriptio*—a prose or verse citation—was placed beneath the *pictura.* The *inscriptio* and *subscriptio* together were called the *scriptura.* The *scriptura* and *pictura* interacted to convey an idea, sentiment, or concept, mainly for moralizing and for intellectual stimulation.

140. See Hessel Miedema, "The Term *Emblema* in Alciati," *Journal of the Warburg and Courtauld Institutes* 31 (1968): 234–50. For a detailed discussion of the emblem and for a basic bibliography on the subject, see Peter M. Daly, *Emblem Theory* (Nendeln, Lichtenstein: KTO Press, 1979).

Emblematic imagery was not confined to collections of emblems, called emblem books, but could be found throughout Baroque literature as *verbal* emblems—forms in which the words alone functioned as both *pictura* and *scriptura*.[141]

A contemporary form related to the emblem was the *impresa,* a badge attached to a shield, hat, or piece of armor.[142] It consisted only of *inscriptio* and *pictura.* Unlike the emblem, the *impresa,* worn by the ecclesiastic and secular elite, usually signified a personal aim or ambition.

Imagini—allegorical figures, usually human in appearance, with symbolic attributes—constituted another form related to the emblem. As a rule, each picture was accompanied by a short motto and explanatory text. Unlike the *scriptura* in the emblem proper, this text was devoted solely to describing the meaning of various symbols.[143] The first anthology of *imagini,* called *Iconologia,* was compiled by Cesare Ripa in 1593. *Iconologia* was published in considerably amplified editions in the course of three centuries in a variety of languages and under different titles and served as the model for similar collections.

Conceived in Italy, the emblem and related forms spread quickly throughout Western Europe and the Slavic countries, including the Ukraine, where they became very popular in the seventeenth and eighteenth centuries. The emblem was an important part of the literary legacy of the seventeenth-century writer, Simeon Polotskii, a graduate of the Kiev Collegium, and survived in the Ukraine up to the end of the eighteenth century in the writings of Grigorii Skovoroda.[144]

141. For a detailed discussion of the verbal emblem (called there the word-emblem), see Peter M. Daly, *Literature in the Light of the Emblem* (Toronto: University of Toronto Press, 1979).

142. For a discussion of the *impresa,* see Robert Klein, "The Theory of Figurative Expression in Italian Treatises on the *Impresa,*" in his *Form and Meaning* (New York: Viking Press, 1979), 3–24. On the relationship of the *impresa* to the emblem, see Daly, *Literature in the Light of the Emblem,* 21–25.

143. Arthur O. Lewis, Jr., "Emblem Books and English Drama: A Preliminary Survey, 1581–1600" (Ph.D. diss., Penn State College, 1951), 23. On the relationships between emblem, *impresa,* and *imagino,* see Elbert N. S. Thompson, "Emblem Books," in his *Literary Bypaths of the Renaissance* (New Haven: Yale University Press, 1924), 29–67.

144. See, respectively, Anthony R. Hippisley, "The Emblem in the Writings of Simeon Polotskij," *Slavic and East European Journal* 15 (1971): 167–83; Dmitrii Chizhevskii, *Filosofiia H. S. Skovorody* (Warsaw, 1934); and I. V. Ivan'o, *Filosofiia i styl' myslennia H. Skovorody* (Kiev: Naukova dumka, 1983).

The emblem appeared in Russia proper in the second half of the seventeenth century, imported from the Ukraine by writers who, like Simeon Polotskii, received their education at the Kiev Collegium. Emblem literature also entered Russia directly from the West. During his Grand Embassy (1697–98), Peter the Great became fascinated by emblems and ordered the publication of an emblem book. The book, based mainly on the collections by Daniel de La Feuille, with the addition of captions in Cyrillic, came out in Amsterdam in 1705 under the title *Symbola et Emblemata.* It eventually became the source of subsequent emblem literature in Russia.[145]

In all likelihood, Gogol's familiarity with the emblem dated from his school years in the Ukraine.[146] He may very well have come across the definition of the emblem in the multilingual emblem book, *Selected Emblems and Symbols,* in the extensive Troshchinskii library.[147] This book, published by Nestor Maksimovich-Ambodik in 1788, contains in the introductory comments the following definition of the emblem: "An emblem is an allusive image or an intricate picture that displays some natural substance, animate creature, or particular story, with a special caption consisting of a brief apothegm."[148]

Gogol could have also encountered a discussion of the emblem in Aleksandr Nikol'skii's *Foundations of Russian Philology,* which was used as a literature textbook in Nezhin Gymnasium. Nikol'skii noted: "Captions are often allegorical, and in this case they are always accompanied by hieroglyphs or visual signs. The Moscow Zaikonospassky Academy has an inscription with the depiction of a candle burning in fog, and the words: 'Non mihi, sed aliis,' i.e., Not for me but for others."[149] Although he did not explicitly use the word, Nikol'skii here described what was in fact an emblem in terms similar to those

145. Fedor Buslaev, "Illiustratsiia stikhotvorenii Derzhavina," in his *Moi dosugi,* 2 vols. (Moscow, 1886), 2:99. See also A. I. Markushevich, "Ob istochnikakh amsterdamskogo izdaniia 'Simvoly i emblemata' (1705 g.)," *Kniga* 8 (1963): 279–90, and Anthony R. Hippisley, "K voprosu ob istochnikakh amsterdamskogo izdaniia 'Simvoly i emblemata' ('Symbola et Emblemata')," *Kniga* 59 (1989): 60–79.

146. For an earlier discussion, see Gavriel Shapiro, "The Emblem and Its Reflection in the Works of Nikolai Gogol," *Comparative Literature* 42 (1990): 208–26. In "The Emblem in Russian Literature," *Russian Literature* 16 (1984): 289–304, Hippisley examined this subject on a limited scale. His survey includes several examples from Gogol's works.

147. See Fedorov, *Katalog,* 183.

148. Nestor Maksimovich-Ambodik, *Emvlemy i simvoly izbrannye* (St. Petersburg, 1788), vi.

149. Nikol'skii, *Osnovaniia,* 2:116.

of Maksimovich-Ambodik: a construction in which words and "visual signs," that is *scriptura* and *pictura,* interact.

Gogol's uses the term "emblem" in a somewhat looser sense in a letter to his mother on December 18, 1835: "On this occasion, I have enclosed some seeds of vegetables—incidentally, this is appropriate for the New Year. It is an emblem and also a wish that you may sow a lot of good things at the beginning of the year and at the same time lead a joyful and happy life, which will last from now forevermore" (10:379).

That Gogol was not only familiar with the emblem as an established form but was aware of its historical transformation—and its degeneration into cliché—is apparent in *Dead Souls,* where he succinctly demonstrates the changes the form had undergone. Thus Chichikov, when introducing himself to new characters, likens his life over and over again—at least eight times—to a ship in a stormy sea and even to a shipwreck.[150] On becoming acquainted with Tentetnikov, Chichikov "compared his life to a ship at sea driven on by treacherous winds" (7:27; Gibian, 294). On another occasion, he says: "What is this ill-luck, tell me, what is it that weighs me down? Each time I am just on the point of plucking the fruit and, so to speak, putting my hand on it, suddenly a storm bursts or a submerged rock comes in the way, and the whole of my ship breaks into splinters" (7:111; Gibian, 390).[151]

Emblems depicting life as a stormy sea and human destiny as a ship appear frequently in emblem books.[152] *Selected Emblems and Symbols* contains an emblem titled "The Ship Cast into Safety by a Storm" (Fig. 31). The caption to this emblem reads: "The end crowns the deed."[153] This emblem is often to be found in Baroque writing too. In

150. Cf. Proffer, *The Simile and Gogol's "Dead Souls"* (The Hague: Mouton, 1967), 61.

151. In his correspondence, Gogol employed the same emblematic image to describe his own destiny. In his letter to Mikhail Pogodin of March 30, 1837, Gogol wrote: "I am homeless, the waves beat and rock me; and I can rely only on the anchor of pride which higher powers have placed in my breast" (11:92; Proffer, 69).

152. For depictions of such emblems, see Arthur Henkel and Albrecht Schöne, *Emblemata, Handbuch zur Sinnbildkunst des XVI. und XVII. Jahrhunderts* (Stuttgart: J. B. Metzlersche Verlagsbuchhandlung, 1967), 1464–68.

153. See Maksimovich-Ambodik, *Emvlemy i simvoly,* 27. Since Maksimovich-Ambodik's English captions are often awkward compared to those in the other languages of the collection—Russian, Latin, French, and German—I have translated the Russian captions into English myself.

We may observe that this emblem, in fact, depicts what Chichikov so much desires but fails to achieve.

Fig. 31. *The Ship Cast into Safety by a Storm*

English literature, it appears, for example, in Sir Henry Godyere's *The Mirrour of Maiestie;* in Polish literature, in Daniel Naborowski's poem "A Thought"; and in Russian literature, in Simeon Polotskii's "Sermon on the Thirty-Fourth Week After the Descent of the Holy Spirit."[154]

This shipwreck emblem, repeated so frequently throughout *Dead Souls,* is clearly Chichikov's *impresa,* which the protagonist has invented for himself and uses to gain the sympathy of the other characters. Gogol's originality lies in thus employing this well-known emblem as an *impresa* for the protagonist's self-characterization and, further, in his use of this *impresa* emblem for the purpose of irony. Although the other characters take Chichikov's *impresa* at face value, the reader sees through his deceit, especially in the last chapter of the first volume, which describes Chichikov's life before the events related in the *poéma;* Chichikov emerges as a rogue who was pun-

154. See, respectively, Rosemary Freeman, *English Emblem Books* (London: Chatto & Windus, 1948), 32–33; Jadwiga Sokołowska and Kazimiera Żukowska, eds., *Poeci polskiego baroku,* 2 vols. (Warsaw: Państwowy Instytut Wydawniczy, 1965), 1:188 and 848; and T. V. Chartoritskaia, comp., *Krasnorechie Drevnei Rusi (XI–XVII vv.)* (Moscow: Sovetskaia Rossiia, 1987), 367. On the ship-in-a-stormy-sea image in Russian Baroque literature, see A. S. Eleonskaia, *Russkaia oratorskaia proza v literaturnom protsesse XVII veka* (Moscow: Nauka, 1990), 79–81.

ished according to his just deserts and not as the unjustly persecuted victim he would like to appear. However, by repeatedly putting this verbal emblem in Chichikov's mouth, Gogol makes it, and demonstrates how the emblem as such becomes, banal and ultimately cliched. The banalization of the emblem that serves as Chichikov's *impresa* builds up the reader's perception of his *poshlost'*.

A particularly striking emblem appears in a crucial episode of *Taras Bulba,* in which Taras reacts to the Cossack leadership's signing a peace agreement with the Poles:

> When the regimental clerk presented the terms of the peace, and the leader signed it, Taras took off his trusty blade, a costly Turkish saber of the finest steel, broke it in two like a stick, and flung the parts far away in different directions, saying: "Farewell! As the two parts of that sword cannot be united and make up one blade again, so shall we comrades never meet again in this world! Remember my farewell words . . ." (At this word his voice rose higher, gathering uncanny strength, and all were confounded at his prophetic words.) "You will remember me at your dying hour! Do you think you have bought peace and tranquillity; do you think you are going to live at ease? A strange sort of ease you will enjoy: they will flay the skin from your head, leader, they will stuff it with chaff, and for years it will be seen at the fairs! Nor will you Cossacks keep your heads! You will perish in damp dungeons, buried within stone walls, if you are not all boiled alive in cauldrons like sheep!
>
> "And you, lads!" he went on, turning to his followers: "who among you wants to die a genuine death, not on the stove or on a woman's bed, or drunk under a tavern fence like any carcass, but an honest Cossack death." (2:167–68; Kent, 2:128)

The reader is held fast by the extraordinary act Taras Bulba performs to prove his point. Gogol demonstrates his hero's unusual strength by stressing the contrast between the high quality of Taras's sword and his ease in breaking it. Taras's act of breaking the sword illustrates his point graphically; his subsequent speech provides the explanation for the act. Serving as *pictura* and *scriptura,* these together constitute a distinct example of the verbal emblem.

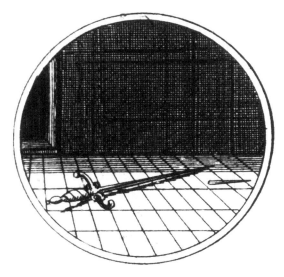

Fig. 32. *A Broken Sword*

We can trace this act of Taras Bulba to the emblem "A Broken Sword" in *Selected Emblems and Symbols,* the caption of which reads "Cannot be soldered together. The loss cannot be made good" (Fig. 32).[155] Commenting on this emblem in his introduction, Maksimovich-Ambodik says, "A broken sword signifies the loss of a good opinion, name, honor, and glory"—all of which Taras's speech, warning the Cossacks that in signing the peace treaty with the Poles they will lose their lives and freedom, that only by fighting the enemy can they preserve their honor and independence, certainly vehemently expresses.[156]

By incorporating this emblem in a tale set in a Ukraine steeped in Baroque culture, Gogol skillfully recreates the atmosphere of the time. Taras Bulba's use of the emblem in his speech to the Cossacks was well founded, for the emblem then had a powerful impact and was a most effective way of influencing opinions.

Although Gogol may have familiarized himself with *Selected Emblems and Symbols* in Troshchinskii's library, he could have become acquainted with the book from other sources, given its great popularity among the gentry of early nineteenth-century Russia, as Ivan

155. Maksimovich-Ambodik, *Emvlemy i simvoly,* 59.
156. Ibid., lv.

Turgenev's *Nest of Gentlefolk* attests.[157] Gogol included the sword emblem only in the 1842 edition of *Taras Bulba*, which he wrote while abroad, and therefore we cannot dismiss the possibility that he found it during that time in one of the Western emblem books.[158]

Whereas the sword episode in *Taras Bulba* makes use of one specific emblem, the whole cycle of *Evenings on a Farm near Dikanka* is pervaded both thematically and structurally by a complex of emblems that share a common motif: the bee.

In emblematic literature, a bee frequently symbolizes the labor of a writer or artist. As Maksimovich-Ambodik explains in his introduction to *Selected Emblems and Symbols*, it is synonymous with artistic craftsmanship.[159] The association of the bee with literary activity goes back to the ancient Greeks, who believed that those who possessed supernatural insight, particularly bards, had been fed by bees during their infancy, which had endowed them, the Greeks believed, with wisdom and eloquence. Moreover, the Greeks viewed the Muses—the patrons of Divine Song—as akin to bees.[160] Among the Roman writers, Lucretius, Horace, and Seneca all compare the act of writing to the activities of bees, emphasizing the processes of gathering and metamorphosis.[161]

Bee symbolism was already prominent in Russian literature before the Baroque period. Maksim the Greek (ca. 1470–1556) describes his own literary fastidiousness: "And I wanted to become like bees that fly over all the flowers but do not collect honey from every one." Also adapting this imagery, Baroque writers sometimes compared collections of their works to a honeycomb—the title Aleksei Korobovskii gave his anthology of epigrams in 1695.[162]

157. See I. S. Turgenev, *Polnoe sobranie sochinenii i pisem*, 28 vols. (Moscow and Leningrad: Akademiia Nauk SSSR, 1960–68), 7:161 and 506–7. Dmitrii Chizhevskii and Mario Praz both note the reference to this emblem book in Turgenev's novel: see Chizhevskii, "Emblematische Literatur bei den Slaven," *Archiv für das Studium der neueren Sprachen und Literaturen* 201 (1964): 175–76, and Praz, *Studies in Seventeenth-Century Imagery* (Rome: Storia e letteratura, 1964), 231.

158. See Henkel and Schöne, *Emblemata*, 1496–99.

159. Maksimovich-Ambodik, *Emvlemy i simvoly*, xlv.

160. Arthur Bernard Cook, "The Bee in Greek Mythology," *Journal of Hellenic Studies* 15 (1985): 7–8.

161. See, e.g., Thomas M. Greene, *The Light of Troy: Imitation and Discovery in Renaissance Poetry* (New Haven: Yale University Press, 1982), 73–74, and Jürgen von Stackelberg, "Das Bienengleichnis," *Romanische Forschungen* 68 (1956): 271–93.

162. D. M. Bulanin, "O nekotorykh printsipakh raboty drevnerusskikh pisatelei," *Trudy Otdela Drevnerusskoi Literatury* 37 (1983): 8 and 13.

Fig. 33. *A Beehive*

Fig. 34. *A Beehive*

Fig. 35. *A Beehive*

In the light of this tradition, it is not surprising that in his *Evenings* Gogol cast a publisher in the role of a beekeeper. Moreover, this character's mention of honey and a honeycomb in the preface to this cycle can be taken as Gogol's coded reference to his own craft of writing and to the cycle as a whole.[163] The beekeeper, Rudyi Panko, says, "and you will find no better honey in any village, I will take my oath on that. Just imagine: when you bring in the comb, the scent in the room is something beyond comprehension; it is as clear as a tear or a costly crystal such as you see in earrings" (1:107; Kent, 1:7).

This beehive imagery takes on still more resonance when we look at the captions of a few beehive emblems that appear in *Selected Emblems and Symbols.* Two emblems emphasize the secret nature of a beehive, one reading, "The secret of this is open to no one," the other, similarly, "Not open to anyone. Nobody can see what is inside" (Figs. 33 and 34).[164] The mysteriousness of the beehive expressed in these two captions can be linked to the atmosphere of mystery pervading the *Evenings.*

163. St. Nicholas, Gogol's patron saint, was, according to folk beliefs, a patron of beekeeping. See B. A. Uspenskii, *Filologicheskie razyskaniia v oblasti slavianskikh drevnostei* (Moscow: Izdatel'stvo MGU, 1982), 84–85. It is thus quite possible that by making Rudyi Panko a beekeeper, Gogol in fact encoded his own name. See Shapiro, "Nikolai Gogol' i gordyi gogol'," 148–49.

164. Maksimovich-Ambodik, *Emvlemy i simvoly,* 119 and 89.

Another beehive emblem relevant to the *Evenings* cycle bears a caption "Bitterness from sweetness. Bitter from sweet" (Fig. 35).[165] This emblem—which includes a Cupid—epitomizes the theme of many stories in the collection in which the happiness and joy of love and friendship are transformed into bitterness and sadness. The first story of the cycle, "The Fair at Sorochintsy," for example, ends with the change from joy to sorrow and emptiness:

> Is it not thus that joy, lovely and fleeting guest, flies from us? In vain the last solitary note tries to express gaiety. In its own echo it hears melancholy and emptiness and listens to it, bewildered. Is it not thus that those who have been playful friends in free and stormy youth, one by one stray, lost, about the world and leave their old comrade lonely and forlorn at last? Sad is the lot of one left behind! Heavy and sorrowful is his heart and nothing can help him! (1:136; Kent, 1:32–33)

A similar change of mood occurs in "The Tale of How Ivan Ivanovich Quarreled with Ivan Nikiforovich," a story that Gogol eventually included in the cycle *Mirgorod*, although it originally appeared in the almanac *The Housewarming* with the subtitle "An Unpublished True Story by the Beekeeper Rudyi Panko." The narration opens with a description, amusing in its exaggerated enthusiasm, of Ivan Ivanovich's winter overcoat but closes with the somber exclamation: "It is a dreary world, gentlemen" (2:276; Kent, 2:214).[166]

Gogol's ingenuity and originality in revivifying hackneyed emblems—such as the shipwreck image—is especially evident in his adaptation of one of the most popular emblems: a moth (or a fly) flying into a candle flame. The title that generally accompanies this image— "Brevis et Damnosa Voluptas"—indicates its didactic significance, which the relevant emblem in *Selected Emblems and Symbols* expresses as "Harmful caprice. My pleasure costs me my life" (Fig. 36).[167]

165. Ibid., 205. See also Henkel and Schöne, *Emblemata,* 921–27. The subject matter of this emblem can be traced to the Alciati collection; see Andreas Alciatus, *Index Emblematicus,* 2 vols., ed. Peter M. Daly, Virginia W. Callahan, and Simon H. Cuttler (Toronto: University of Toronto Press, 1985), emblem 112.

166. This reversal of mood, typical for Gogol's art, was noted by John Mersereau; see John Mersereau, Jr., "Gogol's *Evenings on a Farm near Dikanka,*" in his *Russian Romantic Fiction* (Ann Arbor: Ardis, 1983), 167.

167. See Henkel and Schöne, *Emblemata,* 910–12, and Maksimovich-Ambodik, *Emvlemy i simvoly,* 79.

Fig. 36. *Flies Flying near a Burning Candle*

By Gogol's time, this emblem had already become enervated, a cliché much favored by Romantic literature: Lermontov, for example, employs it in his early poem, *Khadzhi Abrek* (1834), in which Leila's death at the hand of the protagonist is foreshadowed by her being likened as she dances before him to a moth whirling in the rays of a setting sun.[168] Gogol utilizes the same emblem in his fragment "The Maidens Chablov," most probably written in 1839 (see 3:723), in which he notes that the maidens "pondered over their own existence, while a thoughtless and fainthearted one would indiscriminately throw herself into the light like a moth into a candle" (3:335). Gogol's treatment of the motif here is markedly different from that of the Romantic school exemplified by Lermontov's poem. With its strong didactic overtones, it is akin to the way emblem was originally used in emblem books. Still more important, Gogol succeeds in retrieving the emblem from banality by using an antanaclasis to endow it with new meaning: in Russian, *svet* means "light," but in this context it may also mean the "world" in the sense of the "beau monde";

168. See M. Iu. Lermontov, *Polnoe sobranie sochinenii,* 5 vols. (Moscow: Academia, 1935–37), 3:271.

Fig. 37. *Avarice*

thus the *beau monde* can be as dangerous to inexperienced youth as a candle to a moth.[169]

Side by side with emblem books, which tended towards didacticism and uplift, appeared collections of *imagini*. Modeled on Cesare Ripa's *Iconologia*, the *imagini* depicted human vices and virtues. One such collection was put together by Joseph Stöber, and was most likely known to Gogol from Troshchinskii's library.[170] The collection contains an allegory of Avarice (Fig. 37), whose description reads:

> This vice is represented by the image of a wan, lean and disheveled old woman; the rags that cover her and the golden chain that serves as a belt mean that wealth-grubbing enslaves her to the point where she denies herself the most necessary things. On the purse that she grips in her hands is depicted a

169. Gogol's dislike for the *beau monde* is well known. He expressed this prejudice on numerous occasions both in his fiction and his correspondence: see, e.g., 6:175 and Gibian, 187; 8:281 and Zeldin, 88; and 11:91.

170. See Fedorov, *Katalog*, 42.

Greek inscription, Plutos [*sic*], the name of the God of riches. A lean and hungry wolf, which stands near her, signifies insatiability and predacity.[171]

This description of the allegory of Avarice may remind the reader of the portrayal of Pliushkin in *Dead Souls:*

> Near one of the buildings Chichikov soon noticed a figure engaged in an altercation with the peasant who had just arrived. It took him quite a while to distinguish whether the figure was that of a man or woman. The dress it had on was quite indefinable, very like a woman's dressing-gown; on its head was a conical cap such as is worn by country servants. . . . From the keys hanging at her girdle and the way she took the peasant unceremoniously to task, Chichikov concluded that she must be the housekeeper. (6:114; Gibian, 118–19)

Further on, Gogol notes that Pliushkin's face was "that of any other gaunt old man" (6:116; Gibian, 121),[172] and he then draws special attention to Pliushkin's clothes:

> His garb was far more remarkable. There was no means or way of telling what went to the making of his dressing-gown: the sleeves and lapels had grown so dirty and greasy that they looked like boot leather; at the back there were four tails instead of two, and out of them dangled tufts of cotton wool. It was also impossible to make out what he had tied around his neck: a stocking, a garter or a stomach-belt, but it was certainly not a cravat. (6:116; Gibian, 121)

Discussing Pliushkin's transformation into a miser, Gogol later says, "His solitary life only fed his avarice which, as we know, has the appetite of a wolf and grows more insatiable the more it devours" (6:119; Gibian, 124).[173]

171. Joseph Stöber, *Ikonologiia, ob"iasnennaia litsami;* ili, *Polnoe sobranie allegorii, emblem i pr.* (Moscow, 1803), 38–39.

172. In Maksimovich-Ambodik, *Emvlemy i simvoly,* xx, Avarice is described as an old man rather than an old woman.

173. The wolf as a symbol of greed and using the metaphor of the wolf to describe Pliushkin's avarice can be clearly traced to Dante's *Divine Comedy:* "She has a nature so vicious

As can be seen, Pliushkin's portrayal bears a striking affinity to the iconography of Avarice as described by Stöber. To begin with, the very name Pliushkin echoes, perhaps ironically, the name of Plutus, the god of riches, which appears in the description of the allegory. (Gogol could not call his character Plutkin: this would have created an erroneous association with *plut,* Russian for "a rogue.") Perceived by Chichikov as an old woman in threadbare clothes, Pliushkin resembles the image of the allegory; he also resembles her in that he is characterized as lean and wearing a belt, or girdle. The belt of Avarice, however, is a golden chain, which symbolizes her enslavement to the greed for riches; at Pliushkin's waist hang the keys to all his actual wealth, which is why Chichikov at first takes him for a female housekeeper. The irony is that Pliushkin's wealth, because of his morbid miserliness, has turned to dust and ashes. Gogol employed the metaphor of an insatiable wolf; in the allegory, too, there appears a lean and hungry wolf, insatiable and predatory.

Gogol's portrayal of Pliushkin, who became the synonym of extreme miserliness in Russian literature, goes well beyond Stöber's description of Avarice. Gogol deepened and darkened the whole picture. By obscuring even Pliushkin's sex at first, Gogol showed that extreme miserliness had deprived Pliushkin of the important part of his being. Gogol goes on to state outright that Pliushkin "finally turned into a rip on the body of humanity" (6:119).[174]

The importance of the emblem—that integral part of Baroque culture—for Gogol's craftsmanship was expressed specifically in his design for the cover of the first edition of *Dead Souls* (Fig. 38).[175] In

and malignant that her greedy appetite is never satisfied and after food she is hungrier than before" (*Inferno* I, 97–99). Furthermore, the she-wolf is condemned for her bottomless hunger on the verge of Purgatorio, where more examples of avarice are given and where the remorse of misers is shown (see *Purgatorio* XX, 10–12). (Might Gogol have made Pliushkin himself repent of his vice in the third volume of *Dead Souls?* A hint to that effect is given by Gogol in *Selected Passages from Correspondence with Friends.* See 8:280; Zeldin, 87.) And finally, in *Inferno,* Plutus, the god of riches, is addressed as an accursed he-wolf (*maladetto lupo;* VII, 8). For references to *The Divine Comedy,* I have used the bilingual edition: Dante Alighieri, *The Divine Comedy,* 3 vols., trans. John D. Sinclair (New York: Oxford University Press, 1979–80).

174. George Reavey's translation, usually accurate, does not convey here Gogol's metaphor; therefore, in this instance, I have translated this phrase myself.

175. To the best of my knowledge, Gogol was the only Russian writer of the first half of the nineteenth century to have an elaborate book cover of his own design actually appear in print. Less ambitious attempts of this kind were made by other Russian writers, Gogol's contemporar-

this, he was following the common practice of Baroque writers, who designed (or commissioned professional artists to design) frontis-pieces and title pages filled with emblematic meaning, to convey the essence of the contents.[176]

The title—*The Peregrinations of Chichikov, or Dead Souls: A Poéma by N. Gogol*—undoubtedly interacts with its pictorial ele-ments, as was customary with the title pages and frontispieces of Gogol's Baroque predecessors. Gogol's cover is, however, unique in that this kind of interaction takes place on different levels, each of the three main sections of the title—*The Peregrinations of Chichi-kov, Dead Souls,* and *Poéma*—interacting with its immediate picto-rial surroundings.

First, *The Peregrinations of Chichikov:* The carriage at the top of the cover conveys the idea of the protagonist's peregrinations; low buildings, a city gate, a town well at the top left, and a belfry at the top right, symbolize provincial Russia, where the action of the book takes place. The fish lying on a plate and hanging up and the abun-dance of wine bottles and glasses represent the theme of gluttony, so pronounced in this narrative. Recall especially the sturgeon that Sobakevich managed to finish off alone at the party in honor of Chichikov's acquisition of the serfs (see 6:150; Gibian, 159).[177]

Next, *Dead Souls:* The second section of the title is graphically represented by numerous skulls and skeletons. Gogol used the book's cover to create the impression (apparently designed to evade censor-

---

ies. Lermontov designed a cover for his early poem *The Circassians* (1828), and Pushkin drafted the title page for his *Dramatic Fragments* (1830). Both Lermontov's cover and Push-kin's title page remained, however, in manuscript form. See Lermontov, *Polnoe sobranie sochinenii,* 3:13, and Pushkin, *Polnoe sobranie sochinenii,* following 7:98.

176. See Daly, *Literature in the Light of the Emblem,* 180–84. Margery Corbett and Ronald Lightbown provide useful background information about the frontispiece in *The Comely Fron-tispiece: The Emblematic Title-Page in England, 1550–1660* (London: Routledge & Kegan Paul, 1979), 1–47. On the frontispiece in Russia, see A. A. Sidorov, *Russkaia knizhnaia graviura* (Moscow: Akademiia Nauk SSSR, 1951).

Mikhail Markovskii was the first scholar to observe the emblematic nature of Gogol's cover design. See M. N. Markovskii, "Istoriia vozniknoveniia i sozdaniia 'Mertvykh dush,' " in *Pamiati Gogolia,* ed. N. P. Dashkevich (Kiev, 1902), 167–68. While my article, on which the present section is based, was in press, Elena Smirnova's *Poéma Gogolia* was published, in which some of my observations and interpretations regarding Gogol's cover design of *Dead Souls* are confirmed. See Smirnova, *Poéma Gogolia,* 76–78.

177. Cf. Smirnova, *Poéma Gogolia,* 77.

Fig. 38.   Nikolai Gogol's own
cover design for *Dead Souls*

ship) that "dead souls" referred only to deceased serfs; at the same
time, these symbols embody two prominent Baroque themes of special relevance to Gogol's works—*vanitas* and *memento mori*.[178] On
the far left, the large bast shoe, typical peasant footwear, and also the
top boot probably symbolize peasant artisanship, specifically cob-
bling. On the far right, a peasant in a festive outfit, characteristic of
the period in which *Dead Souls* was written,[179] raises a wineglass in
one hand and, in the other, holds a Russian musical instrument resem-
bling a balalaika. In the text, this image is echoed in a conceit comparing Sobakevich's face to a pumpkin, "from which Russians make bala-
laikas" (6:94; Gibian, 96). The narrative counterpart to the graphic

178. See ibid., 77, and Chapter 3 below.
179. Cf. Ivanov, *Russkii narodnyi lubok*, 84, and V. F. Ryndin, ed., *Russkii kostium 1750–*
1917, 5 vols. (Moscow: VTO, 1960–72), 2:170–71.

representations of the peasant as artisan appears in Chichikov's lyrical digression at the beginning of chapter 7 of volume 1, in which he contemplates the fate of the recently acquired dead serfs, among whom are the artisans Maksim Teliatnikov, a cobbler, and Stepan Probka, a carpenter who walked through the provinces with his boots on his shoulder. The latter's surname literally means a "cork" and can also be associated with the barrel on the cover (see 6:136; Gibian, 143).

And finally, *Poéma:* Gogol evidently attached great importance to the fact that *Dead Souls* is a *poéma,* and so it is no accident that the word *poéma* appears in the largest print on the cover. Gogol defines the *poéma* as a genre in his *Textbook of Philology for Russian Youth* (written in 1844–45, published posthumously in 1896), in the section "Smaller Kinds of Epic" (8:478–79). Although Gogol does not use the word *poéma* explicitly and does not mention *Dead Souls* as an example, he is clearly speaking of this genre, which he regarded as an epic such as Homer's *Iliad* or *Odyssey,* albeit on a smaller scale (see 8:478). He maintained that even though *poémas* could be written in prose, they could, nevertheless, be viewed as poetic creations.

The poetic nature of *Dead Souls* is represented on the cover by musical instruments. On the far left, a lyre links Gogol's work to the classical tradition. Typical Russian instruments, such as *svirel'* (a whistle-like flute), *buben* (a tambourine), and *rozhok* (a horn), which Gogol depicted from the top downward on the far right of this section of the cover, perhaps also allude to the Russian national character of *Dead Souls.*[180]

In defining this "smaller epic" genre, Gogol claimed that such works could contain a satirical element. He referred to *Don Quixote,* in which Cervantes ridiculed his contemporaries' belated passion for chivalric adventure (see 8:479). To emphasize the satirical element in *Dead Souls,* Gogol drew two masks of satyrs in his cover design. The masks resemble the heads of the Della Valle Satyrs, which Gogol probably saw in Rome.[181] In the tradition of pictorial art, particularly

180. For the musical instruments, see K. A. Vertkov, G. I. Blagodatov, and E. E. Iazovitskaia, *Atlas muzykal'nykh instrumentov narodov SSSR* (Moscow: Muzyka, 1975), 26, 42, 32–33, and figs. 6–8, 99, and 30–32, respectively. I am indebted to Robert Oldani of Arizona State University for his help in identifying these Russian musical instruments.

181. Cf. Francis Haskell and Nicholas Penny, *Taste and the Antique. The Lure of Classical Sculpture 1500–1900* (New Haven: Yale University Press, 1981), 301–3.

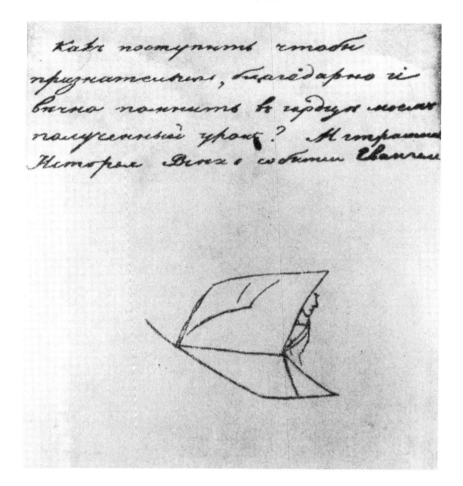

Fig. 39.   Nikolai Gogol. A drawing on one of the dying writer's notes

in frontispieces and title pages, satyrs often symbolized evil passions, and in keeping with this tradition, Gogol's satyric masks embody the passions that, in the words of the *poéma*, "are in the beginning all submissive to man but later grow to be terrible tyrants over him" (6:242; Gibian, 264).

At the bottom of the cover, Gogol placed the head of a sphinx, perhaps wishing to convey the idea of enigmatic wisdom at the base of *Dead Souls.* Konstantin Aksakov was right to raise the point of the

Fig. 40. *The Letters with Which the Book of the World Was Set.* From Johann Arndt, *Sämtliche geistreiche Bücher vom wahren Christenthum* (Frankfurt am Main, 1700)

mystery of Russian life embodied in Gogol's work.[182] By this sphinx, Gogol may furthermore have been suggesting that *Dead Souls* would solve the riddle of his own existence. He expressed this idea to a close friend, Aleksandr Danilevskii, in a letter (May 9, 1842) written shortly after he had designed the cover of his book: "Within a week after this letter you will receive the printed *Dead Souls*—the rather pale threshold of the great *poéma* which is being *formed* within me and which will finally solve the riddle of my existence" (12:58; Proffer, 113).

Emblematic thinking remained an integral part of Gogol's Weltan-

182. Aksakov, "Neskol'ko slov o poéme Gogolia," 47.

schauung up to the last days of his life. Not long before his death, Gogol, having burnt the second volume of *Dead Souls* for the second time, drew a sketch of a man crushed between the covers of a book (Fig. 39). Interpreted emblematically, the book could be the burnt volume of *Dead Souls,* but in a broader sense it signifies Gogol's universe crushing its creator. By this time, Gogol felt that his creative powers were failing.[183]

In this ultimate, and most personal, emblem, Gogol once again demonstrates his affinity with the Baroque world view, for the idea of "the world as a book" was standard in the emblem books of that epoch. A typical example, which depicts the letters with which the Book of the World was set (Fig. 40), appears in Johann Arndt's *Sämtliche geistreiche Bücher vom wahren Christenthum.*[184] The motif was also popular in Slavic Baroque literature. The Czech theologian, pedagogue, and philosopher Jan Amos Komenský (Comenius) employed it in his *Prodromus Pansophiae.* And his contemporary, the Polish poet, Wacław Potocki, encapsulated this concept in his epigram "The World is a Book," a phrase that Simeon Polotskii later adopted as the title for one of his Russian poems.[185]

Concomitant with the motif of the world as a book was the motif of the writer as creator, likened to the Creator. Just as God "wrote" the Book of Nature, the writer creates a universe. Baroque writers acknowledged their subordination to God, but in Gogol's day, in the Romantic period, it was not uncommon for writers to perceive themselves as godlike.[186]

Gogol's own attitude toward his role as writer derived from the Baroque rather than the Romantic perception of the world. Acknowledging the supremacy of the Divine, Gogol viewed himself and his

183. Cf. Zolotusskii, *Gogol',* 502.

184. See Michael Schilling, *Imagines Mundi* (Frankfurt am Main: Lang, 1979), 71 and 276. See also Ernst Robert Curtius, *European Literature and the Latin Middle Ages* (Princeton: Princeton University Press, 1953), 319–26.

185. See, respectively, Dmitrii Chizhevskii, "Das Buch als Symbol des Kosmos" in his *Aus zwei Welten* (The Hague: Mouton, 1956), 90; Wacław Potocki, *Ogród fraszek,* 2 vols. (Lvov, 1907), 1:368–69; P. N. Berkov, "Kniga v poézii Simeona Polotskogo," *Trudy Otdela Drevnerusskoi Literatury* 24 (1969): 264–65; and A. M. Panchenko, "Slovo i Znanie v éstetike Simeona Polotskogo (na materiale 'Vertograda mnogotsvetnogo')," *Trudy Otdela Drevnerusskoi Literatury* 25 (1970): 239.

186. Cf. Imbrie Buffum, *Agrippa d'Aubigné's "Les Tragiques": A Study of the Baroque Style in Poetry* (New Haven: Yale University Press, 1951), 149, and Chizhevskii, *Comparative History of Slavic Literatures,* 144.

writings as part of the Great Plan of the Creator, as we can see in a letter he wrote to Petr Pletnev on May 6, 1851:

> That the second volume of *Dead Souls* is cleverer than the first one, this I can say as a man of taste who can also look at himself like a stranger, so that perhaps Smirnova is partly right; but when I consider the whole process, when I consider how it was created and produced, I see that the only clever one is the One Who creates everything, using us all as building bricks according to His plan, of which He is the only truly intelligent architect. (14:229)

For Gogol, a writer comes closest to understanding the mysteries of Divine Creation when he exercises his own powers of creation; the writer's universe, his book, epitomizes the creation from chaos. Gogol expressed this in a letter (December 2, 1843) to the poet Vasilii Zhukovskii:

> I continue to work, that is, to jot down chaos on paper, a chaos from which the creation of *Dead Souls* should emerge. Labor and patience and even forcing myself have been greatly rewarding. Mysteries are revealed of a kind that the soul hasn't yet heard of. And much in the world becomes clear after this labor. Practicing the art of creation, even a little, one becomes in some measure more susceptible to insights into the great mysteries of God's Creation. (12:239)

Emblematic thinking was a significant part of Gogol's mind. To this, the examples of emblems scattered throughout his oeuvre attest. With his ingenuity and craftsmanship, Gogol endowed the Baroque emblem and its related forms, which had degenerated into cliché by the nineteenth century, with new vitality.

3

Topoi

Aristotle viewed *topoi* as devices enabling an orator to argue most convincingly, but by the time of Rome rhetoricians had already reduced them to set pieces, ready-made arguments.[1] During the Middle Ages, the *topoi* declined further, turning, as Ernst Robert Curtius has shown, into hackneyed themes, clichés.[2] In this chapter, I follow Curtius in viewing various *topoi* as bonds linking various cultures and writers of Western Europe and extend his approach to the Slavic cultures relevant to my study.

In selecting *topoi* for discussion here, I was guided, as with forms, by two considerations: their popularity in the Baroque period and their importance in Gogol's oeuvre. The popularity of these *topoi* in the Baroque period stems from their distinctly manifesting the Weltanschauung of the epoch, particularly such features as its focus on the illusoriness and brevity of existence and its heightened sense of religiosity. The significant role of these *topoi* in Gogol's oeuvre shows his strong debt to the Baroque. At the same time, Gogol, for whom personally these *topoi* were not banalities but rather exalted percepts, demonstrated in his fiction—and here lies his ingenuity—how his characters, incapable of comprehending these notions in their

---

1. For a recent discussion of *topos* in antiquity, see Edward P. J. Corbett, "The *Topoi* Revisited," in *Rhetoric and Praxis,* ed. Jean Dietz Moss (Washington, D.C.: Catholic University of America Press, 1986), 45–49.

2. Curtius, *European Literature,* 70–71.

true magnitude, reduced them to clichés in the Devil-ruled world of *poshlost*. In his artistic "snapshots" Gogol in effect concretely represented the degeneration and banalization of these Baroque *topoi* in his day in the world at large—the same process traced by Curtius approximately a century later in his wide-ranging and extensive scholarly survey from classical antiquity up to Goethe.

It is not surprising, since they manifest the world view of the Baroque period, that the *topoi* we shall examine all exhibit deep inner connections. We start with *theatrum mundi*, the idea that man is an actor on the stage of the world. This perception of human existence as in part illusory is also manifest in the expression "life is a dream"; the transience of man's "part" in the "dream" links these two *topoi* with the theme of *brevitas vitae*. The brevity of human existence presented Baroque man with an antinomy characteristic of that epoch: on the one hand, it drove him toward seeking earthly pleasures—whence the *topos* of *carpe diem,* and on the other, in the atmosphere of heightened religiosity that pervaded the Baroque epoch, this brevity reminded him that such hedonistic pursuits are sheer vanity—whence the *topos* of *vanitas.* The Church at that time promulgated the idea of *vanitas* by reminding its parishioners that due to the brevity of their life they should ponder mortality and think of saving their souls—the idea that lies at the base of *memento mori.* The *topos* of the end of the world is also tightly connected with these other *topoi:* since Baroque man viewed his life as illusory, ephemeral, and in a state of constant flux, he was responsive to the idea that these traits could apply to the entire world. Since life is a dream ending in death, the world too is finite, and all human desires are vain. And since the world was perceived as a play, it would inevitably end dramatically. The Last Judgment, which was to follow the end of the world, was imagined as a closing scene of high pathos.

Theatrum mundi

The idea of the world as a stage is by no means a Baroque invention. The notion that human life resembles a part in a play written and directed by Supreme Forces can be traced to antiquity and appears in the works of Plato, Seneca, and Plotinus. We can find this metaphor in patristic writings, particularly those of Augustine, John Chrysostom, and Synesius, and trace its gradual evolution into the *topos*. But it was the medieval philosopher and humanist John of Salisbury who first coined the phrase *theatrum mundi*.[3] His *Policraticus* (1159), with its pervading notion that the whole world is a stage on which men play various parts while constantly watched by the Spectator, became especially popular in the Late Renaissance and Baroque.[4]

The popularity of *theatrum mundi* in the Baroque is attested to by the motto *totus mundus agit histrionem*, carved over the entrance to the Globe Theatre in London in 1599; some scholars maintain that Jaques's famous "All the world's a stage" speech in *As You Like It* was inspired by this motto.[5] A similar motto—"The world's a stage, / Each plays his role and gets his share"—composed by the Dutch Baroque poet and dramatist Joost van den Vondel (1587–1679) was inscribed over the entrance to the Amsterdam theater in 1638.[6]

The *theatrum mundi* theme was not confined to the stage. The *topos* pervaded the world view of the Baroque (Fig. 41). The Spanish aesthetician Baltasar Gracián (1601–58) entitled a chapter of his *El criticón* "El gran teatro del universo."[7] The Polish poet Zbigniew Morsztyn (1624–98) presented this theme in his poem "Doleful Laments of Apollo and the Muses" (1682):

> All the world's a stage,
> And all the living are characters in the comedy;
>
> .   .   .   .
>
> But this performance often turns to cruel tragedy,
> And those who rise highest in this *theatrum*
> Are most vulnerable to gales and thunderbolts.[8]

3. See John of Salisbury, *Policraticus*, in his *Opera Omnia*, 5 vols., ed. J. A. Giles (Oxford: J. H. Parker, 1848), 3:187. For an English translation, see *Frivolities of Courtiers and Footprints of Philosophers*, trans. Joseph B. Pike (Minneapolis: University of Minnesota Press, 1938), 180.

4. For a historical survey of the *topos*, see Curtius, *European Literature*, 138–42; Warnke, "The World as Theatre," in his *Versions of Baroque*, 66–89; and Peter N. Skrine, *The Baroque* (New York: Holmes & Meier, 1978), 1–24. For the most detailed discussion of the subject, see Lynda G. Christian, *Theatrum mundi* (New York: Garland, 1987).

5. William Shakespeare, *The Complete Works*, ed. George B. Harrison (New York: Harcourt, 1952), 789 and 773.

6. Skrine, *The Baroque*, 10.

7. Curtius, *European Literature*, 141. Cf. the play by Calderón, Gracián's contemporary and countryman, *El gran teatro del mundo* (ca. 1645).

8. For the original, see Zbigniew Morsztyn, *Muza domowa*, 2 vols. (Warsaw: Państwowy

Fig. 41. *Theatrum Vitae Humanae.* From Jean Jacques Boissard, *Theatrum Vitae Humanae* (Metz, 1596)

Gogol's feeling that life is a play full of unexpected reversals resembles the thought in Morsztyn's poem. Gogol expressed this idea in the closing speech of the First Comic Actor in "The Denouement of *The Government Inspector*": "The fact that our lives, which we are in the habit of regarding as comedies, might very well end in the same sort of tragedy that concluded this comedy" (4:130; Ehre, 188)—this fact, he thought, should be of primary concern. The attention to rank present in the Morsztyn poem is absent from this speech. We shall see later, however, that in his treatment of this *topos* Gogol also paid attention to the disparity between the actors' actual roles in the tragicomedy of life and their own aspirations to play a more prominent part on the world stage, despite Morsztyn's warning.

"The Denouement" deserves our attention in another respect. Here Gogol offers a rare model of *theatrum mundi:* the stage is a human soul, and the "actors" are evil human propensities, striving to appear on the stage under a worthy mask and play a noble role. (See the second edition of the close of "The Denouement," 4:135.) According to Gogol's model, which echoes the Baroque's interest in eschatology, the "actors" should undergo inspection and then judgment by the judge—our conscience—at the compelling injunction of the Almighty.

Gogol also employed the *topos* in a more traditional way. He portrayed his characters as "actors" who frequently aspire to impress the "audience" with their "performances." They rehearse their parts carefully and practice acting techniques before appearing on the "stage." For example, in "The Overcoat," the Person of Consequence had the protagonist, Bashmachkin, wait for him for a long time, because he wanted to make an impression on his provincial childhood friend. When he finally let him in, "he turned to him at once and said: 'What do you want?' in a firm and abrupt voice, which he had purposely rehearsed in his own room in solitude before the mirror for a week before receiving his present post and the grade of a general" (3:166; Kent, 2:326–27). We come across another such careful rehearsal in

---

Instytut Wydawniczy, 1954), 2:168. This ambivalence toward life can be traced to "De mundana comedia vel tragedia," a chapter in the *Policraticus* by John of Salisbury. See Tibor Fabiny, "*Theatrum Mundi* and the Ages of Man," in *Shakespeare and the Emblem,* ed. Tibor Fabiny (Szeged: Attila József University, 1984), 288.

Dead Souls, in the episode describing Chichikov's preparation for the governor's ball:

> A whole hour was devoted to the sole object of examining his face in the mirror. An attempt was made to communicate to it a variety of different expressions: now a look of gravity and importance, now one of respect tinged with a smile, now one simply of respect without a smile; the mirror received several bows accompanied by inarticulate sounds somewhat resembling French words, although Chichikov knew no word of French. (6:161; Gibian, 171–72)

Another desire of these "actors" in Gogol's *theatrum mundi* is to take upon themselves larger and more important "roles" in order to imitate the "stars." Consider the titular councilor described in "The Overcoat":

> I have actually been told that a titular councilor who was put in charge of a small separate office, immediately partitioned off a special room for himself, calling it the head office, and posted lackeys at the door with red collars and gold braid, who took hold of the handle of the door and opened it for everyone who went in, though the "head office" was so tiny that it was with difficulty that an ordinary writing desk could be put into it. (3:164; Kent, 2:325)

This story about the titular councilor follows and serves as an illustration for the narrator's comment: "Everyone in Holy Russia has a craze for imitation; everyone apes and mimicks his superiors," a rebuke that could be extended to the whole world.[9]

In Gogol's world, elements of everyday life are presented as distinctly theatrical. For example, in "Nevsky Prospekt," the regular comings and goings of people on the city's main thoroughfare are treated as staged exhibitions that follow one another as rapidly as patterns in a kaleidoscope:

9. Cf. the narrator's remark in "Christmas Eve," written some ten years earlier: "Things are oddly arranged in our world! All who live in it are always trying to outdo and imitate one another" (1:204; Kent, 1:95).

In this blessed period between two and three o'clock in the afternoon, when everyone seems to be walking on Nevsky Prospekt, there is a display of all the finest things the genius of man has produced. One displays a smart overcoat with the best beaver on it, the second—a lovely Greek nose, the third superb whiskers, the fourth—a pair of pretty eyes and a marvelous hat, the fifth—a signet ring on a jaunty forefinger, the sixth—a foot in a bewitching shoe, the seventh—a necktie that excites wonder, and the eighth—a moustache that reduces one to stupefaction. But three o'clock strikes and the display is over, the crowd grows less thick. . . . At three o'clock there is a fresh change. (3:13–14; Kent, 1:211)

Gogol here conveys the impression that the creatures who people the Nevsky Prospekt are like puppets: they emerge on stage at a certain time of the day and then vanish, only to reappear in the same role at the same time the following day.[10] Gogol's portrayal of his characters as automatons is most obvious in "The Nose." In describing the existence of the protagonist, Major Kovalev, prior to the disappearance of his nose, the narrator emphasizes the automatism of his actions, using words and phrases of reiteration such as "always" or "was in the habit of." "Major Kovalev was in the habit of walking every day up and down Nevsky Prospekt. The collar of his shirt front was always extremely clean and well starched" (3:53; Kent, 2:220).[11] Kovalev's *modus operandi* was determined by two or three aspirations: to make a successful career and an advantageous marriage, but to chase attractive women until his matrimonial projects were realized. Kovalev had every reason to hope for success in his undertakings because, in addition to his fashionable whiskers and full, ruddy cheeks, he possessed a good-looking, well-proportioned nose.[12] This conventional appearance of his, and particularly his "moderate" nose, was Kovalev's best recommendation in the world of similar automa-

---

10. On the puppet-like nature of Gogol's characters, see V. V. Rozanov, *O Gogole* (Letchworth, Eng.: Prideaux Press, 1970), 17.

11. Kovalev's surname itself alludes to his automaton nature: *koval'* in Ukrainian, Gogol's native language, means "blacksmith," and indeed he is like a mechanical toy made by a blacksmith. I am grateful to Savely Senderovich for this idea.

12. In the original, Kovalev's nose is called *umerennyi,* which literally means "moderate."

tons, where he quickly established himself and made a circle of acquaintances.

The loss of "such a conspicuous part" (3:61; Kent, 2:227) as a nose in a world of automatons with its emphasis on appearance was tantamount to breaking the windup mechanism of the toy. Kovalev lost the measured automatism so characteristic of him, his motions became abrupt and impetuous: he "jumped out of bed, he shook himself" (3:53; Kent, 2:219–20), or he "ran panting into a little reception room" (3:59; Kent, 2:225). Kovalev's newly dynamic external behavior reflects an internal transformation, which manifests itself in a variety of powerful human emotions previously unknown to him, such as timidity, vexation, despair, strong joy.

Kovalev's partial humanization leads to his being at odds with the world around him; he avoids his cronies and realizes that his social life as well as his career pursuits have come to an abrupt end. He feels misplaced and unhappy in the world of automatons and strives to retrieve his windup mechanism, which would again make him an indistinguishable member of that world. The reinstatement of the nose on Kovalev's face and his subsequent re-automatization, as seen in his repetitive actions at the close of the tale, lead to his happy reestablishment in that environment.

In depicting life as a conflict between human and puppet traits, Gogol betrays contemporaneous Romantic influences, particularly E.T.A. Hoffmann's "The Sandman" (1816).[13] Nevertheless, Gogol's treatment of Kovalev differs considerably from Hoffmann's treatment of Nathaniel: Hoffmann presents Nathaniel's infatuation with the doll Olympia and his subsequent dehumanization as a tragedy that leads to the student's madness and death. Gogol on the other hand initially portrays Kovalev as a complacent automaton; his loss of nose with his subsequent *humanization* is the source of his great unhappiness in the world of automatons. This unhappiness gives place to renewed self-satisfaction only when Kovalev finds his nose and regains his position in the inhuman world surrounding him. Thus it emerges that Kovalev's tragedy is his longing to look and be like everyone else, the quintessence of *poshlost'*.[14] The exclamation of poor de-nosed Kovalev—"The devil wanted to

13. Cf. Dilaktorskaia, *Fantasticheskoe*, 20–21.
14. Cf. Merezhkovskii, *Gogol' i chort*, 4.

have a joke at my expense" (3:60; Kent, 2:227)—underscores the irony of his situation: in fact the Devil was joking when he placed Kovalev, the automaton, in his kindred world of automatons, and not when Kovalev acquired the human qualities that would make him unhappy.

Gogol's presentation of this world of *poshlost'* as a theater directed by the Devil is grounded in pre-Petrine Eastern Slavic traditions. Carnival revels were viewed as reflecting God's permission to the Devil to rule the world for the time of the festivity.[15] Gogol's originality lies in his presenting the world, the theater of *poshlost'*, as ruled by the Devil at all times.

In presenting Kovalev as an automaton Gogol may have been parodying Plato's assertion that a human being is a "divine puppet" (after all, Kovalev's first name was Platon!).[16] In Gogol's tale, when human beings become puppets, their behavior is regulated not by God but by the Devil—the king of *poshlost'*.[17]

In contrast to the characters in the world of *poshlost'*, the characters in the Gogolian epic world are not puppets. They have wills of their own and, despite the narrator's warnings, they are entitled to make their mistakes, even fatal ones, very much like human beings who have freedom of choice in the Universe of the Almighty. This is made particularly clear in the narrator's addresses to his characters. In the last section of the preceding chapter, we saw how Gogol the writer viewed himself as a creator of his world, similar to God, the Creator of the World. Since the world is a play, the writer becomes its playwright, and through his narrator he also at times functions as a stage director. In the tale "A Terrible Vengeance," before Danilo Burulbash is mortally wounded by his father-in-law, the narrator exclaims to Danilo: "Cossack, you go to your doom!" (1:267; Kent, 1:159); in *Taras Bulba*, when Mosii Shilo's life is endangered, the narrator shouts a warning: "Slay him not, Cossack, but rather turn around! The Cossack did not turn, and one of the slain man's servants

---

15. See Iu. M. Lotman, "Gogol' i sootnesenie 'smekhovoi kul'tury' s komicheskim i ser'eznym v russkoi natsional'noi traditsii," *Materialy Vsesoiuznogo simpoziuma po vtorichnym modeliruiushchim sistemam* 1, no. 5 (1974): 131–33. Cf. Fanger, *The Creation of Nikolai Gogol,* 231n.

16. Plato, *The Laws,* trans. Thomas L. Pangle (New York: Basic Books, 1980), 24–25. Also see Curtius, *European Literature,* 138. Cf. Dilaktorskaia, *Fantasticheskoe,* 191 n. 14.

17. For other allusions to Plato in Gogol's works, see Smirnova, *Poéma Gogolia,* 134–36.

stabbed him in the neck with a knife" (2:138; Kent, 2:103). In having the narrator thus address and admonish the heroes, Gogol follows the Western Baroque literary tradition seen for example in the military epic *A Civil War* by the Polish poet Samuel Twardowski (1600–1660). There, in the course of describing the scene of reconciliation between the Poles and the Cossacks, the narrator addresses the Cossack leader, Bogdan Khmel'nitskii, with great indignation and sarcasm: "Now, after shedding so much / Precious Polish noble blood, after so many murders, / You crawl in and weep, o crocodile!"[18] We should note however that Twardowski's narrator, a contemporary and eye-witness of the events described, speaks to a character whose prototype was a historical figure, whereas Gogol's narrator, who is separated from the events described by approximately two centuries and who maintains the distance by referring to this epoch as "that coarse, savage age" (2:164; Kent, 2:125), is appealing to fictional characters originating in Ukrainian folklore. Gogol seems to me to be employing this device of the narrator's emotional involvement in the events depicted in order to transcend the gap in time and create an illusion of authenticity. Furthermore, this device, popular in Baroque military epics such as *A Civil War,* was well suited to *Taras Bulba* and "A Terrible Vengeance," set in the Baroque Ukraine, where this so-called civil war was actually fought.[19]

A corollary to the theme "the world is a stage" is the theme "a stage is the world." In the Baroque period the *topos* was commonly thus reversed.[20] This approach to the *topos* led to downplaying the distinction between the world and the stage, and consequently, between the audience and the actors. One of the ways in which they interacted in the Baroque theater was for the actors to address the audience from

18. For the original, see Samuel Twardowski, *Woyna Domowa Z-Kozaki i Tatary, Moskwą, potym Szwedami, i z-Węgry* (Kalisz, 1681), 1:93.

19. Incidentally, the popularity of *A Civil War* in the Ukraine and its influence on Ukrainian literature enable us to assume that Gogol must have been familiar with this work of the Polish Virgil, either in the original or through its Ukrainian adaptations. On the popularity of *A Civil War* in the Ukraine, see N. I. Petrov, *Ocherki iz istorii ukrainskoi literatury XVIII veka* (Kiev, 1880), 15, and Ryszard Łużny, "Dawne piśmiennictwo ukraińskie a polskie tradycje literackie," in *Z dziejów stosunków literackich polsko-ukraińskich,* ed. Stefan Kozak and Marian Jakóbiec (Wrocław: Zakład Narodowy imienia Ossolińskich, 1974), 31. On Gogol's reading knowledge of Polish, see V. A. Lugakovskii, "Gogol' v pol'skoi literature," *Literaturnyi Vestnik* 1 (1902): 25–28; see also Gogol's letter of April 23, 1838, to Aleksandr Danilevskii, in which he asks his close friend to buy him the recently published *Pan Tadeusz* by Adam Mickiewicz (11:133).

20. See Warnke, *Versions of Baroque,* 69.

the stage. For example, the epilogue of Simeon Polotskii's "Comedy of Prodigal Son," which was modeled on Western Baroque plays, appeals to the spectator to learn the lesson of this parabolic play. Eastern Slavic interludes also incorporated direct addresses by their characters to the audience.[21]

Gogol employs this device in *The Government Inspector.* Liuliukov's congratulations to the mayor's wife and daughter on the occasion of the daughter's expected marriage to Khlestakov are accompanied by his speechless, gesturing appeal to the audience (see 4:85; Ehre, 121); and later the town bureaucrats address the audience indignantly in response to individual insults directed at them in Khlestakov's intercepted letter (see 4:91–92; Ehre, 126–27).

Gogol's handling of the *theatrum mundi* theme was thus enriched by the variety of traditions he drew on, ancient Greek, Western Baroque, pre-Petrine Eastern Slavic, and Romantic. He made a unique contribution to the *topos* in his portrayal of the world of *poshlost'* as the everyday demonic *theatrum mundi* that does not tolerate the presence or expression of authentic human emotions.

Life Is a Dream

The concept of *theatrum mundi* was inseparable in the Baroque period from that of another important *topos*—"life is a dream."[22] Like *theatrum mundi,* this *topos* expressed the Baroque preoccupation with the illusory nature of human life and experience.[23]

We find these *topoi* intertwined in Prospero's closing speech in Shakespeare's final play, *The Tempest:*

> Our revels now are ended. These our actors,
> As I foretold you, were all spirits, and

21. See, respectively, Simeon Polotskii, *Izbrannye sochineniia* (Moscow: Akademiia Nauk SSSR, 1953), 188, and Paulina Lewin, "Stsenicheskaia struktura vostochnoslavianskikh intermedii," in *Russkaia literatura na rubezhe dvukh épokh,* ed. A. N. Robinson, 105–27.

22. For a brief survey of human fascination with dreams from antiquity to the pre-Baroque period, see Michael T. Katz, *Dreams and the Unconscious in Nineteenth-Century Russian Fiction* (Hanover: University Press of New England, 1984), 3–4.

23. See Skrine, *The Baroque,* 144–64, and Warnke, *Versions of Baroque,* 67.

Are melted into air, into thin air.
And, like the baseless fabric of this vision,
The cloud-capped towers, the gorgeous palaces,
The solemn temples, the great globe itself—
Yea, all which it inherit—shall dissolve
And, like this insubstantial pageant faded,
Leave not a rack behind. We are such stuff
As dreams are made on, and our little life
Is rounded with a sleep.

                                    (IV, i, 148–58)[24]

"Life Is a Dream" is the title and central theme of a play by Shakespeare's younger contemporary, Calderón. The protagonist of the play, Sigismundo, the son of Basilio, a Polish king, has been imprisoned in a tower from infancy because his horoscope foretold that he would become a bloody tyrant. In the course of time, Basilio, tormented by pangs of conscience, decides to give his son a chance to disprove his horoscope. By Basilio's order, Sigismundo is transported to the palace while asleep. Upon awakening, he is entrusted with royal authority, but his rule proves disastrous. When he is asleep, he is returned to the tower, where he is told that his royal experience was a dream. In his monologue, Sigismundo concludes that life is a dream: "What is life? A frenzy. What is life? An illusion, a shadow, a fiction, and the greatest blessing [in life] is tiny, for all life is a dream, and dreams are only dreams."[25] We find the *topos* pictorially expressed in a painting by Calderón's countryman and contemporary Antonio de Pereda (ca. 1608–78) entitled *The Knight's Dream* (Fig. 42), perhaps inspired by Calderón's play. The painting portrays a young hidalgo asleep in a chair. On a table in front of him are riches, a skull, and a mask. The skull, *memento mori,* represents the brevity of life; the riches and the skull together symbolize the vanity of earthly pursuits. The mask conveys the idea of *theatrum mundi* and at the same time may suggest the end of the world, when the "play" will be over.[26]

We also find the *topos* "life is a dream" in the Slavic literatures of

24. Shakespeare, *The Complete Works,* 1495.

25. See Hill, 185. For my illustrations of the Baroque themes, I use prose translations from this anthology, which also has the originals.

26. On Pereda and this painting, see August L. Mayer, "Pereda, Antonio," in *Allgemeines Lexikon der bildenden Künstler,* ed. Hans Vollmer (Leipzig: Seemann, 1932), 398.

Fig. 42.   Antonio de Pereda, *The Knight's Dream*. Madrid, Academia de San Fernando

the period, for example, in Zbigniew Morsztyn's poem "On Good-Night": "And that we exist, / We in vain call this life. / This is only a dream, a transient dream, / Allowed to us for a short time."[27] Similarly, the Ukrainian poet Ivan Velichkovskii (d. 1701) remarks in his short poem "Jacob's Ladder," "This world is like a dream."[28] And Gavriil Derzhavin (1743–1816), whose poetry has a Baroque savor, was preoccupied with the *topos* from the early stage of his literary career on, as his 1774 prose translation of Frederick II's "Ode to Maupertius. Life Is a Dream" demonstrates.[29]

The blurred borderline between life and dream, characteristic of the Baroque mentality, already appears in Gogol's early works, such as "A May Night." Levko dreams that he helps a drowned maiden to identify a witch, and that the drowned maiden gives him a note as a

27. For the original, see Zbigniew Morsztyn, *Muza domowa*, 1:219.

28. For the original, see Ivan Velychkovs'kyi, *Tvory* (Kiev: Naukova dumka, 1972), 152.

29. See G. R. Derzhavin, *Sochineniia*, 7 vols. (St. Petersburg, 1868–78), 3:218–20.

reward. Upon awakening, Levko actually finds the note, which miraculously helps him realize his desire—to marry his beloved Ganna (see 1:177; Kent, 1:73–74).

Life and dream are also confounded for Chartkov, the protagonist of "The Portrait " In his dream, Chartkov has a vision of a heavy roll of coins, wrapped in blue paper, with the inscription "1,000 gold coins" on it. Chartkov dreams that this roll was accidentally left by a money-lender whose portrait he purchased earlier that day. Upon awakening, "He could not be certain that it had all been a dream. He could not keep from feeling that there must have been some terrible fragment of reality within the dream" (3:92; Kent, 2:265). And, indeed, later that day Chartkov finds the same roll of money hidden in the portrait frame. The roll, as in the dream, was wrapped in blue paper and marked "1,000 gold coins" (see 3:95, Kent, 2:267).[30]

This ambiguity between life and dream had so strong a hold on Gogol's imagination that it even found expression in his correspondence. In his letter to Vasilii Zhukovskii (October 30, 1837) upon learning of Pushkin's death, Gogol writes:

> If you knew with what joy I abandoned Switzerland and flew to my dear soul, my beauty—Italy. She is mine! No one in the world will take her from me! I was born here—Russia, Petersburg, the snows, the scoundrels, the civil-service department, the professorship, the theater—I dreamed all that. I have awakened in my native land again, and I regret only that the poetic part of the dream—you and the three or four who have left the eternal joy of memory in my soul—was not carried over into reality. There is one more irretrievable thing. . . . Oh Pushkin, Pushkin! What a beautiful dream I was lucky to see in life, and how sad my awakening was. (11:112; Proffer, 72)

Gogol identifies dream and life, life and dream again in his letter of January 18, 1839, to Vera Repnina:

30. Gogol's treatment of dream and reality here differs from that of Pushkin, who in his "The Queen of Spades" (1834) draws a well-defined borderline between Hermann's dreams of winning piles of money in card games and the sobering and, in the end, even maddening reality. See Gillon A. Aitken, trans., *The Complete Prose Tales of Alexandr Sergeyevitch Pushkin* (New York: W. W. Norton, 1966), 286 and 301; for the original, see Pushkin, *Polnoe sobranie sochinenii,* 8:236 and 247–48.

I was reading about your dream with such curiosity that it seemed to me as if I myself were asleep all this time or, to put it better, I could not distinguish it from reality.... As for me, I am so happy now with Zhukovskii's arrival that this alone fills me entirely.... His appearance here is like a dream for me. I am delighted with my dream and am afraid even to think of awakening. (11:193–95)

In depicting the blurred borderline between life and dream Gogol drew on the Baroque tradition felt in contemporary Romantic literature (exemplified in Poe's poem "A Dream Within a Dream.")[31] The attempt to escape the vicissitudes of life into a land of dreams, often by recourse to external means (alcohol or drugs), was however a Romantic novelty, manifested notably in Hoffmann's "The Golden Pot" (1816) and De Quincey's *Confessions of an English Opium Eater* (1822). A similar treatment of "life is a dream" can be found in "Nevsky Prospekt," in the figure of Piskarev, whose world collapses when he realizes that the object of his adoration is a prostitute. He finds shelter in his opium-induced dreams, in which the object of his love appears idealized. Unable to reach a solution to the antinomy of his existence, the "eternal battle between dream and reality," Piskarev escapes into death (3:30; Kent, 1:225).[32]

In the Baroque view of "life is a dream," death is also frequently present, but not in the form of suicide. If life was likened to a dream, then death was viewed as the ultimate slumber (cf. the line quoted above from *The Tempest,* "Our little life is rounded with a sleep").[33] It is not surprising, therefore, that in Baroque literature the borderline between life, perceived as a dream, and death, the ultimate sleep, is also blurred. We find this, for example, in the poem of Zbigniew Morsztyn, "Life Is a Dream and a Shade":

31. Edgar Allan Poe, *Complete Stories and Poems* (New York: Doubleday, 1966), 768.

32. For a detailed discussion of the role of opium-induced dreams in Romantic literature, see Alethea Hayter, *Opium and the Romantic Imagination* (Wellingborough, Eng.: Crucible, 1988). For a comparison of Gogol's tale to Hoffmann's story, De Quincey's novel, and *littérature frénétique,* see, respectively, Mikhail Gorlin, *N. V. Gogol und E. Th. A. Hoffmann* (Leipzig: Harrassowitz, 1933), 48–61, and V. V. Vinogradov, "O literaturnoi tsiklizatsii. Po povodu 'Nevskogo prospekta' Gogolia i 'Ispovedi opiofaga' De Kvinsi," in his *Poétika russkoi literatury* (Moscow: Nauka, 1976), 45–62. For the most recent and detailed study of dreams in Gogol's works, including those of Piskarev, see Katz, *Dreams,* 66–83.

33. This theme of death as an ultimate slumber passed from Baroque to Romantic literature; see, for example, Poe's story "The Sleeper," in his *Complete Stories and Poems,* 745–46.

And you are fast asleep
Though it seems to you that you live.
Life can be called life only in form:
Life is the essence of death,
Life that is equal to a dream.[34]

Gogol too characterizes death as ultimate slumber in an episode in *Taras Bulba* portraying Taras's return to consciousness after being seriously wounded:

> "I have had a long sleep!" said Taras, waking as from a heavy drunken slumber, and trying to recognize the objects around him. A terrible weakness overpowered his limbs. The walls and corners of an unfamiliar room seemed hovering before him. At last he saw that Tovkach was sitting before him and seemed to be listening to every breath he took.
> "Yes," thought Tovkach to himself, "you might perhaps have slept forever!" (2:146; Kent, 2:110)

Gogol thus treats the *topos* "life is a dream" along lines familiar from Baroque literature and adopted later by Romantic literature, blurring the borderline between life and dream and presenting them as two mingled spheres. In the case of Piskarev, Gogol follows Romantic innovation in portraying a drug-induced dream followed by self-inflicted death—a realm the hero, unable to resolve the conflicts in his life, escapes to.

Brevitas vitae

Preoccupation with the brevity and transience of human existence is already to be found in an ancient Egyptian text more than four thousand years old: "Generations pass away and others go on since the time of ancestors. . . . They that build buildings, their places are no more. What has been done with them?"[35] The brevity of human life repeat-

---

34. For the original, see Zbigniew Morsztyn, *Muza domowa*, 2:199.
35. See John A. Wilson, "Egypt," in *Before Philosophy. The Intellectual Adventure of Ancient Man*, ed. Henri Frankfort and Henrietta A. Frankfort (Baltimore: Penguin, 1949), 114.

edly finds striking expression in the Bible: "My days are swifter than a weaver's shuttle" (Job 7:6); "For he remembered that they were but flesh, / a wind that passeth away and cometh not again" (Psalms 78:39). *Brevitas vitae* was also a major *topos* for Greek and Roman philosophers. Seneca entitled one of his works *De brevitate vitae* and discussed the subject in other treatises on numerous occasions.[36]

In the Baroque period, consciousness of the brevity, mutability, and transience of human existence was particularly acute.[37] The great calamities that occurred on the eve of the Baroque and during the period itself—religious wars and plagues that decimated the population of Europe—as well as positive achievements such as the scientific and geographic discoveries all strongly contributed to the sense of a transformation in the world and, as a result, in human life. On the eve of the Baroque, Michel de Montaigne (1533–92) expressed these sentiments: "The world runnes all on wheeles. All things therein move without intermission; yea the earth, the rockes of *Caucasus,* and the Pyramides of *Ægypt,* both with the publike and their own motion. *Constancy it selfe is nothing but a languishing and wavering dance.*"[38]

Indeed, preoccupation with the transience of human existence and with mutability in the world became one of the hallmarks of the Baroque. This acute awareness of impermanence in the world, an awareness which was shared by writers in the late sixteenth, throughout the seventeenth, and on into the eighteenth century, can be considered a typical manifestation of the Baroque mind.[39] The process of flux was viewed in the Baroque age as the only constant in the world, and writers were aware all the time that their entire experience was volatile and undependable.[40] *Brevitas vitae* was also a popular theme in the visual arts. One emblem presents the brevity of life graphically as the short span of an outstretched hand (Fig. 43).

36. On Seneca's *De brevitate vitae,* see Max Pohlenz, *Philosophie und Erlebnis in Senecas Dialogen* (Gottingen: Vandenhoeck & Ruprecht, 1941), 81–84; on Seneca's preoccupation with the *topos* as expressed in his other works, see Anna Lydia Motto, *Guide to the Thought of Lucius Annaeus Seneca* (Amsterdam: Hakkert, 1970), 123.

37. For such awareness in antiquity, see Jeffrey H. Tigay, *The Evolution of the Gilgamesh Epic* (Philadelphia: University of Pennsylvania Press, 1982), 5 n. 2.

38. Michel de Montaigne, *The Essayes,* trans. John Florio (New York: Modern Library, n.d.), 725. The italics are Montaigne's.

39. Buffum, *Agrippa d'Aubigné's "Les Tragiques,"* 93.

40. See Hill, 174.

Fig. 43. *Vita Brevis.* From Juan de Borja, *Empresas Morales* (Prague, 1581)

It is not surprising, therefore, that the theme of the brevity of life was voiced by so many in the Baroque period. In the refrain of his poem "Allegory of the Brevity of Things Human," the Spanish poet Góngora (1561–1627) wrote:

> Learn, flowers, from me, what parts we play
> from dawn to dusk. Last noon the boast

and marvel of the fields, today
I am not even my own ghost.[41]

There is a similar poignant resonance in the poem by the Polish poet
Daniel Naborowski (1573–1640) on the brevity of life:

Our comprehension fades with every hour:
A forebear lived, and you, now heirs are born.
In short—today you're here, tomorrow gone.
But that you were, deceased will be your name;
Sound, smoke, clouds, wind, flash, voice—man's
life resounds.[42]

The theme of life's brevity was common in Ukrainian poetry as
well. In a poem included in the collection *Ethica Hieropolitica,*
published in 1712, an anonymous Baroque poet wrote:

Our life is brief, barren, sad, and full of tears.
But it will serve those who live virtuously.
Life is very short for the vain, and one who lives long
Will vanish too like a many-colored bubble.[43]

And Derzhavin lamented in his "On the Death of Prince Meshcherskii" (1779), which Gogol must have read in the Nezhin Gymnasium:
"No sooner did I see this world / Ere Death began to grind his
teeth."[44]

Gogol himself on learning of the death of Krylov, wrote to Stepan
Shevyrev: "Our life is so brief that there is no time even to grieve"
(December 14, 1844; 12:398). And in a letter to Aleksandr Danilevskii (November 20, 1847) Gogol unburdened himself: "Life is so
brief, and yet I have done almost nothing of what I ought to do"
(13:393).

41. Segel, 201 (199). Segel's anthology has interlinear English translations; if the original
appears on a different page, it is given here in parentheses.

42. Segel, 209 (208).

43. For the original, see Dmitrii Chizhevskii, "Ukraïns'kyi literaturnyi barok," *Pratsy
ukraïns'koho istorychno-filolohichnoho tovarystva v Prazi* 5 (1944): 84.

44. Harold B. Segel, *The Literature of Eighteenth-Century Russia,* 2 vols. (New York: Dutton, 1967), 2:257. For the original, see Derzhavin, *Sochineniia,* 1:54. The poem is included in
one of the books used as a textbook in the Nezhin Gymnasium in Gogol's time; see Nikol'skii,
Osnovaniia, 2:53–54; cf. 10:54 and 397.

Closely linked with the notion of the brevity of life was that of its mutability. An anonymous Ukrainian poet observes, "Time destroys everything and shrouds everything. / Time corrodes everything and terminates everything."[45] A sense of the mutability of human existence and the destructiveness of time also pervades the last poem of Derzhavin:

> Time's river in its ceaseless coursing
> Bears all men's deeds along with it,
> And peoples, governments, and rulers
> Drown in oblivion's abyss.
> But if, through sounds of lyre and trumpet,
> Something should happen to remain,
> Eternity's jaws will consume it—
> 'Twill share the common destiny.[46]

Transformation in the course of time is a constant theme of Gogol's. Occasionally, time makes beneficial changes in human beings, like an artist who eventually approaches perfection in his creation. Gogol expresses this idea in *Taras Bulba,* in the encounter between Andrii and the Polish girl, whom he has not seen for a long time:

> It was not like this that he had imagined seeing her; this was not she, not the lady he had known before; nothing in her was the same, but now she was twice as beautiful and marvelous as before; then there had been something unfinished, incomplete in her, now she was the perfect picture to which the artist has given the finishing touch. (2:101; Kent, 2:72)

But such propitious changes caused by time are the exception. As a rule in Gogol's works, the juxtaposition of *before* and *now,* the contemplation of the mutability of human life, is full of sadness and nostalgia for bygone years, as in a lyrical digression in *Dead Souls:*

45. For the original, see Chizhevskii, "Ukraïns'kyi literaturnyi barok," 89.
46. Segel, *The Literature of Eighteenth-Century Russia,* 2:317. For the original, see Derzhavin, *Sochineniia,* 3:178. For a discussion of Baroque elements in Derzhavin's poetry, see Claude Backvis, "Dans quelle mesure Derzhavin est-il un baroque?" in *Studies in Russian and Polish Literature. In Honor of Wacław Lednicki,* ed. Zbigniew Folejewski (The Hague: Mouton, 1962), 72–104. Gogol was certainly familiar with these "[l]ast verses of Derzhavin," including them in the list of anthological Russian poetry; see 8:488 and 808.

In former years, a long time ago, in the years of my youth, in the years of my irrevocably vanished childhood, I used to experience a feeling of joy whenever I came for the first time to any strange place.... Now I feel quite indifferent when I drive through any new village and it is with indifference that I watch its dreary exterior. To my chilled gaze it looks uninviting and no longer amuses me; and what in bygone years would have provoked a lively animation in my face, laughter and a flow of words, now merely passes by, and my unmoving lips preserve an impartial silence. Oh, my youth! Oh, my spontaneity! (6:110–11; Gibian, 114–15)

A sense of loss with time is also apparent in Gogol's correspondence. In his letter to Nikolai Prokopovich on September 27, 1836, when he was only twenty-seven years old, Gogol wrote: "Alas, we are approaching the years when our thoughts and feelings are turning to the old, to the past, and not to the future. What to do? But the old is beautiful. When, oh when, will we gather and recall Nezhin, and Petersburg, and our youth? Both merry and sad will be our carousal" (11:61).

In "Petersburg Notes of 1836," Gogol exclaims, "Why does our irreplaceable time fly so fast? Who is calling it?" (8:188). This acute awareness of mutability evokes, in his "Sketches for a Play from Ukrainian History," an emotional protest over the flight of time and a demand for the return of past years. His outburst lasts but a moment, however, and is followed by the sober realization of the impossibility of that return: "Give me back, return to me, return to me my youth, the strength of my young powers, myself, myself, fresh, the way I was before. Oh, irretrievable is all that exists in the world" (5:201). This emotional outburst of Gogol's is not unlike the verse of an anonymous Ukrainian Baroque poet: "Past the everboring world / pass our years / Waters divide! separate from the earth, / and return me to the days of my youth!"[47]

The irretrievability of time ties the theme of the transience of life to those of its brevity and mutability. This is how the Italian Baroque poet Francesco Bracciolini (1566–1645) expressed the transient character of human existence in his poem "The Impermanence of

47. Chizhevskii, *A History of Ukrainian Literature,* 288.

Things Mortal": "May will return, and winter will return, / but human warmth, once spent, will ne'er return / to vanish slowly in a second life."[48] The theme of human transience also appears in Polotskii's poem "Man Is a Stranger": "Strangers are we in the world when we are born; / Having briefly lived, we leave for another age,"[49] and in Derzhavin's poem "On the Death of Prince Meshcherskii": "Today a god, tomorrow dust; / Today deceived by flattering hope, / Tomorrow, though, 'Where are you, Man?' "[50]

In the fragment "Nights at the Villa," mourning the premature death of his friend Iosif Viel'gorskii, Gogol wrote: "My dear youth in your bloom! Was it for this? Was the reason why this fresh breath of youth swept over me that I should afterwards plunge suddenly and at once into a deathly chill of emotions, suddenly become older by decades, see my life vanishing yet more desperately and hopelessly?" (3:326).

In his treatment of the themes of brevity, mutability, and transience, Gogol is very close to the tragic view of life of literature before and during the Baroque. Gogol already showed his propensity for viewing life in this way in his early years. Besides his being influenced by the *topos* as such, he probably arrived at this melancholic view of life because of his sometimes poor health, his hypochondria, and the premature death of his father—he more than once compared his own constitution to that of his father.[51]

Carpe diem

The name of this *topos* was taken from the *Odes* of Horace (1:11), who, for his part, drew on the teachings of Epicurus. Unlike Epicurus, however, who taught man to find peace of soul in seeking the plea-

48. Segel, 219.

49. For the original, see Anthony R. Hippisley, "Simeon Polotsky as a Representative of the Baroque in Russian Literature" (Ph.D. diss., Oxford University, 1968), 114.

50. Segel, *The Literature of the Eighteenth-Century Russia*, 2:259. For the original, see Derzhavin, *Sochineniia*, 1:55.

51. See V. I. Shenrok, *Materialy dlia biografii Gogolia*, 4 vols. (Moscow, 1892–97), 4:852; for Gogol's own pronouncements on the subject, see 11:314–15, 12:493, and 13:376.

sures of life and strove to release him from the fear of death, Horace's call to seize the day stemmed from his anguish over the brevity of life. In this regard, Horace was greatly indebted to the poetry of Anacreon and his followers. Anacreontic poetry, best known for its glorification of wine, love, and friendship, was permeated with the fear of aging and mortality.[52]

With the advent of Christianity in Europe, *carpe diem* was invoked as a reaction against the Church's repudiation of vain earthly and fleshly pursuits and against the religious injunction to despise this world to save one's soul, given the inevitability of death and the imminence of the Last Judgment.

It is to be expected that *carpe diem* would be highlighted in the Baroque age, when emphasis on the brevity and illusoriness of life intensified. We find it pictorially represented in the late-sixteenth-century Dutch print entitled *Adolescentia amori* (Fig. 44). The print, first in a series presenting the four ages of man, portrays a young man in the company of Venus and Cupid, who embody the youth's amorous aspirations; he is playing on a lute, while in the background there is merrymaking. The text under the picture confirms that the young man is willing to seek earthly pleasures, but his face is sad and contemplative—an indication that he understands the vain and transient character of life's festivities.

In the literature of the Baroque as well as in the arts, *carpe diem* expressed itself in enjoyment of good food and wines, in praise of friendship, and in seeking for sensual delights—all this in view of the brevity of life. The English poet Robert Herrick (1591–1674) evoked erotic pleasures in his celebrated poem "To the Virgins, to make much of Time":

---

52. On the Stoic aspect of *carpe diem* expressed in Horace's *Odes,* see Quentin F. Wesselschmidt, "Stoicism in the Odes of Horace" (Ph.D. diss., University of Iowa, 1979), esp. 130–31, and R.G.M. Nisbet and Margaret Hubbard, *A Commentary on Horace: Odes, Book 1* (Oxford: Clarendon Press, 1970), 134–42. For a detailed discussion of the *topos* of *carpe diem* from Antiquity through the Baroque, see A. A. Long, *Hellenistic Philosophy: Stoics, Epicureans, Sceptics* (New York: Scribner, 1974); James Ellis Wellington, "An Analysis of the *Carpe Diem* Theme in Seventeenth-Century English Poetry (1590–1700)" (Ph.D. diss., Florida State University, 1956); and Frederick H. Candelaria, "The *Carpe Diem* Motif in Early Seventeenth-Century Poetry with Particular Reference to Robert Herrick" (Ph.D. diss., University of Missouri, 1959).

Fig. 44. Crispin van de Passe, the Elder (inv. Marten de Vos), *Adolescentia Amori* (1596)

> Gather ye Rose-buds while ye may,
>   Old Time is still a flying:
> And this same flower that smiles to day,
>   To morrow will be dying.
>
> . . . .
>
> Then be not coy, but use your time;
>   And while ye may, goe marry:
> For having lost but once your prime,
>   You may for ever tarry.[53]

53. Robert Herrick, *The Poetical Works,* ed. F. W. Moorman (Oxford: Clarendon Press, 1915), 84.

A similar outlook is manifest in the poem "Worldly Pleasure" by the Polish poet Hieronim Morsztyn (ca. 1581–ca. 1623), who encourages man to partake of earthly joys in view of inevitable death:

> My task is to describe the delights of the earth;
>   Let each man have them while he lives, as he wishes.
> For after death, though we believe in eternal joy,
>   It will be quite different from our earthly pleasures.[54]

We find praise of the earthly pleasures of life in Ukrainian Baroque poetry too. Klimentii Zinov'ev (ca. 1650– after 1712) counsels musicians:

> Let them play music untiringly
> And add to the merriment of the young.
> After playing for long enough, let them repose a while
> And let them drink a full glass of vodka each.[55]

A *joie de vivre* that, like this, finds its expression in music and drinking is portrayed in *Taras Bulba* in the episode describing the arrival of Taras and his sons at the Zaporozhian Host:

> Their way was barred again by a crowd of musicians in whose midst a young Cossack was dancing and flinging up his arms, his cap jauntily thrust on one side. He only shouted: "Play faster, musicians! Foma, don't grudge vodka to good Christians!" And Foma, who had a black eye, was ladling out an enormous mugful to every comer at random. (2:63; Kent, 2:40)

The narrator claims that the Cossacks' excessive drinking was part of their festive spirits and the high value they set on camaraderie:

---

54. Bogdana Carpenter, trans., *Monumenta Polonica: The First Four Centuries of Polish Poetry* (Ann Arbor: Michigan Slavic Publications, 1989), 271; for the original, see 270.

55. For the original, see Zinoviiv, *Virshi,* 136. In Russian literature prior to Gogol, Lomonosov demonstrated interest in *Anacreontica* in his "Conversation with Anacreon" (1761), although in the form of polemic with the Greek philosopher; see M. V. Lomonosov, *Polnoe sobranie sochinenii,* 10 vols. (Moscow: Akademiia Nauk SSSR, 1950–59), 8:761–67. Derzhavin also turned his attention to the subject in his "Ancreontic Songs" (1804).

The camp presented an extraordinary spectacle; it was an uninterrupted festivity, a ball that began noisily and never ended. . . . There was a fascinating charm in this carousing. It was not a gathering of people drinking to drown sorrow, but simply the frenzied recklessness of gaiety. . . . The gaiety was drunken and noisy, but for all that it was not the gaiety of the gloomy tavern where a man seeks forgetfulness in dreary and depraving hilarity; it was like an intimate club of school comrades. (2:64–65; Kent, 2:42)

The Cossacks' *carpe diem* attitude to life undoubtedly stemmed, however, from their awareness that "no Dnieper Cossack died a natural death" (2:72; Kent, 2:48). Aware that all would die in combat, aware that death awaited them at any moment, they strove "to seize the day" in the interludes between battles in a frenzy of merrymaking. In Gogol's tale, Ostap and Andrii are observed pondering over their future when they receive their mother's blessing before the battle with the Poles:

What did that blessing predict and tell them? Was it a blessing for victory over the enemy and then a joyous return home with booty and everlasting glory in the songs of the bandore players, or . . . ? But the future is unknown, and it stands before man like the autumn fog that rises from the swamp; in it the birds fly senselessly up and down flapping their wings, not recognizing one another, the dove not seeing the hawk, the hawk not seeing the dove, and not one knowing how far he is flying from his doom. (2:87; Kent, 2:61)

In the spirit of much Baroque literature, Gogol endowed his characters with zest for earthly pleasures; this is seen particularly in those of his works, such as *Taras Bulba,* set in the Baroque Ukraine. It is noteworthy, all the same, that Gogol did not depict the amorous aspect of *carpe diem,* dwelling instead on the Cossacks' glorification of camaraderie as well as their excessive consumption of food and alcohol.[56] In his works set after the Baroque, Gogol presents this *joie*

56. This was noted in a different context by Simon Karlinsky in *The Sexual Labyrinth of Nikolai Gogol* (Cambridge: Harvard University Press, 1976), 80–81.

de vivre as having degenerated into sheer gluttony and gross corpore-ality. Gogol shows these characters' enormous food consumption becoming an end in itself, revealing their spiritual emptiness, the *poshlost'* of their brutal existence. Characters like these—"sky-gazers," as Gogol dubbed them (7:9; Gibian, 273–74)—are already to be found in his *Evenings* cycle, in "Ivan Fedorovich Shponka and His Aunt," for example; in all the tales of the *Mirgorod* cycle except *Taras Bulba;* and in *Dead Souls* as well. (Curiously, eating and drink-ing occupy little space in the Petersburg cycle.) The existence of Petr Petrovich Petukh, a fleeting character in the second volume of *Dead Souls,* centers around food. An extraordinary glutton himself, he "was pondering how he might fatten his guests" (7:55; Gibian, 326). This use of *carpe diem* for satirical effect is indeed Gogol's own special contribution to the *topos.*

Vanitas

Like the other *topoi* we have considered, *vanitas* did not originate in the Baroque period. It is at least as old as the Bible: "Vanity of vanities, saith the Preacher, vanity of vanities; all is vanity" (Ecclesiastes 1:2). This contemplation of the futility of earthly pursuits found its way into the teachings of the Stoics, who, in contrast to Epicurus and his disciples, condemned the quest for pleasure as a manifestation of selfishness. The Stoic primacy of moral sentiments and virtues over hedonistic pursuits became an important aspect of Christian doctrine and is emphasized throughout ecclesiastical literature.[57] This is how the famous French preacher Bossuet (1627–1704) treated the *topos* of *vanitas,* in concert with *brevitas vitae,* "life is a dream," and *memento mori,* in his "The Funeral Oration for Henriette-Anne, Duchess of Orleans," which appeared in *The Collection of Exem-*

---

57. On the Stoic attitude to earthly pursuits and its role in the formation of the Christian world view, I consulted the following studies: William L. Davidson, *The Stoic Creed* (Edinburgh: Clark, 1907); Charles H. Stanley Davis, *Greek and Roman Stoicism and Some of Its Disciples* (Boston: Turner, 1903); Richard Mott Gummere, *Seneca the Philosopher and His Modern Message* (New York: Cooper, 1963); Ludwig Edelstein, *The Meaning of Stoicism* (Cambridge: Harvard University Press, 1966); and Marcia L. Colish, *The Stoic Tradition from Antiquity to the Early Middle Ages* (Leiden: Brill, 1985).

plary Russian and Translated Works in Prose, which was one of
Gogol's textbooks at the Nezhin Gymnasium:

> And so I am also destined to pay the last tribute to Princess
> Henriette-Anne! She recently listened to my words at the
> grave of her mother, and now we speak likewise over her cold
> remains; and my mournful voice is preserved for this lamenta-
> ble service. Oh vanity! Oh nothingness! Oh mortals who do
> not know their fate! . . . In depicting one disaster, I want to
> depict all misfortunes of the human race, and in one death I
> wish to show the decay and nothingness of all our grandeur.
> For the vanity of the world was never so clearly seen, nor so
> solemnly manifested. So this sight assures us that health is only
> a word, life is a dream, glory is only a phantom, and beauty and
> pleasure are only dangerous temptations. All in us is vain ex-
> cept for the sincere acknowledgement of our vanity before
> God, except for the thought that we should hold in contempt
> all our existence.[58]

This moral and ethical precept developed into a *topos* prevalent in
Baroque literature and the arts, one which survived in folk art up to
Gogol's day (see Figs. 45 and 46). The inscription to each picture contains the same famous biblical phrase—"Vanity of vanities, all is vanity,"
whereas the other captions in the pictures remind man of the transito-
riness and brevity of his life. In particular, the ornamental ligatured
caption around the central part of Figure 45 reads: "O son, everything
is so changeful in the world."[59] The transience of human existence,
which drove Baroque man to the enjoyment of earthly pleasures,
could also lead to this opposite conclusion, taught by the Church: the
pursuit of material advantages and earthly pleasures is mere vanity. The
dichotomy between these two attitudes, *carpe diem* and *vanitas,*
nicely reflects the contradictions in the Baroque world view.

58. *Sobranie v proze,* 1:270–71.
59. For a discussion of the *topos* in art and literature, see Jan Białostocki, "Kunst und Vanitas,"
in his *Stil und Ikonographie* (Dresden: Kunst, 1966), 187–230; Franz Bächtiger, "Vanitas—
Schicksalsdeutung in der deutschen Renaissancegraphik" (Ph.D. diss., Ludwig-Maximillian University, Munich, 1970); Ferdinand van Ingen, *Vanitas und Memento mori in der deutschen
Barocklyrik* (Groningen: Wolters, 1966); and Giles R. Hoyt, "Vanity and Constancy," in *German
Baroque Literature,* ed. Gerhart Hoffmeister (New York: Ungar, 1983), 211–32.

Vanitas was prevalent in literature that reflected the outlook of the day. The German poet Andreas Gryphius (1616–64) expressed this theme in his poem "All Is Vanity":

> Wherever you look, you see nothing but vanity on earth. What this one builds today, that one will pull down tomorrow. Where now there are towns, there will be a meadow tomorrow, where a shepherd's child will play with the flocks.[60]

And the Polish poet Daniel Naborowski wrote in his poem "Vanity":

> The world favors vanities
> And all earthly matters;
> One can forever be sure
> That vain vanity triumphs.[61]

In Ukrainian and Russian Baroque literature, however, *vanitas* was not as common a theme as in Western Europe. As Aleksandr Morozov observes, "The tragic idea of *vanitas* was, in general, alien to Russian and Ukrainian Baroque or was expressed *sotto voce* and did not come to the fore as in religious Western European poetry of the 17th century."[62] Nevertheless, we do find echoes of this *topos* in Baroque Eastern Slavic literature, which was strongly influenced by Western European models. In the poetry of Polotskii, who studied in Kiev and, in all likelihood, in Wilno, and whose poetry came under Western European influence there, *vanitas* found expression in the poem "Leech" in the cycle *Garden of Many Flowers:*

> Two leeches are always present within us.
> They ceaselessly declare: "Give me! Give me!"
> One is the desire of the spirit for vanities;
> Another is the lust of the flesh for pleasures.
> They are never sated,
> They do not stop, like the sea that swallows up the rivers.[63]

60. Hill, 187. In this poem *vanitas* is coupled with the theme of the brevity, mutability, and transience of life. The appearance in combination of these and the other themes discussed is characteristically Baroque.

61. For the original, see Sokołowska and Żukowska, eds., *Poeci polskiego baroku,* 1:178.

62. See A. A. Morozov, "Problema barokko v russkoi literature XVII—nachala XVIII veka (Sostoianie voprosa i zadachi izucheniia)," *Russkaia literatura* 3 (1962): 21.

63. For the original, see V. P. Adrianova-Peretts, ed., *Russkaia sillabicheskaia poéziia XVII–XVIII v.v.* (Leningrad: Sovetskii pisatel', 1970), 140.

Fig. 45.   *Vanitas*

In another cycle, *Rifmologion,* Polotskii spoke about the vanity of
man in face of the brevity of his existence, echoing Ecclesiastes:
"Vanity of vanities, all is vanity, / Nothing lasts for long in the world."[64]

   Polotskii's successor, the Russian poet Mikhail Lomonosov (1711–
65), studied not only in Moscow, St. Petersburg, and Kiev, but also in
Marburg, where he became closely acquainted with German late-
Baroque poetry, and in particular with that of Johann Christian Gün-

---

64. Hippisley, "Simeon Polotsky as a Representative," 114. The lines duplicate the opening
of Ecclesiastes. I should like to emphasize that in a time of religious disunity and debates over
ecclesiastical issues, people of the Baroque age showed great interest in the Old Testament.
Besides Ecclesiastes, they were also especially interested in Psalms and the Book of Job. For a
more detailed discussion of this issue, see Skrine, *The Baroque,* 155.

Fig. 46. "Look Closely, Mortal . . ."

ther (1695–1723). Lomonosov dealt with the theme of *vanitas* in his *Concise Guide to Eloquence* (also known as *Rhetoric*).[65] Apostrophizing man as the ignoble nothingness he will inevitably become, the poet rebuked him for vainglory: "Oh you, food for worms! Oh, ashes and despicable dust! / Oh night! Oh vanity! Why are you so proud?"[66] Lomonosov's younger contemporary, the Ukrainian poet and philosopher Grigorii Skovoroda (1722–94), who studied in Kiev and traveled extensively in the West, wrote in the cycle *Garden of Divine Songs* that "our life is all vain rubbish."[67]

Gogol came close to this outlook of Skovoroda in his depiction of characters devoid of spirituality, their lives all "vain rubbish."[68] But Skovoroda is not the only Ukrainian Baroque writer whose works come to mind when considering this aspect of Gogol's outlook. Gogol's depiction in *Dead Souls* of the governor's guests, whom he compares to vain flies (see 6:14; Gibian, 9–10), can be linked to earlier Ukrainian Baroque sermonizing, and in particular to an episode from "The Word on the Second Week after the Holy Spirit Day" by Stefan Iavorskii (1658–1722), in which this preacher compares man's vain pursuits to fish aimlessly swimming.[69]

In this connection, let us consider afresh "The Nose." The life of the protagonist, Major Kovalev, is full of vain intents, such as amorous pursuits and looking for a cushy job. His vanity is emphasized in his frequent gazing at himself in the mirror (see 3:52–53, 54, 68, 73, and 74; Kent, 2:219, 221, 232, 237, and 238). A mirror as a symbol of vanity also appears in Gogol's "The Portrait" and in *Dead Souls* in the description of Chartkov and Chichikov (see 3:97 and 98; Kent, 2:269 and 270; and 6:13, 135, and 161; Gibian, 9, 141, and 171–72).[70] A

65. On Lomonosov's familiarity with German poetry, see Ilya Z. Serman, *Mikhail Lomonosov* (Jerusalem: Hebrew University of Jerusalem, 1988), 56–58.

66. For the original, see Lomonosov, *Polnoe sobranie sochinenii,* 7:292.

67. For the original, see Hryhorii Skovoroda, *Povne zibrannia tvoriv,* 2 vols. (Kiev: Naukova dumka, 1973), 1:81.

68. Students of Gogol have found a number of conceptual similarities between Gogol and Skovoroda. See, for example, Chizhevskii, "About 'The Overcoat,' " 315–16, and Smirnova, *Poéma Gogolia,* 62–63.

69. Smirnova, *Poéma Gogolia,* 63–64. This scholar rightly goes on to say that the didactic spirit of *vanitas* pervades a great deal of Gogol's works. She also interprets the abundance of dishes and bottles on the cover of *Dead Souls* designed by Gogol as the writer's allusion to the theme of *vanitas* (77).

70. In "Nevsky Prospekt," Piskarev's projected portrayal on canvas of Pirogov's "manly face" (3:36; Kent, 1:230) was designed to play the role of his "mirror." Pirogov also demonstrates his

mirror, the image of the ephemeral *par excellence,* became the pre-
eminent symbol in the iconography of *vanitas* in art before and
during the Baroque.[71] Another primary symbol of *vanitas* was the
skull, which also conveyed the idea of transience and linked *vanitas*
to *memento mori.* Such a symbol, I suggest, is the de-nosed Kovalev;
his noselessness and hence likeness to a skull is in some sense a
variation on a well-known motif exemplified in Lucas Furtenagel's
The Portrait of Peter Burgkmair and Anna Allerlaiin (1529, Vienna,
Kunsthistorisches Museum), where the faces appear as death's-heads
in the mirror. This experience of noselessness did not teach Kovalev
or the world surrounding him a lesson. In this sense, it may remind us
of Jan Amos Komenský's ironic allegory, *The Labyrinth of the World
and the Paradise of the Heart* (written in 1623, first published in
1631), which depicts various people strolling conceitedly about,
proud of their physical appearance, carousing, or amassing wealth,
and all disregarding the warnings of Death present among them.[72]

The *topoi* of *vanitas* and *memento mori* appear often and more
clearly in *Dead Souls,* particularly in the second volume, where Gogol's aim is to effect a change in the reader through the example of
the moral transformation of his characters. Of Chichikov first and

---

vanity in a hypocritical remark, parodying Ecclesiastes, about his military rank: " 'O dear, vanity,
all is vanity. What if I am a lieutenant?' " (3:36; Kent, 1:229).

71. See G. F. Hartlaub, *Zauber des Spiegels* (Munich: Piper, 1951), 149–57; Heinrich
Schwarz, "The Mirror in Art," *The Art Quarterly* 15 (1952): 106–9; Erwin Panofsky, *Problems
in Titian, Mostly Iconographic* (New York: New York University Press, 1969), 92–94; and Jan
Białostocki, "Man and Mirror in Painting: Reality and Transience," in *Studies in Late Medieval
and Renaissance Painting in Honor of Millard Meiss,* 2 vols., ed. Irving Lavin and John
Plummer (New York: New York University Press, 1977), 1:71–72.

72. See Jan Amos Komenský (Comenius) *The Labyrinth of the World and the Paradise of
the Heart* (Ann Arbor: University of Michigan Press, 1972), 12–13. A recent study has raised
the possibility that Komenský's *Labyrinth* was known in Russia as early as the second quarter of
the seventeenth century; see V. K. Bylinin, " 'Labirint mira' v interpretatsii russkogo poéta
pervoi poloviny XVII veka," in *Razvitie barokko i zarozhdenie klassitsizma v Rossii XVII–
nachala XVIII vv.,* ed. A. N. Robinson (Moscow: Nauka, 1989), 42–49.

Several scholars have linked Gogol to Komenský, albeit in passing. Thus Chizhevskii associated Gogol's *Selected Passages* with Komenský's *Praxis Pietatis;* Ernest Denis called Komenský
a precursor of great Russian novelists; and V. V. Bibikhin, the author of the comments on
Komenský's *Labyrinth* in the recent Russian edition of his pedagogical works, interpreted this
statement by Denis as an allusion to Gogol.

See, respectively, Chizhevskii, "Neizvestnyi Gogol'," 149; Ernest Denis, *La Bohème depuis la
Montagne-Blanche,* 2 vols. (Paris: Leroux, 1903), 1:225–26; and J. A. Komenský, *Izbrannye
pedagogicheskie sochineniia,* 2 vols. (Moscow: Pedagogika, 1982), 1:612.

foremost: Murazov advises him, "Forget this noisy world and all its whims and temptations" (7:113; Gibian, 392), and at a certain moment, Chichikov seems inclined to follow Murazov's advice, when he has experienced "a state of semi-consciousness such as comes over a man when confronted with black and inevitable death—that monster repugnant to our nature" (7:109; Gibian, 387).

Memento mori

In the Mesopotamian epic, *Gilgamesh,* the protagonist says to his friend Enkidu: " 'Only the gods [live] forever under the sun. / As for men, their days are numbered; / their achievements are a puff of wind.' "[73] Similar observations are found in many other ancient texts. The most important sources in the formation of the *memento mori topos,* however, were the Bible and Roman Stoicism. Regarding the life of man we read in Psalms: "For He knoweth our frame; He remembereth that we are dust" (Psalms 103:14). Seneca meditated increasingly upon death and emphasized the importance of such meditation (e.g., *Epistles* 70:17—18).[74] The *topos* of *memento mori* took shape in the Middle Ages and reached its zenith in art and literature in the Baroque period.[75] The Church actively promulgated this concept in sermons and in eulogies such as Bossuet's, quoted above, as an effective means of weaning people from earthly pleasures by reminding

73. *Gilgamesh,* trans. John Gardner and John Maier (New York: Knopf, 1984), 109. On the awareness of man's mortality in *Gilgamesh,* see Thorkild Jacobsen, *The Treasures of Darkness: A History of Mesopotamian Religion* (New Haven: Yale University Press, 1976), 202—7 and 217—19, and Tigay, *The Evolution of the Gilgamesh Epic,* 50—51 and 164—65.

74. For a detailed discussion of the concept of death and its place in Stoicism, see Ernst Benz, *Das Todesproblem in der stoischen Philosophie* (Stuttgart: Kohlhammer, 1929).

75. For a detailed discussion of the *topos* in art and literature, see André Chastel,"L'art et le sentiment de la mort au XVIIe siècle," *XVIIe Siècle* 36—37 (1957): 287—93; Edelgard Dubruck, *The Theme of Death in French Poetry of the Middle Ages and the Renaissance* (The Hague: Mouton, 1964); Kathleen Cohen, *Metamorphosis of a Death Symbol* (Berkeley and Los Angeles: University of California Press, 1973); Gert Kaiser, "Das *Memento mori,*" *Euphorion* 68 (1974): 337—70; Philippa Tristram, *Figures of Life and Death in Medieval English Literature* (New York: New York University Press, 1976); Gerhild Scholz Williams, *The Vision of Death: A Study of the "Memento Mori" Expressions in Some Latin, German, and French Didactic Texts of the 11th and 12th Centuries* (Goppingen: Kümmerle, 1976); and Kristine Lynn Koozin, "Metaphors of Memento Mori: Still Life Painting and Poetry of Seventeenth-Century Holland" (Ph.D. diss., Ohio University, 1984).

them that life is brief and that they should think of preparing their souls for the Last Judgment and the life to come (see Fig. 47).

We find this aspect of the Baroque world view in the following poem by the French poet Jean-Baptiste Chassignet (ca. 1571–ca. 1635):

> Mortal, think that there lies beneath the roof of a charnel-house a body eaten by worms, defleshed, denerved, where the revealed bones, marrowless and untied, abandon their joints; here one of the hands falls as it rots, the eyes roll back, liquefy into phlegm, and the various muscles form the usual fodder for the greedy worms; the torn belly, bursting with putrescence, infects the neighbouring air with the foul stench, and the half-gnawed nose deforms the face; then, knowing the condition of your fragility, rely on God alone, deeming vanity all which makes you no more knowledgeable, no wiser.[76]

The Polish poet Hieronim Morsztyn more succinctly expresses the same idea in his poem "Time":

> Everything passes with time,
> I am alive, but death is around the corner.
> One man gets on a boat, another—off the boat,
> This one dies, that one is born.[77]

Memento mori was commonplace in Eastern Slavic literature as well. According to Hippisley, this theme was emphasized in the Kiev Collegium. Polotskii, schooled there, wrote a number of poems on the subject, with such titles as "Oblivion of Death," "Memory of Death," and "To Wait for Death."[78] In one of the poems Polotskii wrote: "There is no joy for a warrior when an enemy reaches him with a sword. / Every man look, behind you there is Death with a scythe."[79] The theme was also expressed in the poetry of another

---

76. Hill, 199.

77. For the original, see Sokołowska and Żukowska, eds., *Poeci polskiego baroku*, 1:241–42.

78. Hippisley, "Simeon Polotsky as a Representative," xiii.

79. For the original, see Adrianova-Peretts, ed., *Russkaia sillabicheskaia poéziia XVII–XVIII v.v.*, 153.

Fig. 47. *Memento mori.* From 1702 *Sinodik*

Kiev Collegium graduate, Ivan Velichkovskii, who wrote in his poem "On the Image of the Foppish Youth Secretly Followed by Death":

> It is not good, oh handsome youth, to make merry;
> Look around to see who follows you like a thief.
> This is Death who wants you prematurely in your grave,
> The scythe also knows how to reap beautiful flowers.[80]

The *topos* of *memento mori* stands out in Gogol's works. As I have already suggested, the *topos* is reflected in the skull-like image of the temporarily de-nosed Kovalev, which evokes the well-known iconographical motifs represented in pre-Baroque and Baroque art and literature: a man looking for himself in the mirror but finding only Death reflected in it; Death in the midst of people who ignore its presence; and the like.

Memento mori appears with all its force in *Dead Souls*. The *topos* is already alluded to by the skulls and skeletons on the cover of the first edition. Its importance to this work is confirmed in Gogol's preparatory notes intended for the reprinting of the first volume of *Dead Souls*, in which he set down its central ideas. Among these were "[h]ow the emptiness and impotent idleness of life make way for dull and inexpressive death. How this terrible event happens senselessly. They don't move. Death strikes a motionless world" (6:692).[81]

A significant aspect of *memento mori* was the perception of death as the leveler that does not distinguish between rich and poor, powerful and powerless. Here is how Francesco Bracciolini expressed this idea in his poem "Invincible Death": "Death cannot be by riches held at bay / a single day; and ne'er was farther than / a moment—Ah, days fleeting and so few!"[82] And here is the Polish poet Wacław Potocki (1621–96), who in his poem "What Time Finds, Time Ruins" speaks of men's equality before Time and Death:

> Someone once said, Time's wisdom has no peer.
>   Another, Time's stupidity. And so?
> The former counted divers trades and arts,
>   Which time did exercise men in—and does;

80. For the original, see Velychkovs'kyi, *Tvory*, 135.
81. See Smirnova, *Poéma Gogolia*, 65–66 and 77.
82. Segel, 257 (256).

> The latter—statesmen, states, kings, sages, knights,
> Towns, castles, palaces, which to their harm
> Bequeathed the same uncertain legacy,
> Sank in the silence of eternity.
> You ask, The question then is how resolved?
> Whatever came with time shall in time die.[83]

This aspect of *memento mori* also found expression in Eastern Slavic literature. Polotskii wrote, "Tsar and pauper as equals enter the pit of the grave." Velichkovskii lamented: "No one can hide from you, death! / Oh grief! Tsar and slave have to die." Skovoroda addressed death: "You do not spare a Tsar's head either, / You do not distinguish where a peasant is and where a Tsar— / You devour all, like fire devours straw." And Derzhavin in the poem cited earlier, "On the Death of Prince Meshcherskii," said, "Both king and captive feed the worms."[84]

Contemplation of death as the great leveler can be found in Gogol's "Overcoat." Describing Akakii Akakievich's death, the narrator characterized him as "a creature on whom disease fell as it falls upon the heads of the mighty ones of this world!" (3:169; Kent, 2:329). And the narrator in *Dead Souls,* describing the prosecutor's death, interrupts his sarcastic portrayal with the philosophical comment, "the manifestation of death was as terrible in a small man as in a great one" (6:210; Gibian, 226).[85]

Another important facet of *memento mori* was the idea that man should remember his end and live virtuously, because only such a life will be rewarded by the Almighty. We find this reminder in van den Vondel's poem "On the Death of Maria van den Vondel":

> When mortal life ends under sod
> Begins the unending life in Heaven,
> Known unto angels and to God,
> And only to the blessed given.[86]

83. Ibid., 251.

84. See, respectively, Hippisley, "Simeon Polotsky as a Representative," 108; Velychkovs'kyi, *Tvory,* 136; Skovoroda, *Povne zibrannia tvoriv,* 1:67; Segel, *The Literature of Eighteenth-Century Russia,* 2:258; and Derzhavin, *Sochineniia,* 1:54.

85. Cf. Igor' Zolotusskii, "Troika, kopeika, koleso," in his *Ispoved' zoila* (Moscow: Sovetskaia Rossiia, 1989), 366.

86. Segel, 155 (154).

A similar thought appears in Potocki's poem, "Man's Life": "Who wants to live with God, not burn in hell, / Should think of every single hour his span."[87] And Polotskii instructs his reader: "Be ready to die, and you may receive Eternal Life through death."[88]

Gogol expressed this idea with singular clarity in a letter to his mother on January 25, 1847:

> In the Holy Scriptures it is said that he who remembers his end at every moment will never sin. He who remembers about death and imagines it vividly before his eyes will not desire death, because he sees himself how many good things it is necessary to do to earn a good end and stand before the judgment of the Lord without fear. Until the time when a person becomes accustomed to the thought of death and makes it seem as if it were awaiting him the next day, he will never begin living as one ought to; and he will postpone everything from day to day to a future time. The constant thought of death educates the soul in an amazing way; it lends strength for life and good deeds in life. (13:194; Proffer, 169–70)[89]

Yet another facet of *memento mori* was the concept of *ars moriendi,* or the art of dying well. This emerged in the art and literature of the fifteenth century and remained popular through the Baroque when death and the image of death were omnipresent because of the frequent, devastating plagues. *Ars moriendi* presented the possibility of attaining salvation through deathbed repentance. The Rohan Book of Hours (1418–25) depicts a dying man saying: "Into Thy hands, O Lord, I commend my spirit. You [sic] have redeemed me, O Lord, Thou God of truth," and the figure of God leaning over him and answering: "Do penance for thy sins, and thou shalt be with me in the judgment."[90] One of the ways of "dying well"

87. Ibid., 208.

88. Adrianova-Peretts, ed., *Russkaia sillabicheskaia poéziia XVII–XVIII v.v.,* 154.

89. Cf. Gogol's entry in his 1846–51 notebook: "One has to moderate one's spirit in cheerful moments by considering the most important things in life–death, future life,–so that it will be easier and brighter in difficult moments" (7:383).

90. See T.S.R. Boase, *Death in the Middle Ages* (New York: McGraw-Hill, 1972), 119 and fig. 102. For more information about *ars moriendi* in art and literature, also see Sister Mary Catharine O'Connor, *The Art of Dying Well* (New York: Columbia University Press, 1942), and Émile Mâle, *Religious Art from the Twelfth to the Eighteenth Century* (New York: Pantheon, 1949), 150–55, and Rainer Rudolf, *Ars moriendi* (Cologne: Böhlau, 1957).

in the period of the religious wars that shook Europe was to attain salvation in battle against the infidels (the Moslems) or against a "heretical" Christian denomination. These ideas were expressed in Antonio Possevino's treatise *The Christian Knight* (1569), on which the Polish preacher Piotr Skarga modeled his *Knightly Devotion* (1606).[91] The Polish poet Samuel Twardowski maintained that a hetman [commander-in-chief] ought to die on the battlefield.[92] *Ars moriendi* stands out in the 1842 edition of *Taras Bulba.* (In the 1835 edition it was inconspicuous, and perhaps in underscoring it in the 1842 edition Gogol was influenced by Western sources, literary or pictorial, while he worked abroad.) True to the spirit of the Baroque period, in which the tale was set, Gogol endowed its military characters with the aspiration to die as befits a warrior, a defender of "true" Christianity. The protagonist of the tale, like Twardowski's narrator, calls on Cossacks to die "an honest Cossack death" in battle (2:168; Kent, 2:128), and indeed each Cossack in the tale views it as a great honor to die for the Orthodox faith. The best illustration of this is Kukubenko's death, the graphic description of which bears a striking resemblance to well-known Christian iconographical motifs: the ascension of the soul and its place on the right hand of Christ—the lot accorded the righteous. In this tale, Christ explains to Kukubenko why his soul was so honored: " 'Thou hast not betrayed thy comrades; thou hast wrought no deed of dishonor; thou hast forsaken no man in trouble; thou hast guarded and saved My Church' " (2:141; Kent, 2:106).[93]

This spirit of *miles christianus,* the Christian soldier, which pervades the 1842 edition of *Taras Bulba,* is to be found, albeit figuratively, in other works of Gogol's written in the 1840s, at the time of his heightened religious sensibilities. In "The Rule of Living in the World," Gogol speaks of a contemporary Christian in the military terms so often associated with *ars moriendi,* only this time, unlike in *Taras Bulba,* he envisions this battle allegorically. He views human

---

91. Possevino's treatise, in its turn, was undoubtedly modeled on Erasmus's very influential *Manual of the Christian Knight* (1503).

92. See Stefan Herman, "Śmierć Sarmaty na polu bitwy (Barokowa *ars moriendi*)," *Teksty* 3 (1979): 144–45 and 147.

93. For a detailed discussion of the Kukubenko episode, see Gavriel Shapiro, "A Note on the Connection Between an Episode from Nikolai Gogol's *Taras Bulba* and Visual Art, Mainly Roman Baroque," *Hebrew University Studies in Literature and the Arts* 13 (1985): 214–21.

life as a path, along which man must combat worldly temptations and guard his figure of a true Christian:

> We are called to battle, not to a festival: we shall celebrate victory in the other world. . . . Present amidst the battle, do not lose it from sight even for an hour; preparing for the battle, prepare yourself for it beforehand in order to follow the road soberly, vigilantly, and joyfully. Fear not! For at the end of the road there is God and eternal bliss![94]

Gogol expressed the same thought a few years later, in *Selected Passages from Correspondence with Friends:*

> But remember, we were not at all called into the world for celebrations and banquets. We were called here for battle; we will celebrate the victory *there*. And that is why we must not for a moment forget that we have entered into battle and choose something in which there is less peril; like good soldiers, every one of us must rush there where the battle is blazing. The Heavenly General views all of us from above, and our smallest deed does not escape His gaze. Do not shun the field of battle, and, when in battle, seek out not the enemy's weakness but his strength. (8:368; Zeldin, 198)[95]

By and large, Gogol presented the *memento mori* theme much as it had appeared in Baroque literature. Like Baroque writers, Gogol characterized death as the indiscriminate terminator of human life. He was also preoccupied with the idea frequently highlighted in Baroque writings that man should constantly ponder over his death and lead a virtuous life so that he may fearlessly await his end, but even more important, the end of the world and the Last Judgment. Gogol also introduced into his writings the theme of *ars moriendi* characteristic of the pre-Baroque and Baroque periods with their incessant contemplation of death. His treatment of this concept was twofold: on the one hand, he played it out in literal military terms, as

---

94. As cited by Geir Kjetsaa in his "Gogol' kak uchitel' zhizni: Novye materialy," *Scando-Slavica* 34 (1988): 60.

95. On the connection between the two passages, see Kjetsaa, "Gogol' kak uchitel' zhizni," 63.

in *Taras Bulba,* set in the Baroque Ukraine, conveying the Zeitgeist of that period. On the other hand, in his sermonizing writings he applied such military terms figuratively to the conduct of a contemporary Christian, who must fight the good fight within himself, in order to attain salvation in the next world.

The End of the World

The *topos* of the end of the world, as we find it in the Baroque culture, originated in the Old Testament visions of prophets such as Daniel and Isaiah. With the emergence of Christianity, the Old Testament apprehension of the collapse of the world underwent metamorphosis and received a new interpretation, in particular in the Book of Revelation.[96] In the Baroque period eschatological images derived from the Revelation, such as the 1626 *Death on a Pale Horse* by an anonymous artist of the Kiev school (see Fig. 48), were common.

The Baroque attitude toward the eschaton differed considerably from that of earlier times. Comparing the treatment of this *topos* in the literature of the Late Middle Ages and of the Baroque, Frank J. Warnke maintains that the difference lay in that late medieval literature viewed the world as continuing to develop and to flourish for an indefinite time while individual human bodies decayed, whereas in Baroque literature the destruction of an individual was seen as an omen of the imminent annihilation of the whole world.[97] This idea surfaced in the epigram of the German poet Friedrich von Logau (1604–55) entitled "The Best Thing in the World": "Do you know what I like best in this world? That time consumes itself, and that the world is not going to last forever."[98] The calamities of the world led the Polish poet Samuel Przypkowski (ca. 1592–1670) to the conclusion: "Flood, earthquake, polluted air, / war, famine: what is then left

96. For a historical survey of the eschatological beliefs, see Philip P. Wiener, ed., *Dictionary of the History of Ideas,* 4 vols. (New York: Scribner, 1973), s.v. "Eschatology," and M. H. Abrams, "Apocalypse: Themes and Variations," in *The Apocalypse in English Renaissance Thought and Literature,* ed. C. A. Patrides and Joseph Wittreich (Ithaca: Cornell University Press, 1984), 342–68.

97. Warnke, *Versions of Baroque,* 209.

98. Hill, 217.

Fig. 48. *An Apocalypse Scene: Death on the Pale Horse*

to the world but doom?"[99] Eschatological visions are also manifest in the poetry of Ivan Velichkovskii, in the cycle entitled *Verses on Apocalypse.*[100] For Klimentii Zinov'ev, this kind of apocalyptic world perception is an occasion for human repentance: "The end of the visible world is near: / It is time for sinful man to repent."[101]

Apocalyptic visions, always present in Gogol's thinking, found their outlet in his writings. Konstantin Mochul'skii has observed: "The religious conscience of the writer is apocalyptic: the earth is burning, the skies are folding up, the dead are rising from their graves, monsters are arising from the seeds of our sins."[102] Indeed, in the 1835 edition of "The Portrait," Gogol describes the end of the world in apocalyptic terms, echoing Revelation:

> "My son," he said to me after staring long and almost motionlessly into heaven—"very soon, very soon now the time will come when the Tempter of the human race, the Antichrist, will be born on earth. Terrible will that time be and it will be just before the end of the world. He is rushing on his giant horse, and terrible will be the tortures suffered by those who remain true to Christ." (3:443; Tulloch, 95)

Further on in his monologue, the artist, in a manner well in line with the Baroque emphasis on the flux of existence, accounts for the destruction of the world by the fact that "with every day that passes the laws of nature are becoming weaker and weaker."

In the early eighteenth century there were already predictions by the Swabian mystic Johann Albrecht Bengel (1687–1752) that the end of the world would occur in 1837. At the close of the eighteenth century, Bengel's predictions were accepted by Johann Heinrich Jung-Stilling (1740–1817), whose writings were popularized in Russia by the early-nineteenth-century Freemasons. Jung-Stilling's eschatological teachings were favorably received and became fashionable at the court of Alexander I, and his works were published in Russian in the late 1810s. In all likelihood, Gogol was familiar with the works of Jung-Stilling and was reflecting his widely known es-

99. For the original, see Dmitrii Chizhevskii, "K problemam literatury barokko u slavian," *Litteraria* 13 (1970): 53.

100. See Velychkovs'kyi, *Tvory,* 113–15.

101. Zinoviiv, *Virshi,* 283; see also 290–91.

102. Konstantin Mochul'skii, *Dukhovnyi put' Gogolia* (Paris: YMCA, 1934), 89.

chatological predictions in the 1835 edition of "The Portrait." He did this in *The Government Inspector* (1836) as well but more subtly, and perhaps on this account Gogol deemed it unnecessary to make changes in the publications of that play after 1837.[103] In his 1842 edition of "The Portrait," however, Gogol deleted the obvious allusions to Jung-Stilling's eschatological predictions since they were already outdated.[104]

In *Dead Souls,* besides certain implicit anticipations of the end of the world similar to those in *The Government Inspector,* Gogol took a different approach to this theme.[105] He parodied the eschatological predictions so fashionable at one time in the Russian *beau monde* by showing what a ridiculous form they could take upon reaching the less genteel strata of Russian society:

> The merchants . . . had implicit faith in the predictions of a certain prophet who had already been sitting in jail these last three years. The prophet had appeared no one knows whence, wearing bast-shoes and an unlined sheepskin coat, and smelling terribly of stale fish; and he had announced that Napoleon was Antichrist and was kept on a stone chain, behind six walls and seven seas, but that afterwards he would break his chains and master the whole world. The prophet was very properly jailed for this prediction, but nevertheless he had done his job and set the merchants in a flutter. For a long time after, even while attending to their most profitable deals, they chattered about Antichrist on the way to the tavern for their tea. (6:206; Gibian, 222–23)

With this example Gogol also exposed how a serious theological concept could be vulgarized and made commonplace. In *Selected Passages from Correspondence with Friends* he advocated caution in treating important concepts. In the section entitled "A Question of

---

103. For a recent discussion of the apocalyptic character of the silent scene in *The Government Inspector,* see Iu. V. Mann, " 'Uzhas okoval vsekh . . .' [O nemoi stsene v 'Revizore' Gogolia]," *Voprosy literatury* 8 (1989): 233.

104. See Chizhevskii, "Neizvestnyi Gogol'," 139–41. For a detailed comparative analysis of the two editions of "The Portrait," see Nadezhda Zhernakova, " 'Portret' Gogolia v dvukh redaktsiiakh," *Transactions of the Association of Russian-American Scholars in the U.S.A.* 17 (1984): 23–27.

105. On eschatology in *Dead Souls,* see V. M. Markovich, *Peterburgskie povesti N. V. Gogolia* (Leningrad: Khudozhestvennaia literatura, 1989), 177–84.

Words," Gogol said: "The higher truths are, the more cautious one must be with them; otherwise they are converted into common things, and common things are not believed" (8:231; Zeldin, 23).

Gogol thus treats the theme of the end of the world on two different levels: in the 1835 edition of "The Portrait," he used the popular eschatological predictions of the time for aesthetic and moralistic pronouncements in the solemn spirit of the New Testament, the spirit adopted by Baroque literature. Gogol departed from this tradition in his use of the *topos* in *Dead Souls,* where he was concerned to expose the *poshlost'* of the day. He showed how human beings are capable of debasing any lofty concept by using it trivially—chatting about Antichrist on their way to a tearoom. He satirizes how the merchants, though they believed in the prophecy, were at the same time so deeply immersed in their vain pursuits that they were incapable of thinking about the meaning of their lives, as they should have been moved to do by so ominous a prospect.

The Last Judgment

This *topos* is of course closely related to the preceding one, since according to Christian belief, Doomsday will follow the end of the world. Christian ecclesiastical literature of the Baroque age constantly reminded readers of the ephemeral nature of their existence and the imminence of death and called upon them to detach themselves from earthly pleasures and to do good deeds, in view of the coming Last Day. Thus the Last Judgment *topos* is also connected with the other *topoi* in this chapter: "life is a dream," *brevitas vitae, carpe diem* (through awareness of human physical decay), *vanitas,* and *memento mori.* And also with *theatrum mundi:* Sir Thomas Browne (1605–82), for example, viewed the Last Judgment as the concluding scene of the "play" that is our world: "This is that one day, that shall include and comprehend all that went before it; wherein, as in the last scene, all the Actors must enter to compleat and make up the Catastrophe of this great piece."[106]

106. Sir Thomas Browne, *Religio Medici and Other Writings,* ed. Frank L. Huntley (New York: Dutton, 1951), 53.

The notion of the Last Judgment occupied a very important role in the religious life of the Kievan Rus' in the late tenth century:

> Out of all the depictions whose subject was the last days of the world, the Last Judgment and the future life, those of the Last Judgment should be placed first, as it combined in itself all these events. The significance of its depiction in Old Rus' was enormous; on the strength of this, a Christian missionary converted Prince Vladimir to Christianity. There is no doubt that it produced the same strong impression on the people, both in the period of their conversion to Christianity and in later times. The influence of this depiction on folk poetry is therefore beyond question.[107]

The importance of the Last Judgment in the religious customs of Muscovy is attested to by the "Last Judgment Action" performed once a year on Shrove Sunday as early as the first half of the seventeenth century under the guidance of the highest member of a local clergy. In Moscow, the Action was officiated by the Patriarch himself. Peter the Great put an end to this custom, and the Action was last performed by Patriarch Adrian in 1697.[108] The *topos* survived at least through the mid-nineteenth century, as is clearly demonstrated by pictures dating from then, as well as from the eighteenth century (see Figs. 49 and 50).

The concept of the Last Judgment was equally popular in the Ukraine. According to Vladimir Zavitnevich, "none of the tenets of Christian dogma received such detailed elaboration in Ukrainian everyday life as the Last Judgment. The proof is to be seen in the paintings on this subject available to scholars."[109]

In both the Ukraine and Russia the Last Judgment theme appeared in a variety of literary forms, including drama and meditative poetry. An anonymous late-seventeenth-century Ukrainian author presented

---

107. "Strashnyi Sud," in *Éntsiklopedicheskii slovar'* (St. Petersburg: F. A. Brokgauz and I. A. Efron, 1890–1907), 62:789; also see Fedor Buslaev, "Izobrazhenie Strashnogo Suda," in his *Drevnerusskaia narodnaia literatura i iskusstvo,* 2 vols. (St. Petersburg, 1861), 2:133–54.

108. See "Strashnyi Sud," 791, and Morozov, *Istoriia russkogo teatra,* 310–11.

109. Vladimir Zavitnevich, "Religiozno-nravstvennoe sostoianie N. V. Gogolia v poslednie gody ego zhizni," in *Pamiati Gogolia,* ed. N. P. Dashkevich (Kiev, 1902), 384.

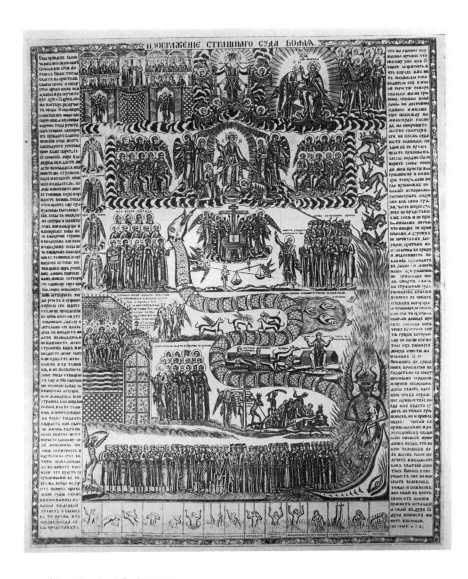

Fig. 49. *The Last Judgment*

Fig. 50. *The Last Judgment*

his own version of the Last Judgment Day in the play *A Short Dialogue About the Sinful Soul Judged by the Impartial Judge, Christ the Savior.* Another dramatic realization of this theme is the play *A Terrible Representation of the Second Advent of the Lord on Earth,* performed in the Moscow Slavic-Greek-Latin Academy in 1702 and apparently written by one of its professors.[110]

In meditative Baroque poetry, treatment of the theme ranged from the elaborate, as in the second book of *Pentateugum* by the Russian poet of Polish origin Andrei Belobotskii (Jan Białobocki, d. early 1700s) entitled *About the Terrible Divine Judgment,* to the epigrammatic, as in Ivan Velichkovskii's "Doomsday": "At that Judgment, when everyone will give an account of everything, will one day be long enough?"[111]

In the light of the great significance of the theme for Christian doctrine and its reflection in literature and art prior to and during the Baroque epoch, it is not surprising that the Last Judgment was of great import in Gogol's works as in his life. In his early childhood he learned about it from his mother in a way that profoundly affected him. Many years later, in a letter of October 2, 1833, he reminded her of this memory from his childhood:

> I asked you to tell me about the last judgment; and so well, so comprehensively, so touchingly did you tell me, a child, about the blessings which await people for a virtuous life—and so strikingly, so terrifyingly did you describe the eternal torments of the sinful—that this shook and awakened all sensitivity within me. That sparked and subsequently produced the most elevated thoughts in me. (10:282; Proffer, 45–46)

Toward the end of his life, at a time of heightened religious sensibilities, the concept of the Last Judgment was especially significant. In *Selected Passages from Correspondence with Friends* (1847), Gogol advised the poet Nikolai Iazykov to

---

110. See, respectively, Petrov, *Ocherki iz istorii ukrainskoi literatury XVII i XVIII vekov,* 137–43, and A. N. Robinson, ed., *P'esy shkol'nykh teatrov Moskvy* (Moscow: Nauka, 1974), 461–63.

111. See, respectively, Adrianova-Peretts, ed., *Russkaia sillabicheskaia poéziia XVII–XVIII v.v.,* 223–30, and Velychkovs'kyi, *Tvory,* 152.

leaf through the Old Testament: there you will find each of our present events, you will see more clearly than day how the present has sinned before God, and the terrible judgment of God upon it so manifestly presented that the present will shake with trembling. . . . Your verses must be in the eyes of everyone like those letters traced in the air which appeared at the feast of Balthazar, which terrified everyone even before they could penetrate their meaning. (8:278; Zeldin, 86)[112]

In a letter to his mother and sisters at the end of March 1849, three years before his death, Gogol wrote, "We are still lucky that God scourges us with misfortunes and, at least sometimes, makes us come to our senses and look upon ourselves. Without this, we would not have come to our senses until the last days of the Last Judgment" (14:114). The theme is also evident in Gogol's notebooks (1842–50), where there is an entry "Drawings of the Last Judgment" (9:573).

As with that of the end of the world, Gogol's treatment of the Last Judgment *topos* was at times serious and then at times satirical. An allusion to the Last Judgment appears in Gogol's early work "A Terrible Vengeance." As Richard A. Peace notes, "The figure of the horseman, the strange clarity of vision, and the phrase 'hour of judgement' (*chas mery*) all give the terrible vengeance a sense of apocalypse."[113] Katerina's warning to her father, the sorcerer—"Father, a terrible judgment is at hand!" (1:259; Kent, 1:151)—also plays a part in evoking this sense.

The Last Judgment theme is present in *The Government Inspector* as well. Donald Fanger maintains that in his earliest draft of the play Gogol developed the situation, in which a group of provincial officials are terror-stricken after they mistake a petty Petersburg clerk for the government inspector, as a parody of the Doomsday. Iurii Mann draws a parallel between the play's closing silent scene and the portrayal of

112. This citation as a manifestation of the Doomsday theme with the reference to Daniel 5 has been noted by Smirnova. She also observed the Balthazar allusion in chapter 10 of *Dead Souls* in the lyrical digression in which the narrator speaks of the chronicle of mankind, which "is shot through with a heavenly fire, that each letter of it screams out, that a piercing finger points from all sides . . ." (6:211; Gibian, 227–28); see Smirnova, *Poéma Gogolia,* 72.

113. Richard A. Peace, *The Enigma of Gogol* (Cambridge: Cambridge University Press, 1981), 23 and 309; also see 286–87.

the Last Judgment in medieval art.[114] One can perceive the episode in *Dead Souls* where the town bureaucrats taking part in the funeral of the prosecutor contemplate the arrival of the new governor-general silently, fearing that he would chastize them for their transgressions (see 6:192–93 and 219; Gibian, 206 and 237), as a variant of this silent scene.[115] Much later on in *Dead Souls,* the speech of the governor-general (the Prince), with which the manuscript of the second volume comes abruptly to an end, includes the phrase, "our dying land" (7:126). Although it is clear in context that the Prince is speaking about Russia, the phrase *zemlia nasha* could be also interpreted in broader terms as "our Earth."[116] Furthermore, this whole speech of the Prince, an impartial and strict judge, with his appeal to his fellow citizens, can be perceived as a model and "general rehearsal" of the Last Judgment, especially given that the Prince was commissioned for his task by the Tsar, whose authority was considered God-given.

The Last Judgment theme also appears in *Dead Souls* in the phrase "great dark jaws" in the description of Pliushkin's garden (6:113; Gibian, 117). In icon painting, particularly Eastern Slavic, as well as in the *lubok,* such "jaws" were common in the iconography of hell, presented as the open, fire-breathing maw of a monstrous serpent (see, for example, Figs. 49 and 50). This image has been interpreted as Gogol's reminder of the retribution awaiting those who, like Pliushkin, have allowed their souls to perish.[117]

An entirely different, satirical treatment of this theme occurs in the dialogue between Pliushkin and his housekeeper Mavra, a dialogue

114. See, respectively, Fanger, *The Creation of Nikolai Gogol,* and Iu. V. Mann, *Poétika Gogolia* (Moscow: Khudozhestvennaia literatura, 1978), 242. For a detailed discussion of the connection between the silent scene in *The Government Inspector* and the Last Judgment theme, see Per-Arne Bodin, "The Silent Scene in Nikolaj Gogol's *The Inspector General,*" *Scando-Slavica* 33 (1987): 5–16.

115. This similarity was properly noted in Bodin, "The Silent Scene," 13. The *poéma* and the play seem still more closely connected when we consider that, at one point, the fear-ridden bureaucrats were thinking: "Chichikov might be the official who had been sent from the governor-general's office to make a secret investigation" (6:193; Gibian, 207).

116. Cf. Belyi, *Masterstvo Gogolia,* 71.

117. See Smirnova, *Poéma Gogolia,* 67–68. The depiction of hell as jaws is found not only in ecclesiastical painting but also in Ukrainian and Russian meditative poetry. Thus, in his *Garden of Divine Songs,* Skovoroda called hell "insatiable" and described its jaws gaping day and night and consuming everything tirelessly (*Povne zibrannia tvoriv,* 1:73 and 87). Derzhavin in his last poem, quoted above, spoke about the jaws of eternity. See Segel, *The Literature of Eighteenth-Century Russia,* 2:317, and Derzhavin, *Sochineniia,* 3:178.

designed to illustrate the man's extreme miserliness coupled with sanctimoniousness:

> "You just wait: on the Day of Judgment the devils will roast you for that on their iron forks! You wait and see how they'll roast you!"
>
> "And why should they roast me if I haven't touched that piece of paper? They might do it for some other woman's failing, but no one has yet accused me of stealing."
>
> "But I tell you the devils will roast you! They will say, 'Here, that's for you, you dishonest woman, for cheating your master!' Yes, they will roast you all right!"
>
> "And I'll tell them they're wrong! Honest, I'm not to blame, I didn't take it. . . . But there it is lying on the table. You're always too quick in blaming people!" (6:127; Gibian, 133)

And Gogol treats the *topos* satirically again when he describes the blacksmiths' charging Chichikov six times the price for the urgent repair of his carriage. Chichikov threatens them with the Last Judgment, a threat they promptly ignore (see 6:217–18; Gibian, 235).

Gogol had already employed the Last Judgment scene for satirical purposes in his *Mirgorod* cycle, in "The Tale of How Ivan Ivanovich Quarreled with Ivan Nikiforovich." In this tale, Gogol underscored the sanctimoniousness of Ivan Ivanovich, who reminded the blaspheming Ivan Nikiforovich of the tortures of the Last Judgment: " 'So you must bring the devil in. Aie, Ivan Nikiforovich! you will remember my words, but then it will be too late; you will suffer in the next world for your ungodly language' " (2:232; Kent, 2:177).

Thus Gogol's employment of this *topos* is twofold. On the one hand, he treated it in accordance with the Baroque literary tradition. On the other, as with the *topos* of the end of the world, he employed it in a unique way: he showed how a serious theological concept could be reduced *ad absurdum*, how shallow use of it can turn it banal. As the examples from *Dead Souls* show, Gogol also employed this *topos* to unmask human pretentiousness and *poshlost'*. The irony of the episode of squabbling between Pliushkin and Mavra is that Pliushkin, the epitome of Avarice (a deadly sin by Christian doctrine), instead of thinking about saving his own soul threatens Mavra with terrible tortures in hell on mere suspicion of stealing a scrap of paper.

And when the swindler Chichikov exploits the Last Judgment threat against the blacksmiths, his use of it is obviously hypocritical and clichéd. Both Pliushkin, the skinflint, squabbling with a servant, and Chichikov, the confidence-trickster, arguing with the blacksmiths, resort to warnings of the Last Judgment, although they themselves, comically enough, are far greater transgressors.

4

Figurative Language

Some of the figures we shall look at in this chapter—anaphora, epiphora, and asyndeton—achieve their effect by repetition and cumulation. Others—antithesis and oxymoron—arrest the reader's attention by means of contrast and incongruity. Chiaroscuro, also based on contrast, constitutes a special case: unlike the other figures, chiaroscuro was introduced first to fine arts by Leonardo da Vinci, then was adopted by literature and became a figure of language only in the Baroque period, vividly demonstrating a fundamental aesthetic principle of the epoch—*ut pictura poesis.* In that period, artists who worked in language were especially attentive to the possibilities of figurative effects based on such principles as *ingenio, acutezza,* and *discordia concors.* The use of wordplay, particularly of antanaclasis and paronomasia, was very widespread in contemporaneous literature. Even more characteristic of the Baroque mentality is the employment of conceit, which although not unknown to antiquity, reached its peak of popularity only during the Baroque.

I selected the figures to discuss by their importance in Gogol's oeuvre and by the relatively little attention they have received in Gogol studies. Gogol used some of these figures in accordance with the Baroque tradition, others he endowed with additional functions, and yet others he employed in a manner all his own. We shall see that Gogol made use of the figurative language popular in the Baroque period to enrich our understanding of his characters and, more important, to explore and deepen semantic aspects of the narrative.

Anaphora and Epiphora

Anaphora, the repetition of a word or a phrase at the beginning of successive lines, can be found at least as early as the Bible: "Give them according to their deeds, and according to the wickedness of their endeavours: give them after the work of their hands" (Psalms 28:4). We frequently come across anaphora in the literature of antiquity, when the rhetoricians asserted that the figure should be employed "for the sake of force and emphasis," as Quintilian summed up in his *Institutio Oratoria* (9, 3:30).[1] A century earlier Virgil employed "here" for this purpose in his *Eclogues:* "Here are cold springs, Lycoris, here soft meadows, here woodland; here, with thee, time alone would wear me away" (10:42–44).[2] In the Middle Ages, Dante, who took Virgil as his guide not only in his imaginary infernal journey but also in his literary undertakings, inscribed over the gates of Hell: "THROUGH ME THE WAY INTO THE WOEFUL CITY, / THROUGH ME THE WAY TO THE ETERNAL PAIN, / THROUGH ME THE WAY AMONG THE LOST PEOPLE" (III, 1–3).[3]

Anaphora was frequently used in Baroque literature for emphasis, as Quintilian had recommended. The German poet Hofmann von Hofmannswaldau (1617–79) employed a tenfold anaphora, "mouth," in his cliché-laden love poem "To a Mouth," emphasizing to excess the subject matter of his poem (excess is a frequent and indeed characteristic feature of the Baroque):

> Mouth! which can cause souls to rush together through desire. Mouth! which is much sweeter than strong wine from heaven. Mouth! which pours out life-giving wine from Alicante. Mouth! which I prefer to the rich treasures of the Indies. Mouth! whose balm can fortify or hurt us. Mouth! which blooms more cheerfully than the splendour of all roses. Mouth! like which and resembling which there is no ruby. Mouth! which the Graces moisten with their springs. Mouth! coral mouth, my only delight! Mouth! let me place one kiss on your ruby [lips].[4]

1. See Quintilian, *The Institutio Oratoria,* 3:463.
2. Virgil, *Works,* 2 vols., trans. H. Rushton Fairclough (Cambridge: Harvard University Press, 1934–35), 1:75.
3. Dante, *The Divine Comedy,* 1:47.
4. Hill, 130.

The Polish poet Daniel Naborowski exploited a fourteenfold anaphora " 'tis naught" in his didactic poem "Honor the Basis of All."[5] And his compatriot Jan Andrzej Morsztyn used a fivefold anaphora in his love poem "To a Young Lady" to emphasize the aloofness of his beloved:

> Hard the iron smelted with great care,
> Hard the diamond hammer never touched,
> Hard the oak tree petrified with age,
> Hard the cliffs aloof from ocean's waves;
> Harder you, whom tears have failed to break,
> Than iron, diamond, solid oak, and cliffs.[6]

In Ukrainian Baroque literature, anaphora appeared especially frequently in *dumy* (lyric-epic songs), a form which reached its peak in the Baroque period. In the *duma* "A Cossack Golota," for example, the protagonist inquires of a Tartar ready to assault him:

> Do you need my fine weapons?
> Do you need my black horses?
> Do you need my expensive clothes?[7]

Anaphora was also often employed in polemical literature; the Ukrainian ecclesiastical writer and preacher Ivan Vishenskii (ca. 1550–after 1621) alternately employed the anaphorae "don't you see how" and "I ask you about the one" in his dispute with the renegade bishops:

> Don't you see how you emit the spirit of the Antichrist, abusive, lying and slanderous. Don't you see how you emit stenchy, hellish pestilence. Don't you see how you slander the Patriarch, as though he arrived ingloriously and uselessly and behaved unwisely upon his arrival. I ask you about the one who is perhaps the wisest, most useful and glorious, like the one who will protect your soul so that it will not be suddenly slain by brigands. I ask you about the one who is perhaps the wisest, most glorious and useful, like the one who warned you

5. Segel, 227 (227–28).
6. Segel, 300.
7. See N. I. Kravtsov and A. V. Kulagina, comps., *Slavianskii fol'klor* (Moscow: Izdatel'stvo MGU, 1987), 237.

against villains so that your spiritual wealth would not be stolen. I ask you about the one who is perhaps the wisest, most glorious and useful, like the one who would teach you how to hide from being murdered by wolves and not to fall into the teeth of temptation. Don't you see how the Patriarch's arrival was and is glorious and useful. Don't you see how the Patriarch is not malevolent, but was and is the wisest among the wisest of this age.[8]

And more than a century later, the Russian poet Lomonosov used the fourfold anaphora in his "The Ode on the Arrival of Her Majesty, the Great Sovereign, the Empress Elizaveta Petrovna from Moscow to St. Petersburg in 1742 after Her Coronation" (1742):

> With you, I will establish the just court,
> With you, I will wipe out greedy hearts,
> With you, I will punish evil,
> With you, I will award virtue.[9]

Epiphora, the counterpart of anaphora, involves the repetition of a word or a phrase at the ends of successive lines. Quintilian described this in his *Institutio Oratoria,* quoting a passage from Cicero's *Pro Milone* (22:59): "Who demanded them? Appius. Who produced them? Appius." Further on, Quintilian indicated that this passage, containing both the anaphora "who" and the epiphora "Appius," illustrates the device known as *complexio.*[10] In the following passage from Cicero's *Philippics,* we find another epiphora: "Men have been brought back from exile by a dead man; citizenship has been given, not only to individuals, but to whole tribes and provinces by a dead man; by boundless exemptions revenues have been done away with by a dead man" (1, 10:24).[11] Like anaphora, epiphora is employed for emphasis: repetition of a word or phrase, whether at the beginning or end of successive lines, in itself arrests the reader's attention.

8. Ivan Vishenskii, *Sochineniia* (Moscow: Akademiia Nauk SSSR, 1955), 72 and 303–6.

9. See Lomonosov, *Polnoe sobranie sochinenii,* 8:85.

10. See Quintilian, *The Institutio Oratoria,* 3:463, and Heinrich Lausberg, *Handbuch der literarischen Rhetorik,* 2 vols. (Munich: Hauber, 1973), 1:321.

11. Cicero, *Philippics,* trans. Walter C. A. Ker (Cambridge: Harvard University Press, 1969), 45.

Epiphora is found in Baroque literature less frequently then anaph-ora. This is especially true in poetry, where the rules of rhyme nor-mally preclude the repetition of the same word or phrase at the end of a line. A rare example of epiphora in Baroque poetry appears in the poem "About Dorothy," in which the Polish poet Hieronim Morsztyn (ca.1580–before 1626) praised, tongue-in-cheek, a woman of loose morals:

> Plenty of joy, plenty of gladness,
>   When I set out to Dorothy.
> Worries and troubles go away,
>   When I come to Dorothy.
> No need to wait for happiness and the Golden Age,
>   When I sit next to Dorothy.
> Gold and precious stones are trifles,
>   When I lie near Dorothy.
> Just about everything except virtue
>   Has my noble Dorothy.[12]

Ivan Vishenskii, the Ukrainian ecclesiastical writer and preacher quoted above, employed an epiphoral phrase full of derision in his "Concise Reply to Piotr Skarga." Responding to Skarga's claim that the Roman Catholic Church alone is steadfast in its truth, Vishenskii scorn-fully inquired: "How come, then, it [the Roman Catholic Church] falsi-fied an unwavering, veritable faith, if the Roman Church is unwaver-ingly veritable? In what way, then, is the Roman Church unwaveringly veritable?"[13] As these very different examples illustrate, the effect which writers strove to achieve by using epiphora varied, as also with anaphora, from mockingly humorous to solemnly didactic.

Gogol was acquainted with both anaphora and epiphora from his

---

12. Sokołowska and Żukowska, eds., *Poeci polskiego baroku,* 1:271–72. There is a double entendre (formally, an example of antanaclasis, discussed at the end of this chapter) in the penultimate line of the poem: the word *cnota* means in Polish both "virtue" and "virginity"; see Jan Stanisławski, *Wielki Słownik Polsko-Angielski,* 2 vols. (Warsaw: Wiedza Powszechna, 1975), 1:137–38.

13. Vishenskii, *Sochineniia,* 153. Piotr Skarga (1536–1612) was a prominent Polish Jesuit polemist and preacher. Vishenskii wrote his "Concise Reply" in response to the second edition of Skarga's famous treatise *On the Order and Unity of the Divine Church under One Pastor and on the Greek and Russian Deviation from This Unity;* see I. P. Eremin, "Kommentarii," in Vishenskii, *Sochineniia,* 316.

school years. Nikol'skii discussed both figures in his *Foundations of Russian Philology,* the textbook used in the Nezhin Gymnasium when Gogol studied there. Nikol'skii called anaphora *edinonachatie* and epiphora *edinozakliuchenie* and illustrated the use of both figures with extracts from Lomonosov's poetry; as an example of anaphora, he used the passage quoted above from the poet's ode, and as one of epiphora he cited Lomonosov's "Paraphrase of Psalm 70" (1751):

> You placed me near the gulf,
> So that I would see my ruin;
> But, having soon relented, You saved
> And from the deep abyss me elevated.
>
> You became famous for Your generosity,
> Wished to comfort me,
> And, having soon relented, You saved
> And from the deep abyss me elevated.[14]

Dumy were for Gogol another source of these figures, particularly anaphora.[15] In his article "The Songs of the Ukraine," Gogol quoted a song with a sixfold anaphora "can it be":

> Can it be that I shall go no more
>   Where I used to go!
> Can it be that I shall love no more
>   Whom I used to love!
> Can it be that I shall go no more
>   Early near the castle!
> Can it be that I shall stand no more
>   With my beloved!
> Can it be that I shall go no more
>   To the woods for hazel-nuts!

14. Lomonosov, *Polnoe sobranie sochinenii,* 8:385; see Nikol'skii, *Osnovaniia,* 2:37–39. The word order of my translation is intended to reflect that of the original.

15. Cf. N. Iu. Shvedova, "Printsipy istoricheskoi stilizatsii v iazyke povesti Gogolia 'Taras Bul'ba,' " *Materialy i issledovaniia po istorii russkogo literaturnogo iazyka,* 5 vols., ed. V. V. Vinogradov (Moscow: Akademiia Nauk SSSR, 1949–62), 3:63–64. Gogol was known as a great connoisseur and collector of Ukrainian and Russian folk songs; for the folk songs collected by Gogol, see Georgievskii, "Pesni, sobrannye N. V. Gogolem."

Can it be that ended are
My maidenly laughs!
(8:93; Tulloch, 189)[16]

Gogol himself employed anaphora and epiphora from the beginning of his writing career. In his first published work, *Hanz Kuechelgarten* (1829), he used the fourfold anaphora "how," reminiscent of
Lomonosov's, "with you":

How poisonous is their breath!
How false is the quivering of their hearts!
How insidious are their minds!
How empty-sounding are their words!
(1:94)[17]

But whereas Lomonosov's anaphora emphasized objectives for Elizabeth's reign didactically, in the guise of divine assurances to the
newly crowned Empress, Gogol's underscores his protagonist's disgust with the "beau monde hateful and feebleminded" (1:93). Another anaphora, found in a series of rhetorical questions rather than
rhetorical exclamations, appears in another passage dominated by a
tone of disgust, this time in *Dead Souls*. There the narrator repeats
"why" to stress his caustic indignation with Manilova at her negligent
housekeeping: "Why, for instance, was the cooking in the kitchen
managed so stupidly and unsystematically? Why was the larder so
empty? Why was the housekeeper a thief? Why were the servants
untidy and drunken? Why did the whole of the domestic staff sleep so
unmercifully and gossip the rest of the time?" (6:26; Gibian, 23).[18]

Gogol also employed anaphora in passages with a lyrical tonality
reminiscent of *duma*. This tonality is heard in *Taras Bulba* where the
writer used the threefold anaphora "will," twice doubling it to give

16. The translation of this song is mine; in his translation of this article by Gogol, Alexander
Tulloch rendered this song in the original Ukrainian.
17. To convey Gogol's figurative language as accurately as possible, I use my own, literal,
translation of passages from *Hanz Kuechelgarten* rather than the rhymed Ardis translation:
Hanz Kuechelgarten, Leaving the Theater & Other Works, ed. Ronald Meyer (Ann Arbor: Ardis,
1990), 20–59.
18. I have reinstated Gogol's initial anaphora "why"; in the Reavey translation of this passage the word "why" and the phrase "for instance" are transposed.

especially forceful emphasis to his narrator's premonitions of the Cossacks' destruction and the subsequent glorification of their deeds in a bandura-player's *duma:*

> Will, will the whole plain with its fields and roads be covered with their bleaching bones, be richly bathed in their Cossack blood and strewn with broken wagons, shattered swords, and splintered lances; far and wide will lie, scattered, their heads with hanging moustaches and long forelocks tangled and stiff with blood. Will the eagles fly down to peck and tear out their Cossack eyes. . . . Will, will the bandore player come with the gray beard over his chest, a white-headed old man, though maybe still full of ripe manhood, prophetic in spirit, and he will say his rich powerful word about them. (2:131–32; Kent, 2:97–98)[19]

Gogol's use of anaphora also extended to texts with a moralizing tonality. We find an example of this in his recently discovered didactic work "The Rule of Living in the World" (its most likely date 1844):

> Despondency is truly a temptation of the spirit of darkness, with which he attacks us, knowing how hard it is for man to struggle with it. Despondency is against God. It is a consequence of our insufficient love for Him. Despondency begets despair, which is a spiritual murder, the most horrible of all evil deeds committed by man, for it cuts off all the ways to salvation and therefore is loathed by God more than all other sins.[20]

The repetition of "despondency" in this passage emphasizes the importance of the subject and echoes Gogol's utter abhorrence of this emotion, which in accordance with Christian tradition he considered a deadly sin.[21]

---

19. I have adjusted the Kent translation, perhaps at the expense of the English syntax, to accentuate the anaphora as it appears in the original. For additional observations on the use of anaphora by Gogol's narrators, see L. I. Eremina, *O iazyke khudozhestvennoi prozy N. V. Gogolia* (Moscow: Nauka, 1987), 30–37.

20. See Kjetsaa, "Gogol' kak uchitel' zhizni," 59.

21. See Morton W. Bloomfield, *The Seven Deadly Sins* (n.p.: Michigan State University Press,

All the examples of Gogol's use of anaphora given so far, despite their appearance in passages with differing tonalities, were used by the narrator, even though at times, as in *Hanz Kuechelgarten,* they conveyed the character's thoughts. The use of anaphora by the character himself is a different matter. We find this in the "Diary of a Madman," a rare instance of first-person narrative in Gogol's oeuvre. This type of narrative penetrates deeper into the character's inner world, and an emphatic literary device like anaphora contributes greatly to this effect. The protagonist and narrator of this tale, Poprishchin, suffers from his inferior status, which does not corre-spond to his pride in his nobility and to his high ambitions, a discrep-ancy that ultimately drives him to madness.[22] Poprishchin's predica-ment is exacerbated by his infatuation with the director's daughter. In one of the entries in his diary Poprishchin shows his longing for this world of the director and his daughter, a world in which he does not belong and to which he has no access:

> I should like to know what he [the director] thinks most about. What is going on in that head? I should like to get a close view of the life of these gentlemen, of all these *équi-voques* and court ways. How they go on and what they do in their circle—that's what I should like to find out! . . . I should like to look into the drawing room, of which one only sees the open door and another room beyond it. Ah, what sumptuous furniture! What mirrors and china! I long to have a look in there, into the part of the house where her Excellency is, that's where I should like to go! (3:199; Kent, 1:245)

1952), 54. For the pictorial representation of the seven deadly sins, including despondency, in Russian Baroque art, see the engraving by Simon Ushakov. The subject was very popular, and *lubok* copies of Ushakov's engraving were made in Gogol's time; see Sytova, *The Lubok,* fig. 108.

22. Poprishchin's hypersensitivity about his status indicates, it seems, that he attained his rank merely through the civil service, in accordance with the Table of Ranks (see Peace, *The Enigma of Gogol,* 300–301). To this allude both his last name, which stems from the Russian *poprishche* meaning "career," "arena of activity" (Peace, *The Enigma of Gogol,* 129), and his first name, Aksentii, which apparently derives from the Latin word *accensus* ("one who attends someone of higher rank"). The latter meaning is especially fitting since Poprishchin "attended" the director by sharpening his quills.

Having no access to the inner chambers of the director's house, Poprishchin attempts to overcome this obstacle in his imagination. We watch his imaginary wandering about the director's house, going from the study, the only room he is allowed into, to the drawing room, then to a room the name of which he does not know, and finally to the most desirable of them all—the boudoir of the director's daughter. The use of the phrase "I should like to" as anaphora, and at times also as epiphora, highlights the intensity of Poprishchin's aspirations. Another epiphora, also conducive to the reader's entering into the protagonist's innermost feelings, appears later on in this narrative. Very distressed by the prospect of the director's daughter's marriage to a court chamberlain, Poprishchin ponders his own low rank of titular councilor, which appears to him as the only obstacle on his way to happiness: "Why am I a titular councilor and on what grounds am I a titular councilor? Perhaps I am not a titular councilor at all? Perhaps I am a count or a general, and only somehow appear to be a titular councilor? . . . I should like to know why I am a titular councilor. Why precisely a titular councilor?" (3:206; Kent, 1:251–52). The emphatic repetition of "titular councilor" underscores Poprishchin's obsession with rank, which he views as the source of his misery, and helps to lay the psychological ground for the "resolution" of this obsession in the character's leap into *mania grandiosa.*

The epiphora device is much in evidence in Gogol's works, both early and late. In a passage of lyrical tonality in "A May Night," a tale of the *Evenings* cycle, Gogol used the sixfold epiphora "night" to highlight the beauty of that time in his native Ukraine: "Do you know the Ukrainian night? Aie, you do not know the Ukrainian night! . . . Heavenly night! Enchanting night! . . . Divine night! Enchanting night!" (1:159; Kent, 1:55).

We find the epiphora "virtuous man," in combination with the anaphora "because," employed sarcastically in *Dead Souls.* Explaining his reasons for taking Chichikov as the protagonist of the *poéma,* the narrator, whose voice in this passage sounds especially close to Gogol's, expresses his resentment at the exploitation of the virtuous man as a literary character, which by Gogol's time could set a reader's teeth on edge: "Because it is time at last to give the poor virtuous man a rest . . . because they make a hypocritical use of the virtuous man; because they do not respect the virtuous man" (6:223; Gibian, 242).[23]

In Gogol's letter to the poet Nikolai Iazykov (September 27, 1841), there is a passage with three repetitions of the phrase "then you do not love me":

> And if, when we bid farewell to each other, a spark of my soul's strength does not pass from my hand into your soul at our handshake, then you do not love me. And if sometime ennui overcomes you and, remembering me, you do not have enough power to overcome it, then you do not love me; and if a momentary ailment makes you heavier and your spirit bows low, then you do not love me. (11:347)

This passage, like "The Rule of Living in the World" cited earlier, is very indicative of Gogol's frame of mind in the 1840s, when he came to believe in his prophetic powers. The letter is pervaded with the tone of a preacher certain of his gift of foresight—"For never has the voice that flies out of my soul deceived me" (11:346)—and his unique role in the destiny of his friends—"From now on, your gaze should be brightly and cheerfully raised upward—our meeting occurred for that reason" (11:347). In this frame of mind Gogol used the epiphora "then you do not love me" to assist his ailing friend to overcome his despondency, which, as we may recall, Gogol viewed as a terrible sin eventually leading to spiritual death.

Gogol employed both anaphora and epiphora throughout his career. He used them for emphasis, along the lines propounded by Quintilian and followed by medieval and Baroque writers. Gogol employed these figures with remarkable diversity in his poetry and prose, fiction and correspondence, in passages with differing tonalities—lyrical, satirical, or moralizing. In addition Gogol used both anaphora and epiphora in the first-person narrative "Diary of a Madman" to highlight important features of Poprishchin's character, contributing to our better understanding of this miserable man's inner world and our knowledge of his most cherished dreams, which, remaining unrealized, drove him to insanity.

23. I have deliberately altered the Reavey translation to show Gogol's use of the epiphora in the original.

Asyndeton

Asyndeton is a figure of cumulation based on the omission of conjunctions between similar parts of a sentence. Among the most widely used were noun and verb asyndetons, but adjectival, adverbial, and other asyndetons were employed as well.

Aristotle said that asyndeton "serves to amplify an idea" (*Rhetoric* 1413b).[24] Cicero employed the figure in his *Philippics,* praising Caesar as a man of "genius, calculation, memory, letters, industry, thought, diligence" (2, 44:116).[25] Quintilian pointed out in his *Institutio Oratoria* that asyndeton "is useful when we are speaking with special vigour" (9, 3:50).[26]

Asyndeton became particularly prominent in literature of the Baroque period. This "heaping up" of words created a striking, cumulative effect in writing that may be compared to the massive shapes and general lavishness in Baroque painting, and also to the multiplication of columns on the façade of a Baroque building.[27] As Harold B. Segel has noted, "This Baroque sense of amplitude, reinforced by the cumulative use of variety and ornament, resulted in the massiveness and physical sumptuousness generally associated with Baroque art."[28]

Lope de Vega used asyndeton in a love sonnet, stringing together a series of extremely diverse adjectives, emphasizing that his lyrical "I" is possessed by complex and contradictory feelings:

> Fall faint, be insolent, or furious,
> gruff-mannered, tender, generous, reserved,
> encouraged, wounded, living, or deceased,
> unfailing, cowardly, brave, traitorous;
>
> not find, not only good, but calm repose;
> appear happy, mournful, humble, proud,
> annoyed to anger, valiant, fugitive,
> offended, satisfied, suspicious . . . [29]

24. Aristotle, *The Rhetoric,* trans. Lane Cooper (New York: Appleton, 1960), 218.

25. Cicero, *Philippics,* 179 and 181.

26. Quintilian, *The Institutio Oratoria,* 3:475.

27. Imbrie Buffum, *Studies in the Baroque from Montaigne to Rotrou* (New Haven: Yale University Press, 1957), 20.

28. Segel, 30.

29. Segel, 286 (285–86).

Jan Andrzej Morsztyn employed a noun asyndeton in his poem "On His Mistress," to arrest the reader's attention and direct it to the beauty of his beloved, claiming that her face and neck were whiter than "marble, milk, swan, pearl, snow, lily."[30]

The Ukrainian writer Ivan Vishenskii also employed a noun asyndeton, coupled with the anaphora "all," to place especially strong emphasis on his warning to the reader against vain pursuits, presenting earthly existence as a catalogue of sinful ailments:

> There is not a single spot free from the sinful disease—all is scab, all is wound, all is swelling, all is rot, all is hellish fire, all is sickness, all is sin, all is untruth, all is slyness, all is cunning, all is perfidy, all is intrigue, all is lies, all is dream, all is shadow, all is vapor, all is smoke, all is vanity, all is futility, all is apparition—nothing is more worthless than reality.[31]

Lomonosov considered asyndeton—he called it *bessoiuzie*—an important rhetorical figure;[32] his esteem for the device is attested to by the numerous examples of it in his own poems. In "An Ode on the Capture of Khotin" (1739), Lomonosov employed a noun asyndeton to glorify Russian warriors, for whom "waters, forest, mounds, rapids, remote steppes" were equally accessible.[33] And Lomonosov's successor, Derzhavin, used both adjectival and noun asyndetons in his poem "On Luck" (1789), to underscore the impermanence, unreliability, and transience of *Fortuna:*

> On a globe-shaped chariot,
> crystal, slippery, fatal,
> After the shining dawn,
> Over the mountains, steppes, seas, forests,
> You gallop around the world every day.[34]

Nikol'skii included the same extract from this poem of Derzhavin's in his *Foundations* to illustrate his discussion of asyndeton. The figure

---

30. Sokołowska and Żukowska, eds., *Poeci polskiego baroku,* 1:721.
31. Vishenskii, *Sochineniia,* 48–49.
32. See Lomonosov, *Polnoe sobranie sochinenii,* 7:257 and 261.
33. See, respectively, Lomonosov, *Polnoe sobranie sochinenii,* 7:261 and 8:20.
34. For the original, see Derzhavin, *Sochineniia,* 1:171.

was also treated in Tolmachev's *Rules of Philology,* another textbook
used in the Nezhin Gymnasium, so that undoubtedly Gogol was already acquainted with asyndeton and its importance in his school-
days, and it is not surprising that it is so frequent in his works.[35] We
come across an asyndeton in his early work *The Hetman* (1830–32):
"As soon as Ostranitsa woke up, he saw the whole homestead filled
with people: moustaches, short overcoats, women's brocade hats,
white kerchiefs, men's blue coats; in a word, the homestead was
nothing else but a toy-shop, or a dish with Russian salad or, even
better, a motley Turkish shawl" (3:298). The effect of this pileup of
nouns is to arrest the reader's attention and direct it to the mixed,
parti-colored crowd perceived by the just-awakened Ostranitsa.

In another early work, "The Fair at Sorochintsy," Gogol compiled
an asyndeton of nouns designating still more diverse elements:
"Oxen, sacks, hay, gypsies, pots, peasant women, cakes, caps—
everything is bright, gaudy, discordant, flitting in groups, shifting to
and fro before your eyes" (1:115; Kent, 1:12). As an epigraph for this
chapter of the tale, Gogol used an extract, which also contains an
asyndeton, from one of his father's comedies (1:115 and 519; Kent,
1:12 n. 6). In his asyndeton Gogol *père* included nouns denoting
quite incongruous kinds of merchandise—wheels, glass, tar, tobacco,
straps, and onions—to convey the very diverse nature of another fair,
but those nouns nonetheless belonged to one and the same semantic
category, objects of trade, whereas Gogol *fils* made *his* catalogue
from nouns denoting still more unequal elements, in order to emphasize not only the diversity of this fair but also, and perhaps mainly, its
discordance.

The early-twentieth-century Gogol scholar Iosif Mandel'shtam, the
first to analyze Gogol's style systematically, noted Gogol's affection
for asyndeton without calling it by its technical name:

> One of the remarkable devices that helps Gogol make his
> language humorous lies in the juxtaposition of the names of
> objects or actions, a juxtaposition that creates an unusually
> rapid change of impressions; a transition from one name to
> another takes place without their being connected in any way,
> a transition that does not rest on any association—neither in

35. See Nikol'skii, *Osnovaniia,* 2:34–35, and Tolmachev, *Pravila,* 2:288–91.

time, nor in place, nor in reason, nor in logic. . . . It is interesting to see how Gogol relishes this manner of depiction, introducing disorder, clearly on purpose, also where it would have been noticeable of its own accord, even without the device.[36]

Mandel'shtam suggests here that Gogol employed this figure to surprise and amuse the reader by bringing together unrelated, incompatible locutions. It seems to me that in employing such diverse words within the asyndeton, Gogol not only surprises and amuses, but also accomplishes other ends. Let me illustrate this.

Often Gogol employed asyndeton with the purpose that Aristotle noted—to amplify ideas. This is how he used it both in the 1835 and the 1842 editions of "The Portrait": "Gold became his passion, his ideal, his fear, his enjoyment, his goal" (3:110 and 420–21; Tulloch, 74, and Kent, 2:281). Here Gogol emphasized that moneygrubbing consumed Chartkov's whole being. There is almost an oxymoron in the series; "fear" and "enjoyment" are a combination reminiscent of Lope de Vega's love sonnet. This underscores how Chartkov the miser was overtaken by conflicting sensations: he relished the sight of the money he had amassed and at the same time was frightened by the possibility of parting with his treasure.

A quite different example of asyndeton, also depicting miserliness, is to be found in the section of *Dead Souls* describing the commodities stored and stacked at Pliushkin's estate. To emphasize the once enormous wealth of this landlord, and then to convey the lively atmosphere of the chip market, which contrasts strikingly with the deadening atmosphere of Pliushkin's estate,[37] Gogol employed two extended asyndetons, resulting in a passage that I am tempted to compare to a luxuriant Baroque building:

> He [Pliushkin] owned over a thousand souls, and few could be found who had so much bread stored in grain, flour, or simply in stacks of corn, such storehouses, barns and drying sheds heaped with such quantities of linen, cloth, cured and uncured sheepskins, dried fish, and every kind of vegetable. If anyone had peeped into his work-yard, where a stock of vari-

---

36. Iosif Mandel'shtam, *O kharaktere gogolevskogo stilia* (Helsinki, 1902), 277–78.
37. Cf. Proffer, *The Simile,* 116.

ous woods and utensils had been got ready but had never been used, he might have imagined himself wafted to the wood-ware market in Moscow, where bustling mothers-in-law make their daily pilgrimage, with their cooks trailing behind them, to effect their household purchases, and where white mounds of every kind of wooden articles fitted together, turned, dovetailed, wickered, lie about—barrels, mincers, tubs, buckets, vessels with spouts and without spouts, loving cups, linden-bark baskets, boxes in which peasant women dump their filaments and other waste, hampers of thin flexible aspen wood, pots of plaited birch-bark and much else serving the use of the rich and poor alike in Russia. (6:116–17; Gibian, 121–22)

Following this passage, Gogol employed two other smaller asyndetons to demonstrate both visually and semantically the worthlessness and pettiness of Pliushkin's current acquisitions in his homestead and inside his home:

Not satisfied with what he had, he used daily to stalk the streets of his village, peeping under the little bridges and planks, and everything he came upon, whether it was an old sole, a bit of peasant woman's dress, an iron nail, a piece of broken earthenware, he carried them all off home and put them in a pile which Chichikov had noticed in the corner. . . . He used to pick up anything he saw on the floor of his room, a piece of sealing wax, a bit of paper, a feather, and put it all away on his desk or on the window-sill. (6:117; Gibian, 122)

These last two asyndetons contrast in their brevity with the massive asyndeton at the beginning of the passage and visually demonstrate, as it were, the consequence of Pliushkin's *vita morbi:* once a prosperous and prudent landlord, he has turned into a pathological miser. Furthermore, the large, compound asyndeton that characterized the affluence of Pliushkin's estate in the earlier days prepares the reader for another contrast, this time strictly semantic; shortly after the passage quoted above Gogol shows that because of his character's parsimony all his wealth has ultimately turned to dust and rot (see 6:119; Gibian, 124).

We have seen how in his early work "The Fair at Sorochintsy" (1831) Gogol employed an asyndeton of jarring elements—human beings, animals, and inanimate objects—to underscore both the diversity and discordance of the fair. In his later works, he frequently pursued another goal when employing this type of asyndeton: by stringing together nouns disjointedly denoting people and objects, he drew the reader's attention to the inhuman, almost inanimate, nature of his characters.[38] Consider this passage from "The Coach" (1836): "In the middle of the square, there are very tiny shops; in them one may always see a bunch of pretzels, a peasant woman in a red kerchief, forty pounds of soap, a few pounds of bitter almonds, buckshot, some cotton material, and two shopmen who spend all their time playing a sort of quoits near the door" (3:178; Kent, 2:241). By including in one and the same asyndeton the peasant woman and the two shopmen together with soap, almonds, and buckshot, Gogol as it were equated them, thereby conveying the idea that the idiocy of life devoid of spirituality was finally soul-destroying—the idea at the root of his *Dead Souls.*

Antithesis

Figures of language such as anaphora, epiphora, and asyndeton arrest the reader's attention by means of repetition and cumulation. Other figures Gogol used, such as antithesis and oxymoron, achieve the same effect by means of contrast and contradiction.

Aristotle recommended antithesis, the juxtaposition of semantically contrasting adjacent clauses or phrases, as pleasing "because things are best known by opposition, and are all the better known when the opposites are put side by side" (*Rhetoric* 1410a).[39] Later, literary authorities of the classical age, such as the anonymous author of *Rhetorica ad Herrennium,* similarly described antithesis as a figure that endows a notion with clarity and force, as well as embellishing discourse. The embellishment was especially prominent in the Ba-

---

38. We observe the same tendency in Gogol's "downward metaphors"; see Chizhevskii, "Neizvestnyi Gogol'," 155.

39. Aristotle, *The Rhetoric,* 204.

roque age; in *The Garden of Eloquence* (1593), Henry Peachem affirmed that antithesis "graceth and bewtifieth the Oration," and in *The Mysterie of Rhetorique Unvailed* (1657), John Smith called the device "a Rhetorical Exornation."[40]

The Baroque propensity for contrast was manifest in the especially frequent use of antithesis in literature. On it Richard Crashaw built his love poem "The Weeper":

> O sweet Contest; of woes
> With loves, of teares with smiles disputing!
> O fair, & Friendly Foes,
> Each other kissing & confuting!
> While rain & sunshine, Cheekes & Eyes
> Close in kind contrarietyes.[41]

Andreas Gryphius, a contemporary German poet, employed it to express religious exaltation in his poem "On the Birth of Jesus," exclaiming: "Night, more than brilliant night! More light than day!"[42]

Antithesis is pervasive in the Slavic literatures of the time. Daniel Naborowski sealed with it his poem "Honor the Basis of All": "Who lives with honor has enough, though naught, / Who dies without it— naught, though he have all."[43] Skovoroda employed it in his epigrammatic statement "Insomuch as evil is hard and bitter, / So goodness is easy and sweet."[44] Derzhavin used antithesis with striking effect in his poem "On the Death of Prince Meshcherskii," pointing to the brevity of life and its reverses of fortune:

> While we—but grandeur mixed with nothing:
> Today a god, tomorrow dust;
> Today deceived by flattering hope,
> Tomorrow, though, "Where are you, Man?"[45]

---

40. Alex Preminger, ed., *Encyclopedia of Poetry and Poetics* (Princeton: Princeton University Press, 1965), 40.

41. Hill, 258.

42. Segel, 107.

43. Segel, 228 (227).

44. Skovoroda, *Povne zibrannia tvoriv,* 2:85.

45. Segel, *The Literature of Eighteenth-Century Russia,* 2:259.

Antithesis is discussed in the literature textbooks Gogol used at the Nezhin Gymnasium—Nikol'skii's *Foundations of Russian Philology,* Tolmachev's *Rules of Philology,* and the *Collection of Exemplary Russian and Translated Works in Prose* (in Sreznevskii's introduction, "An Attempt at Concise Rhetoric"). These textbooks cite Derzhavin's poem "On the Death of Prince Meshcherskii," quoted above, Lomonosov's "Letter on the Use of Chemistry," and a translated passage from Massillon's "Word on the Triumph of Religion."[46]

Gogol viewed antithesis in a more general sense as a very important artistic device. In his article "On Present-Day Architecture," he wrote: "The true effect lies in the sharp antithesis; beauty is never so bright or obvious as it is in contrast" (8:64; Tulloch, 123).[47] It is not surprising therefore that he made use of antithesis from the very beginning of his career. Indeed this particular figure—and the principle of contrast more generally—occupy a very important, perhaps central position in his poetics, a position which deserves separate, more detailed study. Here I can only demonstrate on a limited scale how Gogol employed antithesis in its strict sense and how he experimented with it as a literary device, endowing it with various functions.

Gogol used antithesis, rather conventionally, in his first published work, *Hanz Kuechelgarten:*

> Two years have passed. In peaceful Lünensdorf
> All stands out vividly and flourishes as before;
> The same concerns and the same pastimes
> Excite the quiet hearts of its residents.
> But things are not as before in Wilhelm's family:
> The pastor already left this world long ago.
>
> (1:90)

In this passage, Gogol simply contrasted—and thus emphasized— sorrowful changes in the family of Hanz's beloved with the permanency in the lives of the rest of the villagers.

Several years later, Gogol employed antithesis as a contrasting figure of language in contiguous phrases, coupling it with the two adjec-

---

46. See Nikol'skii, *Osnovaniia,* 2:52–54, Tolmachev, *Pravila,* 1:67–71, and Iosif Sreznevskii, "Opyt kratkoi ritoriki," in *Sobranie v proze,* 2:xiii–lxv.

47. Gogol's predilection for antithesis was noted by Gippius; see his *Gogol',* 81–84.

tival asyndetons, in "Nevsky Prospekt" to emphasize the opposition between an artist of the "Northern Palmyra" and one of Italy: "A Petersburg artist. An artist in the land of snows. An artist in the land of the Finns where everything is wet, flat, pale, gray, foggy. These artists are utterly unlike the Italian artists, proud and ardent as Italy and her skies. The Russian artist on the contrary is, as a rule, mild, gentle, retiring, carefree" (3:16; Kent, 1:213).

But in *Hanz Kuechelgarten* Gogol also used antithesis in a larger sense as a compositional device: still following a rather primitive, Romantic scheme, he juxtaposed the two worlds of "here" and "there"—the small and exclusive world of Lünensdorf, the hero's native village, and the unlimited, enormous world of his wanderings, both in real life and in his dreams.[48]

In "Nevsky Prospekt," Gogol turned again to antithesis as a compositional device, but this time he used it as a polemical tool. He built the narration on a juxtaposition of two plot lines, that of the idealistic, sensitive Piskarev and that of the vulgar, complacent Pirogov. The dissimilarity between the characters, each in his own way failing in his enterprise, was designed to emphasize the main idea of the tale— that in this demonic world, in which appearances differ sharply from reality, "Everything goes contrary to what we expect" (3:45; Kent, 1:237). Gogol's tale drastically deviates from and polemicizes against a Romantic approach, exposing the dreaminess of Piskarev and self-satisfied vulgarity of Pirogov as two sides of pseudo-life and pseudo-culture.[49]

In the *Evenings* cycle, Gogol assigned another role to antithesis—an unconventional, stylistic-compositional role—skillfully exploiting the confrontation in the preface to part 1 between the *panich* and the deacon Foma Grigor'evich (see the *facetia* secton of Chapter 1). The composition of part 1 is based on the alternating, stylistically contrasted narratives, from the bookish style of "The Fair at Sorochintsy" and "A May Night," supposedly told by the *panich,* to the folk style of "St. John's Eve" and "The Lost Letter," ostensibly told by the deacon (see 1:513). Prior to Gogol, the conventional way of constructing a

48. See, Iu. M. Lotman, "Iz nabliudenii nad strukturnymi printsipami rannego tvorchestva Gogolia," *Uchenye zapiski Tartuskogo Gosudarstvennogo Universiteta* 251 (1970): 32.

49. Cf. Dilaktorskaia, *Fantasticheskoe,* 31–32, and Markovich, *Peterburgskie povesti,* 72–74.

cycle was that of Boccaccio's *Decameron,* in which the stories were allegedly told in a circle of friends, whereas Gogol presented it as a contest between the two antagonistic narrators.[50]

Besides its stylistic and compositional role, antithesis also plays an important spatial role in Gogol's oeuvre. To give only one example, an antithesis of this kind is manifest between the two works of the *Mirgorod* cycle, *Taras Bulba* and "The Tale of How Ivan Ivanovich Quarreled with Ivan Nikiforovich." Whereas the artistic universe of the former is the Ukrainian steppe, immeasurable and undivided, reflecting the unselfish world of the Cossack brotherhood, in the latter it is the town of Mirgorod, enclosed and disconnected, indicating the egoistical chaos of the contemporary world.[51]

Gogol also employed antithesis to emphasize transience, mutability, and brevity. I have illustrated this in the preceding chapter with the passage from *Dead Souls* in which the narrator juxtaposes his attitude to life "before" and "now" (see 6:110–11; Gibian, 114–15).

Gogol's preoccupation with drastic changes in human perception of both time and space led him to employ a "chronotopic antithesis."[52] In "Rome," Gogol contrasted the chronotopes of Italy and France and particularly of Rome and Paris as perceived by the Prince, and did this twice: both before and after the Prince's prolonged stay in the French capital. In the beginning, Italy seemed to him a "dark, mouldy corner of Europe where life and every movement died away" (3:226–27), whereas France, and particularly Paris, seemed to him a bright, bustling center of modern European life. Four years later, the Prince's perceptions had changed considerably. By this time, he perceived France as shallow, ostentatious, and discordant, interested in

---

50. Here I disagree with S. A. Fomichev, who thinks that Gogol followed the Boccaccio model; see his "Pushkin i Gogol'," *Zeitschrift für Slawistik* 32 (1987): 79. This antagonism between the narrators is echoed in "St. John's Eve," in which Foma Grigor'evich, clearly aiming at the *panich,* present among the listeners of his story, says: "He [my grandfather] was not like the gabblers nowadays who drive you to pick up your cap and go out as soon as they begin spinning their yarns in a voice which sounds as though they had had nothing to eat for three days" (see 1:137–38; Kent, 1:33–34). For a detailed discussion of the subject, see Gary Duane Cox, "A Study of Gogol's Narrators" (Ph.D. diss., Columbia University, 1978), 37–39 and 50–51.

51. See Iu. M. Lotman, "Khudozhestvennoe prostranstvo v proze Gogolia," in his *V shkole poéticheskogo slova. Pushkin. Lermontov. Gogol'* (Moscow: Prosveshchenie, 1988), 272–78.

52. Bakhtin coined the term "chronotope," defining it as a *Gestalt-Inhalt* literary category and viewing it as "an essential interconnection of temporal and spatial relations, artistically assimilated in literature." See M. M. Bakhtin, "Formy vremeni i khronotopa v romane. Ocherki po istoricheskoi poétike," in his *Voprosy literatury i éstetiki,* 234–35.

things ephemeral and momentary, whereas his native Italy appeared to him profound, natural, and harmonious, focused on the eternal.[53]

In the *Evenings* cycle Gogol also resorted to the so-called negative simile, well known in Eastern Slavic folklore. Gogol was undoubtedly familiar with this antithetic construction, an example of which we find in a Ukrainian song in his own song collection: "It is not the thunder that thunders, it is not the toll that rings, / Vasylko is building a tower-chamber."[54] Andrei Belyi observed Gogol's use of negative simile (without calling it that) when he discussed negation as an underlying principle in "A Terrible Vengeance," citing in abbreviated form this passage that contains a clear example of negative simile, reminiscent of the Ukrainian song I have just quoted: "Those forests on the hills are not forests: they are the hair that covers the shaggy head of the wood demon. . . . Those meadows are not meadows: they are a green girdle encircling the round sky; and above and below the moon hovers over them" (1:246; Kent, 1:138).[55] As in folklore, the negative simile in this passage consists of real and imaginary parts. But in folklore one part replaces and thus cancels the other (in the Ukrainian song, the lofty and imaginary is replaced by the mundane and real), whereas in Gogol's passage there is no cancellation; the two parts, that is, the actual and the illusory, exchange places, as if becoming equal in their reality.[56]

Gogol used antithesis widely in his oeuvre, and it is perhaps no exaggeration to say that the figure became a main "weapon" in his artistic "arsenal." Gogol experimented with it constantly, endowing it with many diverse and important functions, and demonstrated endless ingenuity in handling its traditional forms, such as negative simile, restructuring and assigning it previously unknown roles.

53. Cf. Lucy Vogel, "Gogol' 's *Rome*," *Slavic and East European Journal* 11 (1967): 149–51.

54. Georgievskii, "Pesni, sobrannye N. V. Gogolem," 156. For a discussion of negative simile in Slavic folklore, see D. N. Medrish, "Istoricheskie korni otritsatel'nogo sravneniia," *Russkii fol'klor* 24 (1987): 107–16.

55. See Belyi, *Masterstvo Gogolia*, 57–71.

56. For a discussion of the device in Gogol's works, see D. N. Medrish, "Metaforicheskaia antiteza v fol'klore i literature," *Fol'klor narodov RSFSR* 10 (1983): 116–19.

Chiaroscuro

Chiaroscuro, the interplay of light and shade, another kind of figurative language based on contrast, was also employed by Gogol for emphasis and dramatic impact.[57] The term was coined in the Italian Baroque as late as the end of the seventeenth century,[58] but the problems of light and color were already a concern of philosophers in ancient Greece, as we see in Aristotle and Plato. Aristotle talked of light mainly as a physical reality, whereas Plato primarily interpreted light on the metaphorical-symbolic plane, likening it to a spiritual emanation. These two traditional ways of perceiving light were partly synthesized in the Early Christian period and Middle Ages, in the works of Plotinus, St. Augustine, and Thomas Aquinas.[59]

Leonardo da Vinci, striving for tonal unity to reflect the harmony of nature, developed a system of monochromatic, that is, black and white, underpainting.[60] This method of his appealed to Venetian artists, especially, as Vasari noted, Giorgione.[61] Like Leonardo, Giorgione favored *sfumato*, soft and diffused light, but whereas Leonardo perceived the function of light mainly with respect to forms and sub-

57. The term "chiaroscuro" is sometimes used to define woodcuts in which layers of color are superimposed to achieve fine shading and highlights. I exclude this artistic form from my discussion, focusing instead on chiaroscuro as employed in painting and literature. For the chiaroscuro woodcuts, see Walter L. Strauss, *Chiaroscuro. The Clair-Obscur Woodcuts by the German and Netherlandish Masters of the XVIth and XVIIth Centuries* (Greenwich, Conn.: New York Graphic Society, 1973).

58. See Filippo Baldinucci, *Vocobolario toscano dell'arte del disegno* (Florence, 1681), s.v. "chiaroscuro."

59. For a discussion on the perception of light and color from antiquity to the Middle Ages, see Eva Keuls, "Skiagraphia Once Again," *American Journal of Archaeology* 79 (1975): 1–16, and Jonas Gavel, *Colour. A Study of Its Position in the Art Theory of the Quattro- & Cinquecento* (Stockholm: Almqvist & Wiksell, 1979), 13–43.

60. For a discussion of Leonardo's ideas on light and color, see John Shearman, "Leonardo's Colour and Chiaroscuro," *Zeitschrift für Kunstgeschichte* 25 (1962): 13–47, and Martin Kemp, *Leonardo da Vinci: The Marvelous Works of Nature and Man* (Cambridge: Harvard University Press, 1981).

For background on Renaissance light and color theory and practice I consulted the following sources: Moshe Barasch, *Light and Color in the Italian Renaissance Theory of Art* (New York: New York University Press, 1978); Gavel, *Colour*; and Linda Kay Caron, "The Use of Color by Painters in Rome from 1524 to 1527" (Ph.D. diss., Bryn Mawr, 1981). For the symbolism of light in Renaissance art, see Millard Meiss, "Light as Form and Symbol in Some Fifteenth-Century Paintings," in his *The Painter's Choice* (New York: Harper & Row, 1976), 3–18.

61. See Giorgio Vasari, *Lives of the Artists,* 2 vols., trans. George Bull (New York: Penguin, 1987), 1:272–73.

stances, playing down its role as color, Giorgione viewed light primarily as color and only secondarily as defining forms.[62] Titian,
Giorgione's younger contemporary, adopted many of the techniques
of that time, in particular a combination of golden tones and dark
ones. Recall, for example, the juxtaposition of dark-toned hair and
golden-toned face in Giorgione's *Portrait of a Young Man* (1504?,
Berlin, Staatliches Museum). Striving to create his own dramatic effects rather than to recreate the harmony of Giorgione's style, Titian
gradually turned his predecessor's golden-dark combination into a
resolute contrast. He also forsook *sfumato,* creating instead the impression that the light was falling from above, as in *St. Mary
Magdalen in Penitence* (1532–33, Florence, Pitti Palace).[63]

Titian's use of chiaroscuro for the sake of emphasis and drama was
espoused by the Early Baroque artist Caravaggio, who considerably
modified Titian's technique. He created the impression that the light
in his paintings came from the side, thereby making light and shade
interact as well as contrast. Placing his models indoors, the artist
endowed his canvases, especially in his later works, such as *St. Jerome
Writing* (1605, Rome, Galleria Borghese) or *Sleeping Cupid* (1608,
Florence, Pitti Palace), with a previously unparalleled complexity
and mysteriousness, and at the same time created a strong sense of
intimacy. Caravaggio's innovations in chiaroscuro were further developed by his numerous followers, such as Gerrit van Honthorst, who
favored indoor scenery with artificial light, particularly candlelight.[64]

The Baroque use of chiaroscuro, which began with Caravaggio,
differed considerably from that of the Renaissance. This reflected
changes in world view. In Renaissance art, the *sfumato* technique,
with its soft light diffused on all beneath it, symbolized the ambiguity
of life, the bittersweet melancholy of existence, but without any

62. See S. J. Freedberg, *Painting in Italy: 1500–1600* (New York: Penguin, 1979), 132.

63. Concerning the art of Giorgione and his influence on the art of Titian, I consulted the
following sources: Christian Hornig, *Giorgiones Spätwerk* (Munich: Fink, 1987), and Harold E.
Wethey, *The Paintings of Titian,* 3 vols. (London: Phaidon, 1969–75).

64. On the art of Caravaggio and his contribution to the development of Baroque
chiaroscuro, see Walter Friedlaender, *Caravaggio Studies* (New York: Schocken, 1969), and
Howard Hibbard, *Caravaggio* (New York: Harper & Row, 1983). On artists Caravaggio influenced, see Richard E. Spear, *Caravaggio and His Followers* (New York: Harper & Row, 1975).

For background information on Baroque art, I consulted the following studies: Denis Mahon,
Studies in Seicento Art and Theory (London: Warburg Institute, 1947); Rudolf Wittkower, *Art
and Architecture in Italy 1600–1750* (Baltimore: Penguin, 1965); Victor-L. Tapié, *The Age of
Grandeur: Baroque Art and Architecture* (New York: Praeger, 1966); and John Rupert Martin,
Baroque (New York: Harper & Row, 1977).

sharp dramatic contrast; in Baroque art, on the other hand, light coming from the side interacted intricately with shade, creating a sense of complex drama, discord, mystery, and intimacy.[65] These last two effects were frequently enhanced by depicting an indoor setting with artificial light rather than an outdoor setting as had been the custom in the Renaissance. Furthermore, on the metaphorical plane, the interplay of light and dark in Baroque art often created a dichotomy between the Divine and the demonic, the spiritual and the earthly, a dichotomy reminiscent of medieval Neoplatonic theology.

Baroque literature adopted chiaroscuro, putting into practice in yet another way Horace's motto *ut pictura poesis.* Marino's poem "Titian's Magdalen" exemplifies this influence of pictorial art on literature:

> How beautifully, my lonely shepherdess,
> in that deserted grotto you abide!
> How brightly, where the dark holds greatest sway,
> you light the shadows with celestial rays.[66]

As its title indicates, the poem was inspired by Titian's *St. Mary Magdalen in Penitence.*[67] Marino's Baroque outlook is clear: he draws the reader's attention to an enclosed space (in this case the grotto) and to the interplay of light and dark in the painting, emphasizing, with "celestial rays," how Titian portrayed light dramatically falling from above.[68]

Typical Baroque candlelight chiaroscuro is employed in a verbal "canvas" in Twardowski's *Civil War,* when the king dispelled rumors that he had stealthily quitted the army:

> Taking the reins in his hand, he again mounts the horse,
> And by candlelight he announces to all about his intent
> To stay until the shadows of the frightening night
> Are shattered, and the early Lucifer
> Proclaims the day.[69]

---

65. Cf. Segel, 116.

66. Ibid., 126.

67. See Wethey, *The Paintings of Titian,* 1:143. Although Wethey dates the painting to 1530–35, more recent studies narrow this gap to 1532–33; see Terisio Pignatti, *Titian,* 2 vols. (New York: Rizzoli, 1981), 1:60.

68. For an illuminating discussion of Marino's poetics, see James V. Mirollo, *The Poet of the Marvelous: Giambattista Marino* (New York: Columbia University Press, 1963).

69. Twardowski, *Woyna Domowa,* 1:88.

In this episode, the interplay of candlelight and darkness functions on two planes: the candlelight makes the king's presence physically visible to the troops and helps raise their morale in the terrifying dark of the night; then too, the candlelight and the ensuing light of an early dawn symbolize the light of truth that disperses the darkness of false tidings.

We find verbal chiaroscuro in the Eastern Slavic Baroque literatures as well. Like Twardowski, Ivan Velichkovskii employed the device both visually and metaphorically in his cycle devoted to St. Barbara:

Visited in the dungeon by Christ, the light of the world,
Her wounds were healed by the Doctor of soul and body;
Let me see the Lord in this dark world,
To rid myself of sinful wounds and deadly darkness in my soul.[70]

In the first lines of this stanza, Velichkovskii is referring to the legend according to which St. Barbara, incarcerated by her father, was visited by a priest disguised as a doctor, who baptized her a Christian.[71] We easily visualize the chiaroscuro effect of the scene depicted by Velichkovskii as if in a Baroque painting: the actual darkness of the young woman's confinement is suddenly dispersed by the light emanating from the messenger of Christ, and this light symbolically represents the truth of Christianity that clears away the darkness of Barbara's paganism. This verbal "canvas" impelled the poet's lyrical "I" to contemplate his own fate and to ask God to appear to him in this "dark" world and enlighten his "dark" soul with the "light" of faith.

In *The Life of Iulianiia Lazarevskaia,* written by her son Kallistrat, light and burning candles are seen at night in the storeroom where her corpse was laid, a symbolic testimony to her righteousness. And in the anonymous *Tale of Savva Grudtsyn,* the ailing Savva has a nightly vision of "a Lady from whom emanated light, and who shone with indescribable grace," which indicates that this sinful young

70. Velychkovs'kyi, *Tvory,* 98.
71. See Hall, *Dictionary of Subjects & Symbols in Art,* s.v. "Barbara."

man, who was visited in his dream by the Holy Virgin, is on the road to salvation.[72]

Himself an amateur painter, Gogol was certainly familiar with chiaroscuro and particularly with its use in Baroque art—he studied painting in the early 1830s in the evening classes of St. Petersburg Academy of Fine Arts and later, during his stay abroad, he had close contacts with painters, mainly in Rome.[73] In Gogol's day, given the attraction of the Baroque heritage in the age of Romanticism, chiaroscuro was of interest to writers such as Goethe, Schopenhauer, Mérimée, and to Italian painter-theorists such as Giuseppe Bossi and Girolamo Luigi Calvi.[74] This attraction of the Romantics to chiaroscuro found concrete expression in works of art. An important example of this was Karl Briullov's *The Last Day of Pompeii* (1833), a painting that Gogol welcomed with fervent enthusiasm in his 1834 article of the same name (see 8:107–14; Tulloch, 203–10). In this article Gogol affirmed that the main goal of contemporary artists was to achieve precisely the effect produced in this painting by the interplay of light and shade (see 8:108; Tulloch, 204). The chiaroscuro effect was also not uncommon in literary works of the day: Maturin used candlelight chiaroscuro in his novel *Melmoth, the Wanderer* (1820); Lermontov, Gogol's contemporary, also an amateur painter, employed it in his unfinished early novel, *Vadim* (1832–34).[75]

Gogol's predilection for chiaroscuro has already been pointed out by scholars. Boris Éikhenbaum, in his study of Lermontov (1924),

72. Serge A. Zenkovsky, ed., *Medieval Russia's Epics, Chronicles, and Tales* (New York: Dutton, 1974), 398 and 472. For the original, see M. O. Skripil', comp., *Russkaia povest' XVII veka* (Leningrad: GIKhL, 1954), 46 and 100.

73. For a detailed discussion of Gogol's great interest in art, see A. A. Nazarevskii, "Gogol' i iskusstvo," in *Pamiati Gogolia. Sbornik rechei i statei* (Kiev, 1911), 49–90. About Gogol's life in Rome and his familiarity with the art of the Eternal City, see Richter, "Rom und Gogol'." On Gogol's ties with contemporary artists who worked in Rome, see N. G. Mashkovtsev, *Gogol' v krugu khudozhnikov* (Moscow: Iskusstvo, 1955).

74. See Nancy Jane Gray Troyer, "The Effects of Color and Painting Treatises on Nineteenth-Century Concepts of Color and Chiaroscuro," in her "The *Macchiaioli*: Effects of Modern Color Theory, Photography, and Japanese Prints on a Group of Italian Painters, 1855–1900" (Ph.D. diss., Northwestern University, 1978), 98–130.

75. See Boris Éikhenbaum, "Lermontov," in his *O literature* (Moscow: Sovetskii pisatel', 1987), 252–53. Éikhenbaum was perhaps the first scholar to speak about the interplay of light and dark in early nineteenth-century literature (285–86). As for Lermontov, he also used chiaroscuro in his paintings, particularly in the portrait of his imaginary ancestor, Duke Lerma (1832–33); see V. A. Manuilov, ed., *Lermontovskaia éntsiklopediia* (Moscow: Sovetskaia éntsiklopediia, 1981), following 528.

quoted a passage from "The Fair at Sorochintsy" to demonstrate that writers in the first half of the nineteenth century quite commonly exploited this device. A decade later, Andrei Belyi noted and illustrated Gogol's "rare ability to create a picture consisting of light, darkness, and glitter—with only two strokes of his pen."[76] And Louis Pedrotti, in his study on the fragment "Rome," observed Gogol's use of contrasting light and shade in his portrayal of Annunziata and the Roman landscape.[77]

In this discussion, I shall limit myself to several cases of Gogol's using Baroque chiaroscuro with its artificial light and indoor scenery as exemplified in the paintings of Gerrit van Honthorst. We already see an instance of this in Gogol's early work, *The Hetman:*

> The head of the detachment was moving in silence, and the fickle light of the candlewick, enclosed in a misty circle, threw a pale ghost of light on his face, while the shadow from his enormous moustache was rising and covering everybody in two long bands. Only the crudely carved outline of his face was definably touched by the light and made it possible to discern a deeply insensible expression on his face, revealing that everything gentle had frozen and died in his soul; that life and death made no difference to him; that his greatest delights were tobacco and alcohol; that his paradise was the place where everything rattles and falls from the hand of a drunk. (3:304)

As we see, Gogol employed chiaroscuro here straightforwardly, describing the interplay of light and dark on the facial features of his character in order to expose his coarseness, destructiveness, and overbearing nature, which is symbolized by his overshadowing moustache.

His use of the device was more complex a few years later in "Vii," in the passage describing the church where Khoma was reading the Psalms over the body of the dead witch:

> In the middle of the church stood the black coffin; candles were gleaming under the dark images; the light from them

76. See Éikhenbaum, "Lermontov," 285, and Belyi, *Masterstvo Gogolia,* 132.
77. Louis Pedrotti, "The Architecture of Love in Gogol' 's 'Rome,' " *California Slavic Studies* 6 (1971): 22–23.

only lit up the icon stand and shed a faint glimmer in the middle of the church; the distant corners were wrapped in darkness. The tall, old-fashioned icon stand showed traces of great antiquity; its carved fretwork, once gilt, only glistened here and there with splashes of gold; the gilt had peeled off in one place, and was completely tarnished in another; the faces of the saints, blackened by age, had a gloomy look. (2:206; Kent, 2:157)

Here Gogol endowed the chiaroscuro with definitely symbolic meaning, emphasizing the abnormal darkness and gloom in the church. This prevalence of gloom in the temple of God, a darkness that cannot be overcome by additional light—Khoma lights a great number of candles around the whole church but his efforts avail him nothing—implies that this church is becoming an accursed, godless place overtaken by the Evil Spirit, a foreboding which comes true at the end of the tale (see 2:217; Kent, 2:168).

Another example of Baroque chiaroscuro in Gogol's oeuvre, and perhaps the most outstanding and complex one, appears in the 1842 edition of *Taras Bulba,* in the episode where Andrii and his companion, a Tartar woman, move clandestinely through a tunnel toward the besieged Polish city of Dubno:

Andrei moved slowly in the dark and narrow underground passage, following the woman and carrying the sacks of bread. "Soon we shall be able to see," said his guide. "We are near the spot where I left the candlestick." And in fact the dark earthen walls began to be lighted up with a faint glimmer. They reached a rather wider place which seemed to be a chapel of sorts; anyway there was a little narrow table like an altar fixed to the wall, and a faded, almost completely effaced image of a Catholic Madonna could be discerned above it. A little silver lamp hanging before it gave a faint glimmer. The Tartar woman bent down and picked up from the ground a tall thin copper candlestick, with snuffers, a skewer to push up the wick, and an extinguisher hanging on little chains about it. Picking it up, she lighted it from the little lamp. The light grew brighter and, walking on together, now throwing a brilliant light, now casting a coal-black shadow, they resembled the paintings by Gerardo della Notte. (2:94–95; Kent, 2:67)[78]

Gogol's familiarity with Baroque chiaroscuro is evident in this reference to Gerrit van Honthorst, whom he called by his widespread Italian nickname. This Dutch painter, a follower of Caravaggio, spent the formative years of his artistic life (ca. 1610–20) in Rome. Honthorst also favored chiaroscuro, but unlike Caravaggio, whose source of light was almost never revealed, he favored night scenes (whence his nickname) with artificial light, particularly candlelight.[79] It is noteworthy that Gogol referred to Honthorst only in the 1842 edition of *Taras Bulba;* there is no mention of the Dutch artist in the 1835 edition, or in any other work prior to this period. Since Gogol first arrived in Rome in the spring of 1837, it is almost certain that it was there, in Italy, that he became acquainted with Honthorst's works.[80]

Turning to the episode itself, we see that besides endowing the scene with mystery and drama, the chiaroscuro here bears a symbolic meaning. The narrator's remark about the light and dark successively enveloping Andrii together with his companion, the Tartar maidservant may reinforce the reader's impression of certain similarities between them: indeed, Andrii, a Ukrainian Cossack, is, like the Tartar maid, serving the enemy. Andrii, however, does so voluntarily, a captive of love for his Polish girl, but the Tartar maid does so because of her physical captivity. This association of Andrii with the Tartar maid also suggests a certain effeminacy in him: he forgot the bond of military brotherhood through his love for a woman—a serious transgression of the Cossack code. This effeminacy is foreshadowed at Andrii's first meeting with the Polish girl (and also in his first encounter with her captive Tartar maid), when she mischievously

78. I have altered the last clause of Kent's translation to bring it nearer the original and to convey the Italian version of this Dutch painter's name more correctly.

79. For detailed information about Honthorst, see Jay Richard Judson, *Gerrit van Honthorst* (The Hague: Nijhoff, 1959).

80. In Italy, Gogol could see Honthorst's canvases with candlelight chiaroscuro such as *The Beheading of St. John the Baptist,* Rome, S. Maria della Scala, 1618, or *Merry Company,* Florence, Uffizi Gallery, 1620, in Uffizi since 1773; cf. Judson, *Gerrit von Honthorst,* 158 and 245. For an earlier discussion of Gogol's reference to Honthorst, see Shapiro, "A Note on the Connection Between an Episode from Gogol's *Taras Bulba* and Visual Art, Mainly Roman Baroque," 215–216.

decks him out in woman's clothing and jewelry (see 2:57; Kent, 2:36).[81] The light and dark in this tunnel that connect the Cossack Orthodox world with the Polish Catholic one figuratively suggest that Andrii, abandoning his family, comrades-in-arms, native land, and Orthodox faith, all for his love of the Polish girl, is crossing a moral frontier.[82]

Thus the subtle chiaroscuro symbolism of the tunnel episode alludes to Andrii's moral fall, preparing the reader for the narrator's categorical statement, "And ruined is the Cossack! He is lost for all the chivalry of the Cossacks! He will see the camp no more; nor his father's farms, nor the church of God. The Ukraine will see no more of the bravest of the sons who undertook to defend her" (2:107; Kent, 2:77).[83]

We find another example of chiaroscuro, a unique one, in *Dead Souls,* in the passage describing the first appearance of Ulinka Betrishcheva before Chichikov:

> There was suddenly a rustling sound in the study. The walnut door of a carved cupboard flew open, and on the other side of it a slender, living figure appeared with one hand on the brass knob of the door. If an oil-painting had suddenly been lit up from behind and made transparent, it would not have caused as much surprise as the apparition of this figure. . . . It was as though it had brought a ray of sunshine with it and the gen-

---

81. Cf. Peace, *The Enigma of Gogol,* 50. This passage calls to mind an episode from the life of Heracles: a slave of the queen Omphale, the famous hero was wearing female attire at her whim. See Pierre Grimal, *The Dictionary of Classical Mythology* (New York: Blackwell, 1987), 206.

82. Perhaps the subterranean tunnel itself and the marshland on the way to and inside of it allude to the low moral ground of Andrii's venture. For further discussion of symbolism in this episode, see Guminskii, " 'Taras Bul'ba' v 'Mirgorode' i 'Arabeskakh,' " 251–52.

83. Other details in this episode subtly prepare the reader for the narrator's later pronouncement. For example, the earthen walls of the passage reminded Andrii of the Kiev catacombs (see 2:95; Kent, 2:67–68). Andrii undoubtedly was thinking of the Kiev Monastery of the Caves, or *Kievo-Pecherskaia Lavra* (*laura* in Greek means "a passage"). By having Andrii compare this first and for a long time most famous sanctuary of the Orthodox faith and of the Ukrainian people with the passage to the Polish city of Dubno, Gogol, it seems, intended to demonstrate Andrii's national and religious insensitivity, which would later prove fatal to him. On the importance of the Kiev Monastery of the Caves for Ukrainian Orthodoxy, see George Heard Hamilton, *The Art and Architecture of Russia* (New York: Penguin, 1983), 19 and 419 n. 34, and G. N. Logvin, *Kievo-Pecherskaia Lavra* (Moscow: Iskusstvo, 1958).

eral's frowning study had burst into laughter. (7:40; Gibian, 309)

This example would appear to constitute Gogol's innovation in handling chiaroscuro Before Gogol, both painters and men of letters used the device straightforwardly by depicting an actual interplay of light and shade, whereas here Gogol employed chiaroscuro as an integral part of the metaphor in order to emphasize spiritual radiance emanating from Ulinka—the idealized female character in the *poéma*.

Oxymoron

Oxymoron is yet another figure of language based on the principle of contrast, consisting as it does of two ostensibly contradictory components, usually a noun and an adjective. Unlike antithesis, however, oxymoron does not tend to show the division and categorization of experience but rather its paradoxical fusion.[84]

Horace captured the nature of oxymoron in his pointed query: *"Quid velit et possit rerum concordia discors?"* (*Epist.* 1, 12:19). ("What is the meaning and what the effects of Nature's jarring harmony?")[85] Some centuries later, St. Augustine, marveling at the mystery of his own existence and at the contradictory world that surrounded him, inquired in his *Confessions:* "What is it that I want to say, Lord, save that I do not know whence I came to this place, to this, shall I say rather 'dying life' than 'living death'?" (1:6).[86]

Oxymoron is common, often significant, in medieval literature. In the prologue to the famous early-thirteenth-century poem by Gottfried von Strassburg, *Tristan and Isolde,* we find "sweet grief," "happy distress," and "joyful death." According to some students, oxymoron underlies the very conception of this poem and is the key to its interpretation.[87] At the close of the medieval period, oxymoron was

84. See Preminger, *Encyclopedia,* 595–96, and *Kratkaia literaturnaia éntsiklopediia,* 5:410–11.

85. Horace, *Satires, Epistles and Ars Poetica,* trans. H. Rushton Fairclough (Cambridge: Harvard University Press, 1929), 328–29.

86. Saint Augustine, *The Confessions,* trans. E. M. Blaiklock (Nashville: Nelson, 1983), 19.

87. For a discussion of the importance of oxymoron in this late medieval work, see Laura

frequently used by Petrarch, and literary scholars view it as characteristic of his poetry.[88]

Oxymoron became the expression *par excellence* of the Baroque
period, itself the epitome of paradox and contradiction.[89] Among the
most popular in the literature of the period were expressions such as
"dying life," "sweet wounds of love," and "fiery water."[90] Giambattista
Marino used the "sweet wounds of love" idea in his poem "The Song
of the Kisses": "loving the wounds, / the deeper they are, the more the
pleasing." And Juan de Arguijo (1567–1623) exploited "fiery water"
in his poem "To Narcissus": "He looks again in the spring and sees
(strange case!) that out of it love's fire comes."[91]

In the Baroque literature of the Slavic countries we find Jan
Andrzej Morsztyn employing all three of these oxymora when speaking of the paradoxical nature of love in his "The Wonders of Love":

> My God! I live, and yet without a heart?
> Not living, yet a flame within me burns?
> If with this flame I do myself destroy,
> Why do I lovingly embrace it so?
>
> If thus I live in tears, afire 'midst flame,
> Why make I no attempt to dry the tears
> With fire? And why, since I command the flame,
> Can I not put it out with flowing tears?[92]

And Skovoroda used the "night-sunlight" oxymoron to express his
religious sensibilities in the Nativity poem "In Natalem Iesu":

> Oh night, new, marvelous, wonderful,
> Clearer than the bright midday,

Mancinelli, "Tristan Versus Parzifal. The 'Prologue' to Gottfried von Strassburg's *Tristan*," *Medieval and Pseudo-Medieval Literature,* ed. Piero Boitani and Anna Torti (Tubingen: Narr, 1984),
11–17.

88. See Pierre Barucco, "L'oxymoron pétrarquesque ou de l'amour fou," *Revue des Études
Italiennes* 29 (1983): 117.

89. See Preminger, *Encyclopedia,* 595–96.

90. See Eleanor McCann, "Oxymora in Spanish Mystics and English Metaphysical Writers,"
Comparative Literature 13 (1961): 16.

91. See Segel, 281 (278), and Elias L. Rivers, ed., *Renaissance and Baroque Poetry of Spain*
(New York: Dell, 1966), 240.

92. Segel, 299 (298).

When through the gloom, dark and black,
The not-evening light of the sun has shone.[93]

In his cycle "Death," included in the collection *Garden of Many Flowers* (1678), Polotskii called upon his readers to abandon their vain pursuits and to ponder mortality; to make his point more convincing, he used the implicitly oxymoronic "forceless strength" to emphasize the unpredictability of man's demise, illustrating how death "destroyed a healthy one; forceless, it brought down a forceful one."[94] Lomonosov employed the "fiery water" idea three times in his poem "Morning Meditation on the Majesty of God" (1751), to underscore the unfathomable power of the Almighty:

> There fiery billows lock in struggle
> And, seeking, come upon no shores.
> Contending for a host of ages
> There flaming whirlwinds twist and turn;
> Like water, rocks are boiling there,
> And burning rains come roaring down.[95]

A poem of Derzhavin's, "The Bathhouse of Aristippus," was cited in the discussion on oxymoron in the textbook used by Gogol when a schoolboy, Tolmachev's *Rules of Philology:* "It happens that the purple could be a burden, / And the beauty—unbeautiful." And oxymoron was referred to by Iosif Sreznevskii in his "Attempt at Concise Rhetoric," an introduction to his *Collection of Exemplary Russian and Translated Works in Prose* also used in the gymnasium Gogol attended.[96]

Gogol employed oxymoron frequently. It underlies the paradoxical nature of his oeuvre.[97] At times, his use of the figure is reminiscent

---

93. Skovoroda, *Povne zibrannia tvoriv,* 1:97.

94. Adrianova-Peretts, ed., *Russkaia sillabicheskaia poéziia XVII–XVIII v. v.,* 154.

95. Segel, *The Literature of Eighteenth-Century Russia,* 1:207. For the original, see Lomonosov, *Polnoe sobranie sochinenii,* 8:118; in Russian, the stanza also contains a threefold (not twofold as in Segel's translation) anaphora "there."

96. See Derzhavin, *Sochineniia,* 3:65; Tolmachev, *Pravila,* 2:270–71; and Sreznevskii, "Opyt kratkoi ritoriki," in *Sobranie v proze,* 2:lxvi.

97. See Dmitrii Chizhevskii, "Gogol: Artist and Thinker," *The Annals of the Ukrainian Academy of Arts and Sciences in the U.S.* 2, no. 3 (1952): 266.

of the pre-Baroque and Baroque, when oxymoron was primarily employed to emphasize the complex and often contradictory nature of passion and religion. In *Taras Bulba* Gogol employed an implicit oxymoron "weak strength" when depicting Taras pondering on Andrii's betrayal as a result of his love for the Polish maiden: "He [Bulba] remembered how great is the power of weak woman" (2:113; Kent, 2:81). In describing Chartkov's infatuation with gold, the narrator in "The Portrait" dubs the character and other avarice-stricken people like him "living corpses" (3:110; Kent, 2:281). And in his "Meditations on Divine Liturgy" Gogol conveyed the intricate nature of Eucharist symbolism by employing the implicit oxymoron "incorporeal flesh": "Thus, by removing bread from the bread he [the priest] signifies the removal of the flesh of Christ from the flesh of the Virgin—the birth of the Incorporeal in the flesh."[98] More important, however, Gogol, unlike his Baroque literary predecessors, frequently employed oxymoron to highlight incongruous, comic aspects of life. To this group belong such passages as "a spirited, young, dappled gray horse, only seventeen years old" (3:59; Kent, 2:226) and "Vassily Feodorov, Foreigner" (6:11; Gibian, 6).[99] Gogol also used oxymoron satirically to expose the foibles of Russian life. In the famous "humane" passage of "The Overcoat" the narrator suggests the oxymoron "human inhumanity" when he talks about a certain young man who is deeply touched by Akakii Akakievich's misery and later is constantly shaken by "seeing how much inhumanity there is in a human being" (3:144; Kent, 2:307).[100] And, finally, in *Selected Passages from Correspondence with Friends,* in the section "To One Who Occupies an Important Position," Gogol spoke of the corruption in Russian society: "You already know that guilt has been so split up among everyone that is now impossible to say at first who is the most guilty. There are the guiltlessly guilty and the guilty innocent" (8:351; Zeldin, 176–77).

Following the pre-Baroque and Baroque tradition, Gogol employed the oxymoron to bring out the complex and oftentimes contradic-

98. N. V. Gogol', *Sochineniia,* 7 vols., 10th ed., ed. N. S. Tikhonravov (Moscow, 1889–96), 4:418.

99. For a longer list of such structures, which Chizhevskii dubbed antithetic oxymora, see his "Gogol: Artist and Thinker," 266.

100. I have altered Kent's translation to accentuate the oxymoron Gogol uses in the original.

tory emotions associated with passions and with belief in God. Perhaps his unique contribution lies in his use of the figure to highlight the comically incongruous sides of human life and as a weapon of biting satire.

Conceit

Conceit, farfetched, intricate metaphor, is based on startling comparisons of disparate elements, and thus, like oxymoron, involves paradox. Theoretical works of Baroque aesthetics, such as Giulio Cortese's *Avvertimenti nel poetare* (1591), Camillo Pellegrino's *Del concetto poetico* (1598), Maciej Kazimierz Sarbiewski's *Del acuto et arguto* (1619), Matteo Peregrini's *Delle acutezze* (1639), Baltasar Gracián's *Agudeza y arte de ingenio* (1649), and Emanuele Tesauro's *Il cannocchiale aristotelico* (1654), all treated conceit as an important figure of language and asserted that it called for a writer of great ingenuity and acuity of mind.[101]

Among the first and most prominent Baroque literati to favor the use of conceit was Giambattista Marino. In his poem "On a Lady Sewing," Marino wrote:

> It is an arrow, an arrow, and not a needle which she is using at her work, she whom I adore, the new Arachne of love; with which, while she beautifies and embroiders the beautiful linen, she pierces and runs my heart through in a thousand places. Alas! And that so delicate, bleeding thread which she pulls, cuts, knots, stretches, twists and winds with her beautiful elegant hand, is the thread of my life.[102]

---

101. For a detailed discussion of the conceit, see the following studies: K. K. Ruthven, *The Conceit* (London: Methuen, 1969), Alexander A. Parker, " 'Concept' and 'Conceit': An Aspect of Comparative Literary History," *The Modern Language Review* 77 (1982): xxi–xxxv; Renate Lachmann, "Die 'problematische Ähnlichkeit.' Sarbiewskis Traktat *De acuto et arguto* im Kontext concettistischer Theorien des 17. Jahrhunderts," in *Slavische Barockliteratur II,* ed. Renate Lachmann (Munich: Funk, 1983), 87–114; and J. W. Van Hook, " 'Concupiscence of Witt': The Metaphysical Conceit in Baroque Poetics," *Modern Philology* 84 (1986): 24–38.
102. Hill, 87.

Marino began his poem with conventional metaphors. His lyrical "I" calls his beloved "the new Arachne of love" because, unlike the heroine of mythology, she uses a piercing arrow, as if taken from Cupid's quiver, instead of a needle, to torment his heart. The reader can easily follow this set of "sewing" metaphors, only to be startled at the end of the poem when Marino unexpectedly equates the thread the woman uses for her sewing with the bleeding thread of his hero's life. The striking effect caused by this farfetched metaphor and the sudden change to tragic tonality nicely demonstrate the mechanism of conceit.

Conceit was well known and skillfully used in the Baroque literature of the Slavic countries. Jan Andrzej Morsztyn created an intricate conceit, endowing the Christian symbol of the Cross with erotic meaning, in his sonnet "On the Little Cross on a Certain Lady's Breast."[103] And Stefan Iavorskii built images of different forms of piety by comparing them to various kinds of wine.[104] Lomonosov favored conceit as one of the basics of poetic thinking. He regarded the development of verbal figurative meaning as very important and viewed it, along with wit (a combination of imaginative force and reasoning), as a necessary condition for poetic creation.[105]

In the seventeenth century, the heyday of the Baroque, conceit was primarily used in lyrical poetry and homiletic literature. In the eighteenth century, when the Baroque was gradually winding down and when satire had become a prominent form, conceit was commonly used for satirical purposes.[106]

Gogol became acquainted with the term as a student at the Nezhin Gymnasium. Conceit was mentioned, albeit pejoratively, by Iosif Sreznevskii in his introduction to *The Collection of Exemplary Russian and Translated Works in Verse;* Sreznevskii scorned Marino for

103. See Segel, 301.
104. Chizhevskii, "K problemam literatury barokko u slavian," 29.
105. A. A. Morozov, "Lomonosov i barokko," *Russkaia literatura* 2 (1965): 75. For a discussion of conceit in Eastern Slavic Baroque literature, see Renate Lachmann, "Die Tradition des *ostroumie* und das *acumen* bei Simeon Polockij," in *Slavische Barockliteratur I,* 41–59; Vladimir N. Toporov, "Eine Seite aus der Geschichte des russischen barocken Concettismus: Petr Buslaevs *Umozritel'stvo Duševnoe," in Slavische Barockliteratur II,* 57–86.
106. For a detailed discussion of the conceit in the eighteenth century, see Barbara Jean Seymour, "A Radiant Trail: The Extension of the Conceit Through Eighteenth-Century English Poetry" (Ph.D. diss., University of Oregon, 1985).

making "excessive use of witticisms or *concetti* (flashes of wit) in his works."[107]

Sreznevskii's condemnation of Marino's "excessive" use of conceit did not discourage Gogol. In the early nineteenth century, by which time conceit had fallen into great disrepute and then into near oblivion, Gogol ignored the disparaging remarks of older contemporaries such as Sreznevskii and added the figure to his artistic arsenal.[108] He employed conceit in all three modes mentioned above—lyrical, moralizing, and satirical. Thus in the 1842 edition of *Taras Bulba,* in the lyrical passage describing the death of Kukubenko, a distinguished Cossack, Gogol likened the irreplaceable loss of Kukubenko, "a blow to everyone" (2:141; Kent, 2:106), to the inadvertent breaking of a glass vessel holding precious wine:

> Slowly he [Kukubenko] sank into the arms of the Cossacks who supported him, and the young blood spurted out in a stream like precious wine brought in a glass vessel from the cellar by careless servants who slip at the entrance and shatter the costly flagon, the wine spilling upon the ground; and the master, running up, clutches his head in despair, since he has kept it for the best moment of his life, so that, if God should grant in his old age a meeting with the comrades of his youth, they might celebrate together those old other days when men made merry otherwise and better. (2:141; Kent, 2:105–6)

Like the ecclesiastical preachers, his Baroque predecessors, Gogol also used conceit for sermonizing when he wished to render his thought especially vivid. In the section of *Selected Passages* entitled "On the Essence of Russian Poetry and on Its Originality," Gogol wrote: "The Russian people needed an abrupt change and the European enlightenment was the flint on which it was necessary to strike with all our slumbering mass. The flint may enkindle the tinder, but, so long as you have not struck it, the tinder will not take fire. The

---

107. Iosif Sreznevskii, "Opyt rossiiskoi piitiki," in *Sobranie v stikhakh,* 1:xlviii.

108. The reception of the conceit in the early nineteenth-century Russian literary criticism is discussed by Stefano Garzonio in his "Concetti kak odin iz intertekstov russkoi liriki" (Paper presented at the Fourth World Congress of Soviet and East European Studies, Harrogate, England, July 1990). At the close of this paper, the Italian scholar addresses, albeit in passing, the matter of Gogol's use of conceits in his works (29).

spark suddenly flashed from the people" (8:370; Zeldin, 200).[109] This extended metaphor conveys the quintessence of conceit, which might itself be likened to a spark produced by two materials struck against each other. Gogol's conceit is testimony that once the spark of meaning has been produced, the materials of the comparison are no longer merely what they were, just as the Russian and European civilizations were no longer the same after the spark of the Petrine reforms.[110]

Gogol's use of conceit for satirical purposes is especially frequent in *Dead Souls*. In his depiction of Pliushkin, Gogol compares his unfeeling hero to a drowning man who is beyond rescue:

> And suddenly a sort of beaming warmth passed over that wooden face, expressing not so much feeling as a pale reflection of it, and as a phenomenon this was not unlike a drowning man unexpectedly reappearing on the surface amid the joyful shouts of the crowd gathered on the bank of a river. But vainly do his brothers and sisters throw a rope into the water and wait for the drowning man's back or exhausted arms to appear again—he has shown himself for the last time. After that all is darkness, and the still surface of the elements bespeak an even greater void and terror. So it was with Plyushkin's face: the instant of feeling was succeeded by an even more callous and meaner mask. (6:126; Gibian, 132)

Gogol here employs conceit with great power in portraying the petrifaction of Pliushkin's soul.

His predilection for this figure is manifest in his frequent employment of it in his correspondence, where, as elsewhere in his fiction, he favored the use of a conceit drawn from school life. In a letter of his to Vasilii Zhukovskii at the end of February 1839, Gogol wrote:

109. Gogol argued in this passage in support of Petrine reforms, thus polemicizing with the Slavophiles. In the subsequent passage, however, Gogol also scorned the Westernizers when he suggested that the Russians needed European enlightenment to examine themselves rather than to copy Europe (8:370; Zeldin, 200).

110. The comparison of conceit to a spark produced by two materials was made by Helen Gardner in her introduction to *The Metaphysical Poets* (London: Oxford University Press, 1961), xxiii. In my view, B. J. Seymour is justified in correcting Gardner, who asserted, "After the flash the stones [*sic*] are just two stones," by insisting instead that after this spark "everything changes, blazes up, takes on new energy." See Seymour, 192.

I should have been entirely happy if something of that tedious
feeling had not interfered with my delight. It was the same
feeling that a schoolboy has when his teacher goes for a walk
into the countryside with all his classmates and leaves him
alone in the small school yard as punishment for his laziness.
He watches the evening fade, and through it, with the eyes of
imagination, he envisages a meadow in the distance, sunlight
on it, a group of friends, a ball flying upward, merry cries. He
sees everything and doesn't want to tear himself away from his
vision, rubbing his sour stubborn phiz with his fist and sleeve
and not taking his eyes off the steadily setting sun. (11:201)

Gogol's contemporaries, Konstantin Aksakov and Stepan Shevyrev,
were among the first critics to note his employment of conceit,
without calling it that (they called it simile, a practice that continues
among critics and literary scholars to this day). In enthusiastic praise
for *Dead Souls,* Aksakov asserted that when Gogol drew comparisons
for the purpose of illustration, he would leave the main line of the
narrative until he had exhausted the subject matter of the comparisons. Expressing admiration for Gogol's "wonderful similes,"
Shevyrev somewhat contradictorily observed that, on the one hand,
Gogol knew how to incorporate them into the *poéma* without de-
stroying its unity, while on the other hand, the similes constituted
separate, complete pictures, in drawing which Gogol was carried
away in the spirit of true epic writers like Homer and Dante.[111] Sixty
years after Shevyrev and Aksakov, Iosif Mandel'shtam criticized Gogol
for precisely what those earlier critics had praised: "superfluous enthusiasm for similes, elaborately developed at the expense of the
main subject of comparison."[112] Mandel'shtam illustrated his point
with several quotations from *Dead Souls* and summed up: "In general, it must be concluded: Gogol was carried away by the word; it
frequently guided him instead of his being in control of it."[113] Half a
century later, Viktor Vinogradov came closer to understanding conceit, when he noted its "acute suddenness of disparity and semantic
novelty of convergence," the characteristic features of conceit. As to

111. Shevyrev, "Pokhozhdeniia Chichikova," 359–60.
112. Mandel'shtam, *O kharaktere gogolevskogo stilia,* 77.
113. Ibid., 78–79.

the function of Gogol's conceits, Vinogradov observed that they "serve the purpose of a satirical illumination of reality. At the same time, they themselves reflect a piece of the same Russian reality."[114]

Over the last twenty-five years, several scholars, Western and Soviet, have addressed the issue of Gogol's employment of conceit, though still without calling it that. The most basic study on the subject thus far is the monograph by Carl R. Proffer, who, dubbing it Homeric simile, made the first attempt to explain the function of conceit in Gogol's works.[115] Proffer's most important contribution to our understanding of Gogol's use of conceit is his demonstration that Gogol did not employ it thoughtlessly, that Gogol was not carried away by his descriptions, as Aksakov, Shevyrev, and Mandel'shtam have maintained, but endowed them with a very significant compositional role—to illuminate characters, their interrelations, and the underlying themes of a work by means of an extended comparison, ostensibly unrelated to the main plotline.[116] A good illustration of this compositional role of conceit is provided by the "school" conceit in chapter 9 of *Dead Souls,* discussed in the *vertep* section of Chapter 2. This conceit, in which the bewildered town fathers are compared to a schoolboy on whom classmates played a prank known as "hussar," besides its satirical overtones, underlines the themes permeating the *poéma*—mistaken identities and counterfeit truths.[117]

Conceits appear predominantly in Gogol's later works. Proffer traces this to Gogol's fascination with Homer in the late 1830s and 1840s. I should like to point out, additionally, that these were the years of Gogol's stay abroad, when he was exposed to Western, particularly Italian, Baroque literature, as we learn from his correspondence, for example, his letter to Mariia Balabina of April 1838 (11:143). Furthermore, these were the years of his heightened inter-

114. V. V. Vinogradov, "Iazyk Gogolia i ego znachenie v istorii russkogo iazyka," *Materialy i issledovaniia po istorii russkogo literaturnogo iazyka,* ed. Vinogradov, 3:31.

115. See Proffer, *The Simile.*

116. It is quite possible that Gogol's rather cool response to Aksakov's brochure on *Dead Souls* was in part caused by Aksakov's lack of comprehension of the important functions that Gogol bestowed on conceit in it; see 12:186–87.

117. See Proffer, *The Simile,* 87–88, and Woodward, *Gogol's "Dead Souls,"* 204–14 and passim. It seems to me that Proffer partly missed the point when he equated Gogol's conceits, with their complex function, to Homer's straightforward similes, designed "to stress one common characteristic." See C. M. Bowra, *Tradition and Design in the "Iliad"* (Oxford: Clarendon, 1930), 116 and 126.

est in ecclesiastical writers such as Stefan Iavorskii and Lazar' Baranovich (see 9:561 and 12:219), who frequently employed conceits in their sermons.[118]

In sum, Gogol, drawing on the example of his Baroque predecessors, employed conceit for lyrical and moralizing purposes. His predilection for it was so strong that he used it repeatedly even in his correspondence. His unique contribution to the use of conceit was his endowing it with important compositional functions and, what is more, exploiting it alongside the main plotline for the satirical presentation of Russian "reality."

Wordplay

The generic term "wordplay" comprises a number of figures of language; I shall focus here on the two most frequently used— antanaclasis and paronomasia. Antanaclasis involves the repetition of homonyms—words of the same spelling or sound but with different meaning—whereas paronomasia involves the repetition of words only partially similar in sound and, as in antanaclasis, dissimilar in meaning. Antanaclasis and paronomasia combine in themselves the characteristics of almost all figures of speech that I have previously discussed: like anaphora and epiphora, they entail phonetic repetition; like antithesis and chiaroscuro, they involve contrast, here between the phonetic resemblance and semantic dissimilarity; finally, like oxymoron and conceit, they are based on paradoxical verbal collisions that generate new understanding.[119]

We find antanaclasis and paronomasia discussed in Aristotle's *Rhetoric* (1401b and 1412b) and in Quintilian's *Institutio Oratoria* (9, 3:66–68).[120] Classical writers used these devices in serious works,

118. Smirnova, *Poéma Gogolia,* 63–64.

119. Roman Jakobson defined paronomasia as "a semantic confrontation of phonemically similar words irrespective of any etymological connection." See Roman Jakobson, *Selected Writings,* 7 vols. (The Hague: Mouton, 1971–85), 2:354. For an illuminating discussion on paronomasia and antanaclasis, see Jonathan Culler, "The Call of the Phoneme: Introduction," in *On Puns: The Foundation of Letters,* ed. Jonathan Culler (New York: Blackwell, 1988), 1–16.

120. Aristotle, *The Rhetoric,* 173 and 213–14; Quintilian, *The Institutio Oratoria,* 3:484–85.

although they also not uncommonly employed them for comic effect. Medieval writers also used these forms of wordplay, thereby exploiting in their turn the manifold semantic possibilities that these two figures provide.[121]

Given the characteristic emphasis of the Baroque period on surprise and paradox, it is not extraordinary that antanaclasis and paronomasia were in frequent use.[122] A distinguishing feature of the Baroque was its employment of wordplay in depicting tragic situations and events. Shakespeare, for example, endowed antanaclasis and paronomasia with gruesome significance. We find the former in *Romeo and Juliet* when Mercutio, mortally wounded, says to his friends, "Ask for me tomorrow and you shall find me a grave man" (3, 1:100–102), and the latter in the famous pun in *Macbeth,* when immediately after the murder of Duncan Lady Macbeth says,

> If he do bleed,
> I'll gild the faces of the grooms withal,
> For it must seem their guilt.
> (2, 2:54–56)[123]

This employment of antanaclasis and paronomasia to add force to the tragic did not prevent Baroque writers, including Shakespeare, from also using them to enhance the comedic and even the obscene.[124] Antanaclasis and paronomasia appeared frequently in the Slavic

121. For a discussion of the diverse use of wordplay, particularly paronomasia and antanaclasis, in antiquity and the Middle Ages, see J. J. Glück, "Paronomasia in Biblical Literature," *Semitics* 1 (1970): 50–78; Frederick Ahl, *Metaformations: Soundplay and Wordplay in Ovid and Other Classical Poets* (Ithaca: Cornell University Press, 1985); Laura Kendrick, *The Game of Love. Troubadour Wordplay* (Berkeley and Los Angeles: University of California Press, 1988); R. A. Shoaf, "The Play of Puns in Late Middle English Poetry: Concerning Juxtology," in *On Puns,* ed. Culler, 44–61.

122. For a discussion of wordplay in the Baroque period, see Sister Miriam Joseph, *Shakespeare's Use of the Arts of Language* (New York: Columbia University Press, 1947); M. M. Mahood, *Shakespeare's Wordplay* (London: Methuen, 1957); Edward Le Compte, *A Dictionary of Puns in Milton's English Poetry* (New York: Columbia University Press, 1981); Robert Garapon, *La fantaisie verbale et le comique dans le théâtre français du moyen âge à la fin du XVIIe siècle* (Paris: Armand Colin, 1957); Zoe Samaras, *The Comic Element of Montaigne's Style* (Paris: Nizet, 1970), 116–48; Ames Haven Corley, "Word-Play in *The Don Quixote*" (Ph.D. diss., Yale University Press, 1914).

123. See Shakespeare, *The Complete Works,* 492 and 1197. Cf. Buffum, *Agrippa d'Aubigné's "Les Tragiques,"* 101–2.

124. Preminger, *Encyclopedia,* 681.

Baroque literatures, as a rule for humorous or satirical purposes. In Polish literature, we find such antanaclasis for example in a two-line epigram by Stanisław Serafin Jagodyński (fl. ca. 1600–ca. 1650), in which he employed the word *talent* in its two meanings—as a coin of ancient Greece and Rome and as a great ability for something: "*Czemu ten dyskurs groszem, nie talentem zdobią? / Bo i talenta wszystkie na grosz dzisia robią.*"[125] ("Why is this discourse rewarded with a penny and not with a talent? / Because nowadays everyone has a pennyworth of talent.") Paronomasia was a favorite with Wespazjan Kochowski (1633–1700), who made the following pun: "*Gdzie wino dobre, wieszać nie potrzeba wieńca.*" ("Where wine is good, there is no need for a wreath.") On another occasion, apparently displeased over social gatherings, Kochowski sardonically remarked: "*Ktoś wyłożył biesiadą, że bies siada na niej.*"[126] ("Someone explained that a party is the place where the Devil is present.")

In Ukrainian Baroque literature, we find Ivan Velichkovskii, who was especially fond of verbal games, employing an antanaclasis, coupled with antithesis (God-wise/godless), in the following verse, colored with the religious intolerance characteristic of the Baroque: "*Sitse kto bogomudru Varvaru venchaet, / pobedy na bezbozhnykh varvarov da chaet.*" ("The one who crowns God-wise Barbara, / Let him expect victory over godless barbarians.") Velichkovskii was also fond of paronomasia, an example of which we find in his epigram: "*Magnas, iak magnes. Dovod takyi na to, / zhe tot zhelezo, a ov tiagnet zlato.*"[127] ("A magnate is like a magnet. The following argument supports this: / That one attracts iron whereas this one—gold.")

Velichkovskii's sarcastic remark about a magnate is echoed in Derzhavin's poem of that name, in which the poet employed both antanaclasis and paronomasia, together with the anaphora *kol'* ("if") and the asyndeton in the last line, in his portrayal of an ideal magnate—a model that contrasts with the corrupt ruling bureaucracy depicted in the preceding lines of the poem:

> Ia kniaz'—kol' moi siiaet dukh;
> Vladeletz—kol' strast'mi vladeiu;

125. Sokołowska and Żukowska, eds., *Poeci polskiego baroku*, 1:341.
126. See ibid., 2:247, and Chizhevskii, "K problemam literatury barokko u slavian," 33.
127. Velychkovs'kyi, *Tvory*, 99 and 150.

Boliarin—kol' za vsekh boleiu,
Tsariu, zakonu, tserkvi drug.[128]

(I'm a prince if my spirit is shining;
A master if I master my passions;
A warrior if I worry about everyone,
A friend of the tsar, law, church.)

Gogol, whose outstanding receptiveness to language was perhaps enhanced by his being bilingual in Ukrainian and Russian, was undoubtedly familiar with wordplay from his childhood. He may have been introduced to it formally by Tolmachev's *Rules.*[129] He used it commonly to ridicule the world he had created, frequently resorting to the collision of homonyms (antanaclasis), as remarked by Viktor Vinogradov.[130] Western scholars have also noted Gogol's predilection for antanaclasis. In his discussion of "Vii," Richard Peace pointed to Gogol's punning use of the word "philosopher" as the equivalent of a Stoic and as the seventh and penultimate grade in the Kiev Academy (see 2:747). This wordplay, according to Peace, was intended to be ironical, since the "philosopher," Khoma Brut, was almost completely devoid of any thought processes.[131] Paul Debreczeny discerned another antanaclasis in "The Tale of How Ivan Ivanovich Quarreled with Ivan Nikiforovich": "The phrase *korpus gorodnichego* (256), with its double meaning of both 'torso' and 'regiment' makes a pun [and also fun, if I may be allowed a paronomastic wordplay myself] out of a Gallicism by continuing the preceding leg-infantry metaphor."[132]

Indeed, as these scholars have observed, Gogol frequently employed antanaclasis for derision, at times with biting overtones of satire. He so uses *istoriia,* which means in Russian both "history" and "incident," in his narrator's sarcastic characterization of the scandalous Nozdrev: "In a sense Nozdrev was an historical character. There was always some 'history' attached to any gathering at which he assisted. Something always happened: either he would

128. Derzhavin, *Sochineniia,* 1:433.
129. Tolmachev, *Pravila,* 2:293.
130. See Vinogradov, "Iazyk Gogolia i ego znachenie v istorii russkogo iazyka," 33.
131. Peace, *The Enigma of Gogol,* 60.
132. Paul Debreczeny, "Gogol's Mockery of Romantic Taste: Varieties of Language in the Tale of the Two Ivans," *Canadian-American Slavic Studies* 7 (1973): 335.

have to be conducted from the room by gendarmes or his own friends would be obliged to push him out" (6:71; Gibian, 72). We find an antanaclasis with the same caustic tonality in the 1842 edition of *Taras Bulba,* which Gogol worked on simultaneously with *Dead Souls:* poking fun at the ostentatiousness of the Poles, Popovich, a Cossack, uses an antanaclasis *krasnyi* in two senses, "handsome—pretty" and "handsome—plentiful," when he inquires: "Ah, handsome coats on all the army, but I should like to know whether there is handsome power in the army" (2:116; Kent, 2:84).[133]

Derision was by no means the only role of antanaclasis in Gogol's works. As I have shown in the emblem section of Chapter 2, Gogol employed an antanaclasis *svet* with the two meanings, "light" and "beau monde," in the fragment "The Maidens Chablov," endowing the figure with a definitely moralizing function.

In *Dead Souls,* Gogol bestowed yet another, compositional function on antanaclasis: the title is not only an oxymoron, but also contains a homonymical wordplay, since the Russian word *dusha,* as Gogol scholars have repeatedly noted, means both a "soul" and a "serf." This wordplay indicates the two levels on which *Dead Souls* can be read: the superficial level as a narrative about the protagonist's acquisition of serfs, actually deceased but formally alive by the last census records, and the deeper, existential level as a narrative about the petrified souls of its personages—the leitmotif of the work.[134]

An important compositional function in *Dead Souls* is also allotted to another word—*pritcha.* As I remarked when discussing *facetia,*

133. I have altered Kent's translation, replacing the word "red" with the more suitable word "handsome," because there is no indication in the text that the Poles indeed wore red coats; in addition, I have also kept Gogol's epiphora "army."

134. This ambiguity of the word *dusha* ("soul"/"serf") resulted in the ambivalence of the censors toward *Dead Souls.* This ambivalence is reflected in Gogol's letter of January 7, 1842, to Petr Pletnev, a critic and a literary scholar, a letter in which he mockingly described the censors' dealing with his work:

> No sooner had Golokhvastov, the acting president, heard the title than he shouted in the voice of an ancient Roman: *"Dead Souls!* No, I will never allow this—the soul is immortal, there cannot be any dead soul; the author is taking up arms against immortality." Only with some effort, finally, could the intelligent president understand that it was about serfs not yet taken from the tax rolls. (12: 28–29; Proffer, 105)

Gogol ridiculed Golokhvastov and others like him, notably in volume 2 of *Dead Souls,* in the person of Koshkarev's secretary (see 7:66; Gibian, 338).

with this antanaclasis Gogol was alluding to the allegorical nature of the *poéma,* since *pritcha* means both a "perplexing matter" and a "parable"; hence if we take into account the double entendre of the phrase *mertvye dushi,* the query *"Chto za pritcha éti mertvye dushi?"* could mean both "What is the perplexing problem presented by these dead serfs?" and "What sort of a parable is this *Dead Souls?"*

A special case is Gogol's antanaclasis based on his own surname. One example appears in the 1842 edition of "The Portrait" in the phrase *proshelsia gogolem,* meaning idiomatically "strutted," but perhaps also "walked in a Gogol-like manner"—a curious example of the author's concealed self-ridicule. Another, and very different, example appears in the 1842 edition of *Taras Bulba,* based on the fact that *gogol'* is a "golden-eye duck": "The river glimmers like a mirror, resounding with the ringing cry of the swans, and the proud golden-eye duck soars swiftly above it, and many marsh birds, and red-breasted sandpipers and other wildfowl abound among its reeds and on its banks" (2:172; Kent, 2:131–32). As I have suggested elsewhere, this antanaclasis prompted Gogol to lay claim in a very intricate manner to his prophetic role in contemporary Russia.[135]

Gogol employed paronomasia less frequently than antanaclasis and usually only for satirical purposes. In *Dead Souls,* Selifan, Chichikov's illiterate coachman, refers to his master as *skoleskoi sovetnik* (6:41; Gibian, 38),[136] a distorted form of Chichikov's rank—*kollezhskii sovetnik* ("collegiate councilor"). This mispronunciation by an uneducated serf, is employed by Gogol as an ingenious device to expose Chichikov; the Russian word *skoleskoi* evokes a whole series of paronomastic associations: *skol'zkii* ("slippery") and *koleso* ("a wheel"), apparently alluding to Chichikov's being physically and morally a smoothie and to his peregrinations in pursuit of enrichment (as implied by the Russian verb *kolesit'*), and *okolesitsa* ("nonsense, absurdity"), hinting at the outcome of his dubious venture and at the way it looked to the town.[137]

Gogol's predilection for this figure is confirmed by some of his

135. For a detailed discussion of antanaclasis based on Gogol's surname, see Shapiro, "Nikolai Gogol' i gordyi gogol'," 145–59.

136. Reavey's translation does not reflect Selifan's mispronunciation of Chichikov's rank.

137. For more on Chichikov's associations with a wheel, see Belyi, *Masterstvo Gogolia,* 43, 95, and 102.

preparatory notes. For example, in his 1842—44 notebook there are the following two entries: *"moshinal'nyi chelovek—moshennik"* and *"maral'—zapachkannost'* " (9:549). The first phrase contains a twofold paronomasia. The nonexistent word *moshinal'nyi* evokes *moshna* ("a purse"), implying that a *moshennik* (a "rogue") like Chichikov strives to fill his purse by all means. Another obvious paronomastic reading of this entry, *moshinal'nyi—mashinal'nyi* ("mechanical, automatic"), perhaps suggests that cheating is so deeply rooted in a rogue's nature the he does it automatically, so to speak.[138]

The second 1842—44 notebook paronomasia is based on a misspelling of the word *moral'* ("moral") and implies that a "misspelled," distorted moral leads to *zapachkannost'* ("sullying") of the soul.[139] Gogol employed this paronomasia in his "Leaving the Theater After a Performance of a New Comedy" (1842); this supplement to *The Government Inspector* presented a series of spectators' dialogues, in which they gave their impressions of the play. A merchant says: *"Ono zdes' bol'she, tak skazat', s maral'noi storony. . . . A na schet maral'nosti, tak i za dvorianami éto voditsia"* (5:163). ("It is in here more, so to speak, from the sullied side. . . . And as regards to sullying, the noblemen are also doing this.")

As we see, Gogol often employed paronomasia disguised as misspelling or mispronunciation by his less-educated characters, a device which enabled him to expose characters and phenomena satirically. At times, however, he incorporated paronomasia as a quip made by one of his better-educated characters; an example of such an expression is "Sprechen Sie Deutsch, Ivan Andreutsch?" (6:156; Gibian, 166), with which the town bureaucrats always addressed the postmaster. According to the narrator of *Dead Souls,* this wordplay illustrated "a family atmosphere" among the town fathers, but Gogol apparently used it primarily to ridicule Russians of the Alexandrine reign for their fascination with mysticism particularly common in the works of German

138. Some hundred years later in their novel *The Golden Calf* (1931), Il'ia Il'f and Evgenii Petrov utilized this notebook entry of Gogol's: after receiving 50,000 rubles from Bender, Balaganov steals a worthless purse in a crowded streetcar and, when caught red-handed, claims that he did it "mechanically." See Il'f and Petrov, *The Golden Calf* (New York: Random, 1962), 353; for the original, see Il'ia Il'f and Evgenii Petrov, *Dvenadtsat' stul'ev. Zolotoi telenok* (Moscow: Khudozhestvennaia literatura, 1959), 623.

139. The word *maral'* suggests, of course, the verb *marat',* that is, "to sully."

writers, favored by the postmaster, such as Eckartshausen's *Key to the Mysteries of Nature* (ibid.).[140]

Occasionally, Gogol has a narrator instead of characters use paronomasia for the same satirical ends. For example, in volume 2 of *Dead Souls,* the narrator calls Tentetnikov "*mirnyi i smirnyi khoziain*" ("a mild and gentle host") (7:30; Gibian, 297). Considering the previous description of this character, it is clear that Gogol employed the paronomasia as a sarcastic euphemism for Tentetnikov's idleness.

Thus Gogol's use of the figures of antanaclasis and paronomasia, especially the former, was extensive. Although he resorted to paronomasia less frequently, usually for satirical purposes, he employed it ingeniously in a variety of ways—as "mispronunciation" by his less-educated characters, a friendly quip of his better-educated personages, and a narrator's matter-of-fact remark—in each case with strong satirical overtones that contradict the seeming innocence.

140. This and other works by Eckartshausen (all together twelve entries!) were part of the Troshchinskii library; see Fedorov, *Katalog,* 34–35.

Afterword

In this study, I have attempted to demonstrate Gogol's propensity for the Baroque, a propensity that took shape in his native Ukraine and later developed during his stay in Russia and in the West. My main object has been to show that in drawing on the Baroque cultural heritage, Gogol, quite in the spirit of that epoch, exhibited remarkable versatility and ingenuity.

To this, Gogol's adaptation of the Baroque forms attests, first of all. Especially innovative was his "fusion" of *facetia* and parable, two artistic structures popular during the Baroque period, resulting in a new complex figure to which he assigned a significant compositional and semantic role in his fiction. Not only did Gogol incorporate *facetiae* functioning as parables within the texts, but also various of his separate works can in their entirety be so described. On the surface they appear merely as amusing anecdotes, but their allegorical subtexts were the means by which Gogol intended to drive home his moralizing messages.

Gogol's attitude toward the Baroque cultural heritage was never static. It evolved and changed as he matured artistically and in response to his newly emerging creative needs. His use of *vertep* constitutes a distinct example of this. Thus in his early works set in the seventeenth- and eighteenth-century Ukraine, Gogol on the whole retained the coarseness of *vertep* personages in order to convey the spirit of the Baroque of his native land. In later works, although he continued drawing on *vertep,* Gogol muffled its traits in his characters. This is perhaps because their noticeable *vertep* "ancestry" would have been out of place in nineteenth-century Russia, but, more important, because at this stage Gogol was aiming for a deeper, psychological portrayal of his characters; for this, *vertep*-like stock figures would clearly have been inappropriate.

The discussions of both *lubok* and the emblem have shown us, among other things, how Gogol applied certain Baroque techniques to his oeuvre. Particularly noteworthy is his use of the *lubok* turn-over device, which involved a striking change in a picture when it was turned upside down or otherwise adjusted. Gogol employed this turnover technique in such works as "The Nose" and *Dead Souls,* where his characters appeared to the world surrounding them in various incongruous and often even contradictory hypostases; thus the nose in that tale either crops up baked in bread, or enters the picture as a high-ranking official, or reappears on the face of Major Kovalev, its original owner; and Chichikov, the protagonist of *Dead Souls,* at one moment seems to the town bureaucrats a true million-aire and then a forger of banknotes, at one moment Napoleon and then Captain Kopeikin, a participant in the war against Napoleon. In his employment of this "turnover" technique, Gogol apparently as-pired to achieve goals similar to that of *lubok:* to draw the reader's attention to the multifacetedness of experience, thereby forcing him to seek the complex meaning beyond the superficial veneer of charac-ters and events. To the same end, Gogol appropriated the common Baroque practice of prefacing a written work with an emblematic frontispiece or title page when he himself designed the cover for the first edition of *Dead Souls*—the only such (published) cover in Rus-sian literature of his day. The emblematic nature of his cover design for *Dead Souls* was intended to prepare the reader for the complex, metaphorical, and edifying character of its contents.

In his employment of *topoi,* Gogol demonstrated no less original-ity. Although for Gogol himself these were sublime ideas, he showed in his fiction how his characters, incapable of comprehending these ideas in their true magnitude, reduced them to commonplaces. In *Dead Souls,* for example, Gogol depicted merchants chattering super-ficially about eschatological prophecies and the Antichrist on their way to a tearoom. There and elsewhere, Gogol depicted graphically in his fictional world the same process which the German literary historian Curtius, in his detailed and extensive survey ranging from classical antiquity up to Goethe, pointed to in the literary tradition at large: the transformation of these high concepts into hackneyed themes.

And finally, as I have attempted to show, Gogol's resourcefulness is also manifest in his exploitation of figurative language. Asyndeton, for example: one of the most likely sources of Gogol's familiarity with this figure was his father's comedies—he included an excerpt, with asyndeton, from one of them as an epigraph for a chapter of his "The Fair at Sorochintsy." But unlike the asyndeton he quotes, which listed different kinds of merchandise to indicate merely the great assortment of another fair, Gogol, in an asyndeton of his own within this story, strung together nouns denoting much more unequal, incongruous elements, such as human beings, animals, and inanimate objects, to emphasize not only this fair's diverse but mainly its discordant nature. Several years later, in "The Coach," Gogol employed the same type of asyndeton for a different, sententious purpose: to suggest that an unspiritual existence is pernicious for the soul, degrading a human being almost to the level of an inanimate object. Quite different and much more intricate is the asyndeton Gogol uses in *Dead Souls* to demonstrate, both visually and semantically, the effect of Pliushkin's morbid miserliness.

Conceit, another figure of language, is very much in evidence in the second edition of *Taras Bulba* and in *Dead Souls* (both published in 1842), on which Gogol worked simultaneously while in Italy. Gogol's broad use of the conceit in these two later works could be linked to his being exposed then and there to Italian Baroque literature, particularly to the poetry of Giambattista Marino, the champion of this literary figure. (It is absent from the first edition of *Taras Bulba* written prior to Gogol's departure for Italy.) Gogol's use of the conceit in *Taras Bulba* and in *Dead Souls* is markedly different: in *Taras Bulba* it appears as an ornamental device designed to convey the spirit of the Baroque Ukraine—the setting of this military epic, whereas in *Dead Souls* this extended metaphor allows Gogol to portray a great deal more of Russian "reality" than the main plotline permits. This is in accordance with his desire "to show all Russia—at least from one side" (10:375; Proffer, 52). The conceits in *Dead Souls,* furthermore, illuminate the interrelations of characters and allude to the underlying themes.

And conceit, that Baroque figure *par excellence,* is perhaps the most fitting to end this book with. In volume 2 of *Dead Souls,* Gogol portrayed Kostanzhoglo, an ideal landowner, whose resourcefulness enabled him, in his own words, "to make a profit on all sorts of rubbish" (7:68; Gibian, 341); thus Kostanzhoglo greatly profited from glue made of fish refuse that had been dumped on his land for years.

As I have attempted to demonstrate, it was rather Gogol the writer who most significantly accomplished a feat like that he ascribed to his unrealistic character: indeed it was he who very "profitably" adapted "all sorts of rubbish" of the Baroque cultural heritage to his own creative economy, to paraphrase the title of Vladislav Khodasevich's book on Pushkin, owing to the unparalleled *ingenio* and *acutezza* of his creative mind.

Bibliography

PRIMARY SOURCES

Gogol and His Contemporaries

Belinskii, V. G. *Polnoe sobranie sochinenii.* 13 vols. Moscow: Akademiia Nauk SSSR, 1953–59.

Dal', Vladimir. *Poslovitsy russkogo naroda.* 2 vols. Moscow: Khudozhestvennaia literatura, 1984.

Gogol', N. V. *Arabesques.* Trans. Alexander Tulloch. Ann Arbor: Ardis, 1982.

———. *The Complete Tales.* 2 vols. Ed. Leonard J. Kent. Chicago: University of Chicago Press, 1985.

———. *Dead Souls.* Ed. George Gibian. New York: W. W. Norton, 1985.

———. *Letters.* Ed. and trans. Carl R. Proffer. Ann Arbor: University of Michigan Press, 1967.

———. *Polnoe sobranie sochinenii.* 14 vols. Moscow and Leningrad: Akademiia Nauk SSSR, 1937–52.

———. *Selected Passages from Correspondence with Friends.* Trans. Jesse Zeldin. Nashville: Vanderbilt University Press, 1969.

———. *Sochineniia.* 7 vols. 10th ed. Ed. N. S. Tikhonravov. Moscow, 1889–96.

———. *The Theater of Nikolay Gogol. Plays and Selected Writings.* Ed. Milton Ehre. Chicago: University of Chicago Press, 1980.

Herzen (Gertsen), A. I. *Sobranie sochinenii.* 30 vols. Moscow: Akademiia Nauk SSSR, 1954–66.

Hohol', V. O. *Prostak.* Kiev, 1910.

Lermontov, M. Iu. *Polnoe sobranie sochinenii.* 5 vols. Moscow: Academia, 1935–37.

Poe, Edgar Allan. *Complete Stories and Poems.* New York: Doubleday, 1966.

Pushkin, A. S. *Polnoe sobranie sochinenii.* 17 vols. Moscow and Leningrad: Akademiia Nauk SSSR, 1937–59.

———. *The Complete Prose Tales.* Trans. Gillon A. Aitken. New York: W. W. Norton, 1966.

Turgenev, I. S. *Polnoe sobranie sochinenii i pisem.* 28 vols. Moscow and Leningrad: Akademiia Nauk SSSR, 1960–68.

The Baroque and Other Subjects

Adrianova-Peretts, V. P., ed. *Russkaia demokraticheskaia satira XVII veka.* Moscow: Nauka, 1977.

———. *Russkaia sillabicheskaia poéziia XVII–XVIII v.v.* Leningrad: Sovetskii pisatel', 1970.

Afanas'ev, A. N. *Narodnye russkie skazki.* 3 vols. Moscow: Nauka, 1984–85.

Alciatus, Andreas. *Index Emblematicus*. 2 vols. Ed. Peter M. Daly, Virginia W. Calla-
   han, and Simon H. Cuttler. Toronto: University of Toronto Press, 1985.
Alighieri, Dante. *The Divine Comedy*. 3 vols. Trans. John D. Sinclair. New York:
   Oxford University Press, 1979–80.
Aristotle. *The Rhetoric*. Trans. Lane Cooper. New York: Appleton, 1960.
Augustine, Saint. *The Confessions*. Trans. E. M. Blaiklock. Nashville: Nelson, 1983.
Baldinucci, Filippo. *Vocobolario toscano dell'arte del disegno*. Florence, 1681.
Bebel, Heinrich. *Facetien*. Leipzig: Hiersemann, 1931.
Bracciolini, Poggio. *Facezie*. Milan: Rizzoli, 1983.
Browne, Sir Thomas. *Religio Medici and Other Writings*. Ed. Frank L. Huntley. New
   York: Dutton, 1951.
Carpenter, Bogdana, trans. *Monumenta Polonica: The First Four Centuries of Polish
   Poetry*. Ann Arbor: Michigan Slavic Publications, 1989.
Chartoritskaia, T. V., comp. *Krasnorechie Drevnei Rusi (XI–XVII vv.)*. Moscow:
   Sovetskaia Rossiia, 1987.
Cicero. *Philippics*. Trans. Walter C. A. Ker. Cambridge: Harvard University Press,
   1969.
Climacus, John, Saint. *The Ladder of Divine Ascent*. Trans. Colm Luibheid and Nor-
   man Russell. New York: Paulist Press, 1982.
Derzhavin, G. R. *Sochineniia*. 7 vols. St. Petersburg, 1868–78.
Donne, John. *Complete Poetry*. New York: New York University Press, 1968.
Gilgamesh. Trans. John Gardner and John Maier. New York: Knopf, 1984.
Grzeszczuk, Stanisław, ed. *Antologia literatury sowiźrzalskiej XVI i XVII wieku*.
   Wrocław: Zakład Narodowy imienia Ossolińskich, 1966.
Herrick, Robert. *The Poetical Works*. Ed. F. W. Moorman. Oxford: Clarendon Press,
   1915.
Hill, J. P., and E. Caracciolo-Trejo, eds. and trans. *Baroque Poetry*. London: Dent,
   1975.
Horace. *Satires, Epistles and Ars Poetica*. Trans. H. Rushton Fairclough. Cambridge:
   Harvard University Press, 1929.
John of Salisbury. *Frivolities of Courtiers and Footprints of Philosophers*. Trans.
   Joseph B. Pike. Minneapolis: University of Minnesota Press, 1938.
———. *Opera Omnia*. 5 vols. Ed. J. A. Giles. Oxford: J. H. Parker, 1848.
Kapnist, Vasilii. *Izbrannye proizvedeniia*. Leningrad: Sovetskii pisatel', 1973.
Komenský (Comenius), Jan Amos [Ia. A. Komenskii]. *Izbrannye pedagogicheskie
   sochineniia*. 2 vols. Moscow: Pedagogika, 1982.
———. *The Labyrinth of the World and the Paradise of the Heart*. Ann Arbor:
   University of Michigan Press, 1972.
Kravtsov, N. I., and A. V. Kulagina, comps. *Slavianskii fol'klor*. Moscow: Idzatel'stvo
   MGU, 1987.
Krylov, I. A. *Basni*. Moscow and Leningrad: Akademiia Nauk SSSR, 1956.
Krzyżanowski, Julian, and Kazimiera Żukowska-Billip, eds. *Dawna facecja polska
   (XVI–XVIII w.)*. Warsaw: Państwowy Instytut Wydawniczy, 1960.
Lomonosov, M. V. *Polnoe sobranie sochinenii*. 10 vols. Moscow: Akademiia Nauk
   SSSR, 1950–59.
Maikov, Vasilii. *Izbrannye proizvedeniia*. Moscow and Leningrad: Sovetskii pisatel',
   1966.
Makhnovets', L. Ie., ed. *Davnii ukraïns'kyi humor i satyra*. Kiev: Derzhavne
   vydavnytstvo khudozhn'oï literatury, 1959.
Maksimovich-Ambodik, Nestor. *Emvlemy i simvoly izbrannye*. St. Petersburg, 1788.

Montaigne, Michel de. *The Essayes.* Trans. John Florio. New York: Modern Library, n.d.

Montanus, Martin. *Schwankbücher (1557–1566).* Tubingen: Literarischer Verein in Stuttgart, 1899.

Morsztyn, Zbigniew. *Muza domowa.* 2 vols. Warsaw: Państwowy Instytut Wydawniczy, 1954.

Murner, Thomas. *Schelmenzunft.* Hamburg: Hauswedell, 1968.

Olearius, Adam. *The Travels of Olearius in Seventeenth-Century Russia.* Trans. and ed. Samuel H. Baron. Stanford: Stanford University Press, 1967.

Plato. *The Laws.* Trans. Thomas L. Pangle. New York: Basic Books, 1980.

Polotskii, Simeon. *Izbrannye sochineniia.* Moscow: Akademiia Nauk SSSR, 1953.

Potocki, Wacław. *Ogród fraszek.* 2 vols. Lvov, 1907.

Quintilian. *The Institutio Oratoria.* 4 vols. Trans. H. A. Butler. Cambridge: Harvard University Press, 1920–22.

Rivers, Elias L., ed. *Renaissance and Baroque Poetry of Spain.* New York: Dell, 1966.

Robinson, A. N., ed. *P'esy shkol'nykh teatrov Moskvy.* Moscow: Nauka, 1974.

Segel, Harold B., ed. *The Baroque Poem.* New York: Dutton, 1974.

———. *The Literature of Eighteenth-Century Russia.* 2 vols. New York: Dutton, 1967.

Shakespeare, William. *The Complete Works.* Ed. George B. Harrison. New York: Harcourt, 1952.

Skovoroda, Hryhorii. *Povne zibrannia tvoriv.* 2 vols. Kiev: Naukova dumka, 1973.

Skripil', M. O., comp. *Russkaia povest' XVII veka.* Leningrad: GIKhL, 1954.

Sobranie obraztsovykh russkikh sochinenii i perevodov v proze. 6 vols. St. Petersburg: Obshchestvo Liubitelei Otechestvennoi Slovesnosti, 1822–24.

Sobranie obraztsovykh russkikh sochinenii i perevodov v stikhakh. 6 vols. St. Petersburg: Obshchestvo Liubitelei Otechestvennoi Slovesnosti, 1821–24.

Sokołowska, Jadwiga, and Kazimiera Żukowska, eds. *Poeci polskiego baroku.* 2 vols. Warsaw: Państwowy Instytut Wydawniczy, 1965.

Stöber, Joseph. *Ikonologiia, ob"iasnennaia litsami; ili, Polnoe sobranie allegorii, emblem i pr. Sochinenie poleznoe dlia risovshchikov, zhivopistsov, graverov, skulptorov, stikhotvortsev, uchenykh liudei, a osoblivo dlia vospitaniia iunoshestva, soderzhashchee 225 figur gravirovannykh g. Shtioberom.* Moscow, 1803.

Sumarokov, A. P. *Polnoe sobranie vsekh sochinenii v stikhakh i proze.* 10 vols. Moscow, 1781–82.

The Life of Lazarillo of Tormes. Trans. Robert S. Rudder. New York: Ungar, 1973.

Twardowski, Samuel. *Woyna Domowa Z-Kozaki i Tatary, Moskwą, potym Szwedámi, i z-Węgry, Przez lat Dvvanascie Zá Pánowánia Nayjásnieyszego Iana Kazimierza Krola Polskiego Tocząca się.* In four parts. Kalisz, 1681.

Vasari, Giorgio. *Lives of the Artists.* 2 vols. Trans. George Bull. New York: Penguin, 1987.

Velychkovs'kyi, Ivan. *Tvory.* Kiev: Naukova dumka, 1972.

Virgil. *Works.* 2 vols. Trans. H. Rushton Fairclough. Cambridge: Harvard University Press, 1932.

Vishenskii, Ivan. *Sochineniia.* Moscow: Akademiia Nauk SSSR, 1955.

Zenkovsky, Serge A., ed. *Medieval Russia's Epics, Chronicles, and Tales.* New York: Dutton, 1974.

Zinoviiv, Klymentii. *Virshi. Prypovisti pospolyti.* Kiev: Naukova dumka, 1971.

SECONDARY SOURCES

Gogol and His Contemporaries

Aksakov, K. S. "Neskol'ko slov o poéme Gogolia 'Pokhozhdeniia Chichikova, ili Mertvye dushi.' " In *Russkaia éstetika i kritika 40–50-kh godov XIX veka,* comp. V. K. Kantor and A. L. Ospovat, 42–53. Moscow: Iskusstvo, 1982.

Asoian, A. A. "Dante i 'Mertvye dushi' Gogolia." In his *Dante i russkaia literatura 1820–1850-kh godov,* 37–47. Sverdlovsk: Sverdlovskii Gosudarstvennyi Pedagogicheskii Institut, 1986.

Bakhtin, M. M. "Rable i Gogol' (Iskusstvo slova i narodnaia smekhovaia kul'tura." In his *Voprosy literatury i éstetiki,* 484–95. Moscow: Khudozhestvennaia literatura, 1975.

Baróti, T. "Traditsiia Dante i povest' Gogolia 'Rim.' " *Studia Slavica* 29 (1983): 171–83.

Belyi, Andrei. *Masterstvo Gogolia.* Moscow: GIKhL, 1934.

Bezushko, Volodymyr. *Mykola Hohol'.* Winnipeg: Kul'tura i osvita, 1956.

Bodin, Per-Arne. "The Silent Scene in Nikolaj Gogol's *The Inspector General.*" *Scando-Slavica* 33 (1987): 5–16.

Bogojavlensky, Marianna. *Reflections on Nikolai Gogol.* Jordanville, N.Y.: Holy Trinity Monastery, 1969.

Borghese, Daria. *Gogol a Roma.* Florence: Sansoni, 1957.

Borisova, V. V., and S. M. Shaulov. "Dostoevskii i barokko (Tipologicheskii aspekt problemy mira i cheloveka)." In *Kontseptsiia cheloveka v russkoi literature,* ed. B. T. Udodov, 77–88. Voronezh: Izdatel'stvo Voronezhskogo Universiteta, 1982.

Chicherin, A. V. "Dostoevskii i barokko." In his *Ritm obraza. Stilisticheskie problemy,* 181–92. Moscow: Sovetskii pisatel', 1973.

Chizhevskii, Dmitrii [Dmitry Chizhevsky]. "About Gogol's 'Overcoat.' " In *Gogol from the Twentieth Century,* ed. Robert A. Maguire, 295–322. Princeton: Princeton University Press, 1974.

———[Dmitry Čiževsky]. "Gogol: Artist and Thinker." *The Annals of the Ukrainian Academy of Arts and Sciences in the U.S.* 2, no. 3 (1952): 261–78.

———. "Neizvestnyi Gogol'." *Novyi Zhurnal* 27 (1951): 126–58.

Chudakov, G. I. *Otnoshenie tvorchestva N. V. Gogolia k zapadnoevropeiskim literaturam.* Kiev, 1908.

Clyman, Toby W. "The Hidden Demons in Gogol''s *Overcoat.*" *Russian Literature* 7 (1979): 601–10.

Cox, Gary Duane. "A Study of Gogol's Narrators." Ph.D. diss., Columbia University, 1978.

Debreczeny, Paul. "Gogol's Mockery of Romantic Taste: Varieties of Language in the Tale of the Two Ivans." *Canadian-American Slavic Studies* 7 (1973): 327–41.

Dilaktorskaia, O. G. *Fantasticheskoe v "Peterburgskikh povestiakh" N. V. Gogolia.* Vladivostok: Izdatel'stvo Dal'nevostochnogo Universiteta, 1986.

Dreizin, Felix. "Nationalities in *Taras Bulba.*" In his *The Russian Soul and the Jew. Essays in Literary Ethnocriticism,* 9–59. Lanham, Md.: University Press of America, 1990.

Éikhenbaum, Boris. "Lermontov." In his *O literature,* 140–286. Moscow: Sovetskii pisatel', 1987.

Eremina, L. I. *O iazyke khudozhestvennoi prozy N. V. Gogolia*. Moscow: Nauka, 1987.

Erlich, Victor. *Gogol*. New Haven: Yale University Press, 1969.

Évarnitskii, D. I. "Preobrazhenskaia tserkov' v m. Bol'shikh-Sorochintsakh, Poltavskoi gubernii, gde krestili N. V. Gogolia." *Istoricheskii Vestnik* 2 (1902): 667–78.

Fanger, Donald. *The Creation of Nikolai Gogol*. Cambridge: Belknap Press, 1979.

Fedorov, E. Ia. *Katalog antikvarnoi biblioteki, priobretennoi posle byvshego ministra D. P. Troshchinskogo*. Kiev, 1874.

Fomichev, S. A. "Pushkin i Gogol'." *Zeitschrift für Slawistik* 32 (1987): 78–85.

Frantz, Philip E., comp. *Gogol: A Bibliography*. Ann Arbor: Ardis, 1989.

Fusso, Susanne Grace. "Čičikov on Gogol: The Structure of Oppositions in *Dead Souls*." Ph.D. diss., Yale University, 1984.

———. "*Mertvye Dushi*: Fragment, Parable, Promise." *Slavic Review* 49 (1990): 32–47.

Georgievskii, G. P. "Pesni, sobrannye N. V. Gogolem." In *Pamiati V. A. Zhukovskogo i N. V. Gogolia*, 3 vols., ed. A. N. Veselovskii, 2:125–412. St. Petersburg, 1907–9.

Gerbel', N. V., ed. *Gimnaziia vysshikh nauk i Litsei kniazia Bezborodko*. St. Petersburg, 1881.

Gippius, Vasilii. *Gogol'*. Leningrad: Mysl', 1924.

Gorlin, Mikhail. *N. V. Gogol und E. Th. A. Hoffmann*. Leipzig: Harrassowitz, 1933.

Gukovskii, G. A. *Realizm Gogolia*. Moscow and Leningrad: GIKhL, 1959.

Guminskii, V. M. " 'Taras Bul'ba' v 'Mirgorode' i 'Arabeskakh.' " In *Gogol': Istoriia i sovremennost'*, comp. V. V. Kozhinov, E. I. Osetrov, and P. G. Palamarchuk, 240–58. Moscow: Sovetskaia Rossiia, 1985.

Hayter, Alethea. *Opium and the Romantic Imagination: Addiction and Creativity in De Quincey, Coleridge, Baudelaire, and Others*. Wellingborough, Eng.: Crucible, 1988.

Ivanov, V. V. "Ob odnoi paralleli k gogolevskomu Viiu." *Trudy po znakovym sistemam* 5 (1971): 133–42.

Kadlubovskii, A. P. *Gogol' v ego otnosheniiakh k starinnoi malorusskoi literature*. Nezhin, 1911.

Kamanin, I. M. "Nauchnye i literaturnye proizvedeniia N. V. Gogolia po istorii Malorossii." In *Pamiati Gogolia*, ed. N. P. Dashkevich, 75–132. Kiev, 1902.

Karlinsky, Simon. *The Sexual Labyrinth of Nikolai Gogol*. Cambridge: Harvard University Press, 1976.

Karpenko, A. I. *O narodnosti N. V. Gogolia*. Kiev: Izdatel'stvo Kievskogo Universiteta, 1973.

Karpuk, Paul A. "Gogol's Unfinished Novel 'The Hetman.' " *Slavic and East European Journal* 35 (1991): 36–55.

———. "N. V. Gogol's Unfinished Historical Novel 'The Hetman.' " Ph.D. diss., University of California, Berkeley, 1987.

Katz, Michael T. *Dreams and the Unconscious in Nineteenth-Century Russian Fiction*. Hanover: University Press of New England, 1984.

Kaukhchishvili, Nina. "O khudozhestvennykh priemakh u Gogolia." *Transactions of the Association of Russian-American Scholars in the U.S.A.* 17 (1984): 49–67.

Kjetsaa, Geir. "Gogol' kak uchitel' zhizni: Novye materialy." *Scando-Slavica* 34 (1988): 55–67.

Krivonos, V. Sh. *"Mertvye dushi" Gogolia i stanovlenie novoi russkoi prozy*. Voronezh: Izdatel'stvo Voronezhskogo Universiteta, 1985.

Little, T. E. "Gogol and Romanticism." In *Problems of Russian Romanticism,* ed. Robert Reid, 96–126. Brookfield, Vt.: Gower, 1986.

Lotman, Iu. M. "Gogol' i sootnesenie 'smekhovoi kul'tury' s komicheskim i ser'eznym v russkoi natsional'noi traditsii." *Materialy Vsesoiuznogo simpoziuma po vtorichnym modeliruiushchim sistemam* 1, no. 5 (1974): 131–33.

———. "Iz nabliudenii nad strukturnymi printsipami rannego tvorchestva Gogolia." *Uchenye zapiski Tartuskogo Gosudarstvennogo Universiteta* 251 (1970): 17–46.

———. "Khudozhestvennoe prostranstvo v proze Gogolia." In his *V shkole poéticheskogo slova. Pushkin. Lermontov. Gogol',* 251–93. Moscow: Prosveshchenie, 1988.

Lugakovskii, V. A. "Gogol' v pol'skoi literature." *Literaturnyi Vestnik* 1 (1902): 16–43.

Mandel'shtam, Iosif. *O kharaktere gogolevskogo stilia.* Helsinki, 1902.

Mann, Iu. V. "Évoliutsiia gogolevskoi fantastiki." In *K istorii russkogo romantizma,* ed. Iu. V. Mann I. G. Neupokoeva, and U. R. Fokht, 219–58. Moscow: Nauka, 1973.

———. "Khudozhestvennaia simvolika 'Mertvykh dush' Gogolia i mirovaia traditsiia." In his *Dialektika khudozhestvennogo obraza,* 237–63. Moscow: Sovetskii pisatel', 1987.

———. *Poétika Gogolia.* Moscow: Khudozhestvennaia literatura, 1978.

———. *Smelost' izobreteniia.* Moscow: Detskaia literatura, 1985.

———. " 'Uzhas okoval vsekh . . .' [O nemoi stsene v 'Revizore' Gogolia]." *Voprosy literatury* 8 (1989): 223–35.

———. *V poiskakh zhivoi dushi. "Mertvye dushi": pisatel'—kritika—chitatel'.* Moscow: Kniga, 1984.

Manuilov, V. A., ed. *Lermontovskaia éntsiklopediia.* Moscow: Sovetskaia éntsiklopediia, 1981.

Markovich, V. M. *Peterburgskie povesti N. V. Gogolia.* Leningrad: Khudozhestvennaia literatura, 1989.

Markovskii, M. N. "Istoriia vozniknoveniia i sozdaniia 'Mertvykh dush.' " In *Pamiati Gogolia,* ed. N. P. Dashkevich, 133–226. Kiev, 1902.

Mashkovtsev, N. G. *Gogol' v krugu khudozhnikov.* Moscow: Iskusstvo, 1955.

Matskin, Aleksandr. *Teatr moikh sovremennikov: Iz starykh i novykh tetradei.* Moscow: Iskusstvo, 1987.

Merezhkovskii, D. S. *Gogol' i chort.* Moscow: Skorpion, 1906.

Mersereau, John, Jr. "Gogol's *Evenings on a Farm near Dikanka.*" In his *Russian Romantic Fiction,* 163–73. Ann Arbor: Ardis, 1983.

Mochul'skii, Konstantin. *Dukhovnyi put' Gogolia.* Paris: YMCA Press, 1934.

Mykhed, P. V. "V. T. Narizhnyi i barokko (Do pytannia pro styl' pys'mennyka)." *Radians'ke literaturoznavstvo* 11 (1979): 74–83.

Nabokov, Vladimir. *Nikolai Gogol.* New York: New Directions, 1961.

Nazarevskii, A. A. "Gogol' i iskusstvo." In *Pamiati Gogolia. Sbornik rechei i statei,* 49–90. Kiev, 1911.

Ohloblyn, Oleksander. "Ancestry of Mykola Gogol (Hohol)." *The Annals of the Ukrainian Academy of Arts and Sciences in the U.S.* 12, nos. 1–2 (1969–72): 3–43.

Peace, Richard A. *The Enigma of Gogol. An Examination of the Writings of N. V. Gogol and Their Place in the Russian Literary Tradition.* Cambridge: Cambridge University Press, 1981.

Pedrotti, Louis. "The Architecture of Love in Gogol"s 'Rome.'" *California Slavic Studies* 6 (1971): 17–27.

Peretts, V. N. "Gogol' i malorusskaia literaturnaia traditsiia." In *N. V. Gogol'. Rechi, posviashchennye ego pamiati, v publichnom soedinennom sobranii otdeleniia russkogo iazyka i slovesnosti, razriada iziashchnoi slovesnosti Imperatorskoi Akademii Nauk i Peterburgskogo Universiteta, 21 fevralia 1902 goda,* 47–55. St. Petersburg, 1902.

Petrov, N. I. "Novye materialy dlia izucheniia religiozno-nravstvennykh vozzrenii N. V. Gogolia." *Trudy Kievskoi Dukhovnoi Akademii* 6 (1902): 270–317.

Pliashko, L. A. *Gorod, pisatel', vremia. Nezhinskii period zhizni N. V. Gogolia.* Kiev: Naukova dumka, 1985.

Proffer, Carl R. "Gogol's *Taras Bulba* and the *Iliad.*" *Comparative Literature* 17 (1965): 142–50.

————. *The Simile and Gogol's "Dead Souls."* The Hague: Mouton, 1967.

Radtsig, S. I. "Gogol' i Gomer." *Vestnik Moskovskogo Universiteta* 4 (1959): 121–28.

Richter, Sigrid. "Rom und Gogol'; Gogol's Romerlebnis und sein Fragment 'Rim'." Ph.D. diss., University of Hamburg, 1964.

Rozanov, M. G. "Persidskoe posol'stvo v Rossii 1829 goda (Po bumagam grafa P. P. Sukhtelena)." *Russkii Arkhiv* 2 (1889): 209–60.

Rozanov, V. V. *O Gogole.* Letchworth, Eng.: Prideaux Press, 1970.

Rozov, V. A. "Traditsionnye tipy malorusskogo teatra XVII–XVIII vv. i iunosheskie povesti N. V. Gogolia." In *Pamiati Gogolia. Sbornik rechei i statei,* 99–169. Kiev, 1911.

Samyshkina, A. V. "K probleme gogolevskogo fol'klorizma (dva tipa skaza i literaturnaia polemika v 'Vecherakh na khutore bliz Dikan'ki')." *Russkaia literatura* 3 (1979): 61–80.

Saprykina, E. Iu. "Gogol' i traditsii ital'ianskoi satiry." In *Gogol' i mirovaia literatura,* ed. Iu. V. Mann, 62–83. Moscow: Nauka, 1988.

Saunders, David B. "Contemporary Critics of Gogol's *Vechera* and the Debate about Russian *Narodnost'* (1831–1832)." *Harvard Ukrainian Studies* 5 (1981): 66–82.

Setchkarev, Vsevolod. *Gogol: His Life and Works.* New York: New York University Press, 1965.

Shamim, Ali Asgahr. *Iran dar dawrah-i saltanat-i Qajar.* Teheran: Ibn Sina, 1964.

Shapiro, Gavriel. "The Emblem and Its Reflection in the Works of Nikolai Gogol." *Comparative Literature* 42 (1990): 208–26.

————. "The Hussar: A Few Observations on Gogol's Characters and Their *Vertep* Prototype." *Harvard Ukrainian Studies* 9 (1985): 133–38.

————. "Nikolai Gogol' i gordyi gogol': Pisatel' i ego imia." *Russian Language Journal* 43 (1989): 145–59.

————. "A Note on the Connection Between an Episode from Nikolai Gogol's *Taras Bulba* and Visual Art, Mainly Roman Baroque." *Hebrew University Studies in Literature and the Arts* 13 (1985): 214–21.

————. "The Role of *Facetiae* in Gogol's Early Works." *Transactions of the Association of Russian-American Scholars in the U.S.A.* 17 (1984): 69–74.

Shapiro, Marianne. "Gogol and Dante." *Modern Language Studies* 17, no. 2 (1987): 37–54.

Shenrok, V. I. *Materialy dlia biografii Gogolia.* 4 vols. Moscow, 1892–97.

Shevyrev, S. P. "Pokhozhdeniia Chichikova, ili Mertvye dushi. Poéma N. Gogolia. Stat'ia vtoraia." *Moskvitianin* 8 (1842): 346–76.

Shvedova, N. Iu. "Printsipy istoricheskoi stilizatsii v iazyke povesti Gogolia 'Taras Bul'ba.'" In *Materialy i issledovaniia po istorii russkogo literaturnogo iazyka,* 5 vols., ed. V. V. Vinogradov, 3:45–67. Moscow: Akademiia Nauk SSSR, 1949–62.

Siniavskii, Andrei. *V teni Gogolia.* London: Overseas Publications Interchange, 1975.

Smirnova, E. A. "O mnogosmyslennosti 'Mertvykh dush.'" *Kontekst* (1982): 164–82.

———. *Poéma Gogolia "Mertvye dushi."* Leningrad: Nauka, 1987.

Speranskii, M. N., ed. *Gogolevskii sbornik.* Kiev, 1902.

Stender-Petersen, Adolf. "Gogol und die deutsche Romantik." *Euphorion* 24 (1922): 628–53.

Turbin, V. N. *Geroi Gogolia.* Moscow: Prosveshchenie, 1983.

———. *Pushkin. Gogol'. Lermontov. Ob izuchenii literaturnykh zhanrov.* Moscow: Prosveshchenie, 1978.

Vaiskopf, Mikhail. "Put' palomnika (O masonskikh i teosofskikh istochnikakh Gogolia)." In *Russian Literature and History: In Honour of Professor Ilya Serman,* ed. Wolf Moskovich, 52–61. Jerusalem: Hebrew University of Jerusalem, 1989.

Veselovskii, A. N. "Mertvye dushi." In his *Étiudy i kharakteristiki,* 557–609. Moscow, 1894.

Vinogradov, V. V. "Iazyk Gogolia i ego znachenie v istorii russkogo iazyka." In *Materialy i issledovaniia po istorii russkogo literaturnogo iazyka,* 5 vols., ed. V. V. Vinogradov, 3:4–44. Moscow: Akademiia Nauk SSSR, 1949–62.

———. "O literaturnoi tsiklizatsii. Po povodu 'Nevskogo prospekta' Gogolia i 'Ispovedi opiofaga' De Kvinsi." In his *Poétika russkoi literatury,* 45–62. Moscow: Nauka, 1976.

———. "Siuzhet i kompozitsiia povesti Gogolia 'Nos.'" In his *Poétika russkoi literatury,* 5–44. Moscow: Nauka, 1976.

Vogel, Lucy. "Gogol''s *Rome.*" *Slavic and East European Journal* 11 (1967): 145–58.

Vulikh, N. V. "Antichnye motivy i obrazy v povesti Gogolia 'Taras Bul'ba.'" *Russkaia literatura* 1 (1984): 143–53.

Woodward, James B. *Gogol's "Dead Souls."* Princeton: Princeton University Press, 1978.

———. "The Symbolic Logic of Gogol''s *The Nose.*" *Russian Literature* 7 (1979): 537–64.

Zavitnevich, Vladimir. "Religiozno-nravstvennoe sostoianie N. V. Gogolia v poslednie gody ego zhizni." In *Pamiati Gogolia,* ed. N. P. Dashkevich, 338–424. Kiev, 1902.

Zeldin, Jesse. *Nikolai Gogol's Quest for Beauty.* Lawrence: Regents Press of Kansas, 1978.

Zhernakova, Nadezhda. "'Portret' Gogolia v dvukh redaktsiiakh." *Transactions of the Association of Russian-American Scholars in the U.S.A.* 17 (1984): 23–47.

Zhitetskii, Ignatii. "Gogol'—propovednik i pisatel'." *Zhurnal Ministerstva Narodnogo Prosveshcheniia* 8 (1909): 314–50, and 9 (1909): 24–78.

Zolotusskii, Igor'. *Gogol'.* Moscow: Molodaia gvardiia, 1979.

———. "Troika, kopeika, koleso." In his *Ispoved' zoila,* 357–82. Moscow: Sovetskaia Rossiia, 1989.

The Baroque and Other Subjects

Abrams, M. H. "Apocalypse: Themes and Variations." In *The Apocalypse in English Renaissance Thought and Literature,* ed. C. A. Patrides and Joseph Wittreich, 342–68. Ithaca: Cornell University Press, 1984.

———. *A Glossary of Literary Terms.* New York: Holt, Rinehart and Winston, 1971.

Ahl, Frederick. *Metaformations: Soundplay and Wordplay in Ovid and Other Classical Poets.* Ithaca: Cornell University Press, 1985.

Averintsev, S. S. "Pritcha." *Kratkaia literaturnaia éntsiklopediia,* 9 vols., 6:20–21. Moscow: Sovetskaia éntsiklopediia, 1962–78.

Backvis, Claude. "Dans quelle mesure Derzhavin est-il un baroque?" In *Studies in Russian and Polish Literature. In Honor of Wacław Lednicki,* ed. Zbigniew Folejewski, 72–104. The Hague: Mouton, 1962.

Bächtiger, Franz. "Vanitas—Schicksalsdeutung in der deutschen Renaissancegraphik." Ph.D. diss., Ludwig-Maximillian University, Munich, 1970.

Bakhtin, M. M. "Formy vremeni i khronotopa v romane. Ocherki po istoricheskoi poétike." In his *Voprosy literatury i éstetiki,* 234–407. Moscow: Khudozhestvennaia literatura, 1975.

Bakhtin, Vladimir, and Dmitrii Moldavskii, comps. *Russkii lubok XVII–XIX vv.* Moscow and Leningrad: IZOGIZ, 1962.

Balashov, N. I., and Ia. V. Staniukovich. "Obraz v poézii pol'skogo romantizma." In *Slavianskie literatury: VII mezhdunarodnyi s'ezd slavistov. Doklady sovetskoi delegatsii,* ed. M. P. Alekseev et al., 338–56. Moscow: Nauka, 1973.

Barasch, Frances K. "Definitions: Renaissance and Baroque, Grotesque Construction and Deconstruction." *Modern Language Studies* 13, no. 2 (1983): 60–67.

Barasch, Moshe. *Light and Color in the Italian Renaissance Theory of Art.* New York: New York University Press, 1978.

Barucco, Pierre. "L'oxymoron pétraquesque ou de l'amour fou." *Revue des Études Italiennes* 29 (1983): 109–21.

Bazhan, M. P., ed. *Istoriia ukraïns'koho mystetstva.* 6 vols. Kiev: Akademiia Nauk URSR, 1966–70.

Benz, Ernst. *Das Todesproblem in der stoischen Philosophie.* Stuttgart: Kohlhammer, 1929.

Berkov, P. N. "Kniga v poézii Simeona Polotskogo." *Trudy Otdela Drevnerusskoi Literatury* 24 (1969): 260–66.

———. "Materialy dlia bibliografii literatury o russkikh narodnykh (lubochnykh) kartinkakh." *Russkii fol'klor* 2 (1957): 353–62.

Białostocki, Jan. "Kunst und Vanitas." In his *Stil und Ikonographie,* 187–230. Dresden: Kunst, 1966.

———. "Man and Mirror in Painting: Reality and Transience." In *Studies in Late Medieval and Renaissance Painting in Honor of Millard Meiss,* 2 vols., ed. Irving Lavin and John Plummer, 1:61–72 and 2:23–26. New York: New York University Press, 1977.

Bilets'kyi, O. I., et al., eds. *Materialy do vyvchennia istorii ukraïns'koï literatury.* 5 vols. Kiev: Radians'ka shkola, 1959–66.

Bloomfield, Morton W. *The Seven Deadly Sins.* N.p.: Michigan State University Press, 1952.

Boase, T.S.R. *Death in the Middle Ages.* New York: McGraw-Hill, 1972.

Bowen, Barbara C. "Two Literary Genres: The Emblem and the Joke." *The Journal of Medieval and Renaissance Studies* 15 (1985): 29–35.

Bowra, C. M. *Tradition and Design in the "Iliad."* Oxford: Clarendon Press, 1930.
Britanishskii, V. L. "Pol skie romantiki o pol'skom barokko." *Sovetskoe slavianove-denie* 1 (1972): 78–89.
Brooks, Jeffrey. *When Russia Learned to Read. Literacy and Popular Literature, 1861–1917.* Princeton: Princeton University Press, 1985.
Buffum, Imbrie. *Agrippa d'Aubigné's "Les Tragiques": A Study of the Baroque Style in Poetry.* New Haven: Yale University Press, 1951.
————. *Studies in the Baroque from Montaigne to Rotrou.* New Haven: Yale University Press, 1957
Bulanin, D. M. "O nekotorykh printsipakh raboty drevnerusskikh pisatelei." *Trudy Otdela Drevnerusskoi Literatury* 37 (1983): 3–13.
Buslaev, Fedor. "Illiustratsiia stikhotvorenii Derzhavina." In his *Moi dosugi,* 2 vols., 2:70–166. Moscow, 1886.
————. "Izobrazhenie Strashnogo Suda." In his *Drevnerusskaia narodnaia literatura i iskusstvc,* 2 vols., 2:133–54. St. Petersburg, 1861.
Bylinin, V. K. " 'Labirint mira' v interpretatsii russkogo poéta pervoi poloviny XVII veka." In *Razvitie barokko i zarozhdenie klassitsizma v Rossii XVII–nachala XVIII vv.,* ed. A. N. Robinson, 42–49. Moscow: Nauka, 1989.
Candelaria, Frederick H. "The *Carpe Diem* Motif in Early Seventeenth-Century Poetry with Particular Reference to Robert Herrick." Ph.D. diss., University of Missouri, 1959.
Caron, Linda Kay. "The Use of Color by Painters in Rome from 1524 to 1527." Ph.D. diss., Bryn Mawr College, 1981.
Chastel, André. "L'art et le sentiment de la mort au XVIIe siècle." *XVIIe Siècle* 36–37 (1957): 287–93.
Chizhevskii, Dmitrii [Dmitrij Tschižewskij]. "Das Barock in der russischen Literatur." In *Slavische Barock-Literatur I* (*Forum Slavicum* 23), ed. Dmitrii Chizhevskii [Dmitrij Tschižewskij], 9–39. Munich: Fink, 1970.
———— [Dmitrij Čiževskij]. "Das Buch als Symbol des Kosmos." In his *Aus zwei Welten,* 85–114. The Hague: Mouton, 1956.
———— [Dmitrij Čiževskij]. *Comparative History of Slavic Literatures.* Nashville, Tenn.: Vanderbilt University Press, 1971.
———— [Dmitrij Tschižewskij]. "Emblematische Literatur bei den Slaven." *Archiv für das Studium der neueren Sprachen und Literaturen* 201 (1964): 175–84.
———— [Dmytro Chyzhevs'kyi]. *Filosofiia H. S. Skovorody.* Warsaw, 1934.
———— [Dmitrij Čiževskij]. *History of Russian Literature: From the Eleventh Century to the End of the Baroque.* The Hague: Mouton, 1960.
———— [Dmytro Čyževs'kyj]. *A History of Ukrainian Literature: From the 11th to the End of the 19th Century.* Littleton, Col.: Ukrainian Academic Press, 1975.
————. "K problemam literatury barokko u slavian." *Litteraria* 13 (1970): 5–59.
————. [Dmytro Chyzhevs'kyi]. "Ukraïns'kyi literaturnyi barok." *Pratsy ukraïns'-koho istorychno-filolohichnoho tovarystva v Prazi* 3 (1941): 41–108, and 5 (1944): 78–142.
Christian, Lynda G. *Theatrum Mundi. The History of an Idea.* New York: Garland, 1987.
Cohen, Kathleen. *Metamorphosis of a Death Symbol.* Berkeley and Los Angeles: University of California Press, 1973.
Colish, Marcia L. *The Stoic Tradition from Antiquity to the Early Middle Ages.* Leiden: Brill, 1985.

Cook, Arthur Bernard. "The Bee in Greek Mythology." *Journal of Hellenic Studies* 15 (1895): 1–24.

Cooper, Richard. "Les 'contes' de Rabelais et l'Italie: Une mise au point." In *La nouvelle française à la Renaissance,* ed. Lionello Sozzi, 183–207. Geneva and Paris: Slatkine, 1981.

Corbett, Edward P. J. "The *Topoi* Revisited." In *Rhetoric and Praxis,* ed. Jean Dietz Moss, 45–59. Washington, D.C.: Catholic University of America Press, 1986.

Corbett, Margery, and Ronald Lightbown. *The Comely Frontispiece: The Emblematic Title-Page in England, 1550–1660.* London: Routledge & Kegan Paul, 1979.

Corley, Ames Haven. "Word-Play in *The Don Quixote.*" Ph.D. diss., Yale University, 1914.

Crossan, John Dominic. *Cliffs of Fall. Paradox and Polyvalence in the Parables of Jesus.* New York: Seabury Press, 1980.

Culler, Jonathan. "The Call of the Phoneme: Introduction." In *On Puns: The Foundation of Letters,* ed. Jonathan Culler, 1–16. New York: Blackwell, 1988.

Curtius, Ernst Robert. *European Literature and the Latin Middle Ages.* Princeton: Princeton University Press, 1953.

Daly, Peter M. *Emblem Theory.* Nendeln, Lichtenstein: KTO Press, 1979.

———. *Literature in the Light of the Emblem.* Toronto: University of Toronto Press, 1979.

Davidson, William L. *The Stoic Creed.* Edinburgh: Clark, 1907.

Davis, Charles H. Stanley. *Greek and Roman Stoicism and Some of Its Disciples.* Boston: Turner, 1903.

Denis, Ernest. *La Bohème depuis la Montagne-Blanche.* 2 vols. Paris: Leroux, 1903.

Derzhavina, O. A. *Fatsetsii. Perevodnaia novella v russkoi literature XVII veka.* Moscow: Akademiia Nauk SSSR, 1962.

Dubruck, Edelgard. *The Theme of Death in French Poetry of the Middle Ages and the Renaissance.* The Hague: Mouton, 1964.

Duchartre, Pierre-Louis. *L'imagerie populaire russe et les livret gravés, 1629–1885.* Paris: Gründ, 1961.

Dzhivelegov, A. K. *Ital'ianskaia narodnaia komediia.* Moscow: Akademiia Nauk SSSR, 1954.

Edelstein, Ludwig. *The Meaning of Stoicism.* Cambridge: Harvard University Press, 1966.

Eleonskaia, A. S. *Russkaia oratorskaia proza v literaturnom protsesse XVII veka.* Moscow: Nauka, 1990.

Ellenius, Allan. "Reminder to a Young Gentleman. Notes on a Dutch Seventeenth-Century *Vanitas.*" In *Idea and Form. Studies in the History of Art,* ed. Nils Gösta Sandblad, 108–26. Stockholm: Almqvist & Wiksell, 1959.

Fabiny, Tibor. "*Theatrum Mundi* and the Ages of Man." In *Shakespeare and the Emblem: Studies in Renaissance Iconography and Iconology,* ed. Tibor Fabiny, 273–336. Szeged: Attila József University, 1984.

Fomenko, V. M. "Rosiis'ka narodna kartynka na Ukraïni." *Narodna tvorchist' ta etnohrafiia* 3 (1982): 54–61.

Freedberg, S. J. *Painting in Italy: 1500–1600.* New York: Penguin, 1979.

Freeman, Rosemary. *English Emblem Books.* London: Chatto & Windus, 1948.

Friedlaender, Walter. *Caravaggio Studies.* New York: Schocken, 1969.

Galagan, G. P. "Malorusskii vertep." *Kievskaia Starina* 10 (1882): 1–38.

Garapon, Robert. *La fantaisie verbale et le comique dans le théâtre français du moyen âge à la fin du XVIIe siècle.* Paris: Armand Colin, 1957.

Gardner, Helen. *The Metaphysical Poets.* London: Oxford University Press, 1961.

Garzonio, Stefano. "Ccncetti kak odin iz intertekstov russkoi liriki." Paper presented at the Fourth World Congress of Soviet and East European Studies, Harrogate, England, July 1990.

Gavel, Jonas. *Colour. A Study of Its Position in the Art Theory of the Quattro- & Cinquecento.* Stockholm: Almqvist & Wiksell, 1979.

Glück, J. J. "Paronomasia in Biblical Literature." *Semitics* 1 (1970): 50–78.

Graciotti, Sante. "Il ruolo della letteratura faceta umanistica italiana nelle 'facezie' polacche e russe." In *Mondo slavo e cultura italiana: Contributi italiani al IX Congresso Internazionale degli Slavisti. Kiev, 1983,* ed. Jitka Kresalkova, 162–87. Rome: Il Veltro Editrice, 1983.

Graham, Stephen. *With the Russian Pilgrims in Jerusalem.* London: Macmillan, 1916.

Greene, Thomas M. *The Light of Troy: Imitation and Discovery in Renaissance Poetry.* New Haven: Yale University Press, 1982.

Grimal, Pierre. *The Dictionary of Classical Mythology.* New York: Blackwell, 1987.

Grushevskii, Mikhail. "Ostrianin." In *Éntsiklopedicheskii slovar' Russkogo Bibliograficheskogo Instituta Granat,* 30:709–11.

Gudzii, N. K. "Fatsetsiia." *Literaturnaia éntsiklopediia,* 11 vols., 11:672–73. Moscow: GIKhL, 1929–39.

Gummere, Richard Mott. *Seneca the Philosopher and His Modern Message.* New York: Cooper, 1963.

Hall, James. *Dictionary of Subjects & Symbols in Art.* New York: Harper & Row, 1979.

Hamilton, George Heard. *The Art and Architecture of Russia.* New York: Penguin, 1983.

Hanzal, Josef. *Od baroka k romantismu: Ke zrození novodobé české kultury.* Prague: Academia, 1987.

Harkins, William E. "Lubok." In *Handbook of Russian Literature,* ed. Victor Terras, 266–67. New Haven: Yale University Press, 1985.

Hartlaub, G. F. *Zauber des Spiegels.* Munich: Piper, 1951.

Haskell, Francis, and Nicholas Penny. *Taste and the Antique: The Lure of Classical Sculpture 1500–1900.* New Haven: Yale University Press, 1981.

Henkel, Arthur, and Albrecht Schöne. *Emblemata, Handbuch zur Sinnbildkunst des XVI. und XVII. Jahrhunderts.* Stuttgart: J. B. Metzlersche Verlagsbuchhandlung, 1967.

Herman, Stefan. "Śmierć Sarmaty na polu bitwy (Barokowa *ars moriendi*)." *Teksty* 3 (1979): 139–48.

Heusser, Nelly. *Barock und Romantik.* Leipzig: Huber, 1942.

Hibbard, Howard. *Caravaggio.* New York: Harper & Row, 1983.

Hippisley, Anthony R. "The Emblem in Russian Literature." *Russian Literature* 16 (1984): 289–304.

———. "The Emblem in the Writings of Simeon Polotskij." *Slavic and East European Journal* 15 (1971): 167–83.

———. "K voprosu ob istochnikakh amsterdamskogo izdaniia 'Simvoly i emblemata' ('Symbola et Emblemata')." *Kniga* 59 (1989): 60–79.

———. "Simeon Polotsky as a Representative of the Baroque in Russian Literature." Ph.D. diss., Oxford University, 1968.

Hopwood, Derek. *The Russian Presence in Syria and Palestine, 1843–1914: Church and Politics in the Near East.* Oxford: Clarendon Press, 1969.

Hordyns'kyi, Iaroslav. *Z ukraïns'koï dramatychnoï literatury XVII–XVIII st.* Lvov: Naukove tovarystvo imeni Shevchenka, 1930.

Hornig, Christian. *Giorgiones Spätwerk.* Munich: Fink, 1987.

Hoyt, Giles R. "Vanity and Constancy." In *German Baroque Literature,* ed. Gerhart Hoffmeister, 211–32. New York: Ungar, 1983.

Ingen, Ferdinand, van. *Vanitas und Memento mori in der deutschen Barocklyrik.* Groningen: Wolters, 1966.

Ivanov, E. P. *Russkii narodnyi lubok.* N.p.: IZOGIZ, 1937.

Ivan'o, I. V. *Filosofiia i styl' myslennia H. Skovorody.* Kiev: Naukova dumka, 1983.

Jacobsen, Thorkild. *The Treasures of Darkness: A History of Mesopotamian Religion.* New Haven: Yale University Press, 1976.

Jakobson, Roman. *Selected Writings.* 7 vols. The Hague: Mouton, 1971–85.

Joseph, Sister Miriam. *Shakespeare's Use of the Arts of Language.* New York: Columbia University Press, 1947.

Judson, Jay Richard. *Gerrit van Honthorst.* The Hague: Nijhoff, 1959.

Kaiser, Gert. "Das *Memento mori.*" *Euphorion* 68 (1974): 337–70.

Kelly, Catriona. *Petrushka. The Russian Carnival Puppet Theatre.* Cambridge: Cambridge University Press, 1990.

Kemp, Martin. *Leonardo da Vinci: The Marvelous Works of Nature and Man.* Cambridge: Harvard University Press, 1981.

Kendrick, Laura. *The Game of Love. Troubadour Wordplay.* Berkeley and Los Angeles: University of California Press, 1988.

Keuls, Eva. "Skiagraphia Once Again." *American Journal of Archaeology* 79 (1975): 1–16.

Klein, Robert. "The Theory of Figurative Expression in Italian Treatises on the *Impresa.*" In his *Form and Meaning: Essays on the Renaissance and Modern Art,* 3–24. New York: Viking, 1979.

Koozin, Kristine Lynn. "Metaphors of Memento Mori: Still Life Painting and Poetry of Seventeenth-Century Holland." Ph.D. diss., Ohio University, 1984.

Krzyżanowski, Julian. "Barok na tle prądów romantycznych." In his *Od średniowiecza do baroku,* 7–53. Warsaw: Rój, 1938.

Kuz'mina, V. D. *Russkii demokraticheskii teatr XVIII veka.* Moscow: Akademiia Nauk SSSR, 1958.

———. "Skazka o Bove-koroleviche v russkikh i ukrainskikh izdaniiakh XVIII–nachala XIX veka." In her *Rytsarskii roman na Rusi,* 61–107. Moscow: Nauka, 1964.

Kyryliuk, Ie. P. *Istoriia ukraïns'koï literatury.* 8 vols. Kiev: Naukova dumka, 1967–71.

Lachmann, Renate. "Die 'problematische Ähnlichkeit.' Sarbiewskis Traktat *De acuto et arguto* im Kontext concettistischer Theorien des 17. Jahrhunderts." In *Slavische Barockliteratur II* (*Forum Slavicum* 54), ed. Renate Lachmann, 87–114. Munich: Fink, 1983.

———. "Die Tradition des *ostroumie* und das *acumen* bei Simeon Polockij." In *Slavische Barockliterature I* (*Forum Slavicum* 23), ed. Dmitrii Chizhevskii [Dmitrij Tschižewskij], 41–59. Munich: Fink, 1970.

Lausberg, Heinrich. *Handbuch der literarischen Rhetorik.* 2 vols. Munich: Hauber, 1973.

Lea, K. M. *Italian Popular Comedy.* 2 vols. New York: Russell & Russell, 1934.

Le Compte, Edward. *A Dictionary of Puns in Milton's English Poetry*. New York: Columbia University Press, 1981.

Levin, Iu. I. "Logicheskaia struktura pritchi." *Trudy po znakovym sistemam* 15 (1982): 49–56.

Lewin, Paulina. "Barokko v literaturno-ésteticheskom soznanii prepodavatelei i slushatelei russkikh dukhovnykh uchilishch XVIII veka." *Wiener Slavistisches Jahrbuch* 23 (1977): 180–98.

———. "Stsenicheskaia struktura vostochnoslavianskikh intermedii." In *Russkaia literatura na rubezhe dvukh épokh*, ed. A. N. Robinson, 105–27. Moscow: Nauka, 1971.

Lewis, Arthur O., Jr. "Emblem Books and English Drama: A Preliminary Survey, 1581–1600." Ph.D. diss., Penn State College, 1951.

Likhachev, D. S. "Barokko i ego russkii variant XVII veka." *Russkaia literatura* 2 (1969): 18–45.

Likhachev, N. P. *Materialy dlia istorii russkogo ikonopisaniia*. 2 vols. St. Petersburg, 1906.

Linnemann, Eta. *Parables of Jesus*. London: S.P.C.K., 1966.

Lipking, Joanna Bridzle. "Traditions of the *Facetiae* and Their Influence in Tudor England." Ph.D. diss., Columbia University, 1970.

Logvin, G. N. *Kievo-Pecherskaia Lavra*. Moscow: Iskusstvo, 1958.

Long, A. A. *Hellenistic Philosophy: Stoics, Epicureans, Sceptics*. New York: Scribner, 1974.

Lotman, Iu. M. "Khudozhestvennaia priroda russkikh narodnykh kartinok." In *Narodnaia graviura i fol'klor v Rossii XVII–XIX vv. (K 150-letiiu so dnia rozhdeniia D. A. Rovinskogo)*, ed. I. E. Danilova, 247–67. Moscow: Sovetskii khudozhnik, 1976.

Łużny, Ryszard. "Dawne piśmiennictwo ukraińskie a polskie tradycje literackie." In *Z dziejów stosunków literackich polsko-ukraińskich*, ed. Stefan Kozak and Marian Jakóbiec, 7–36. Wrocław: Zakład Narodowy imienia Ossolińskich, 1974.

McCann, Eleanor. "Oxymora in Spanish Mystics and English Metaphysical Writers." *Comparative Literature* 13 (1961): 16–25.

Mahon, Denis. *Studies in Seicento Art and Theory*. London: The Warburg Institute, 1947.

Mahood, M. M. *Shakespeare's Wordplay*. London: Methuen, 1957.

Mâle, Émile. *Religious Art from the Twelfth to the Eighteenth Century*. New York: Pantheon, 1949.

Mancinelli, Laura. "Tristan Versus Parzifal. The 'Prologue' to Gottfried von Strassburg's *Tristan*.' In *Medieval and Pseudo-Medieval Literature*, ed. Piero Boitani and Anna Torti, 11–17. Tubingen: Narr, 1984.

Maravall, José Antonio. *Culture of the Baroque: Analysis of a Historical Structure*. Minneapolis: University of Minnesota Press, 1986.

Markovs'kyi, Ievhen. *Ukraïns'kyi vertep*. Kiev: Vseukraïns'ka Akademiia Nauk, 1929.

Markushevich, A. I. "Ob istochnikakh amsterdamskogo izdaniia 'Simvoly i emblemata' (1705 g.)." *Kniga* 8 (1963): 279–90.

Martin, John Rupert. *Baroque*. New York: Harper & Row, 1977.

Mayer, August L. *Geschichte der spanischen Malerei*. Leipzig: Klinkhardt & Biermann, 1922.

———. "Pereda, Antonio." In *Allgemeines Lexikon der bildenden Künstler*, ed. Hans Vollmer, 398. Leipzig: Seemann, 1932.

Medrish, D. N. "Istoricheskie korni otritsatel'nogo sravneniia." *Russkii fol'klor* 24 (1987): 107–16.

———. "Metaforicheskaia antiteza v fol'klore i literature." *Fol'klor narodov RSFSR* 10 (1983): 112–19.

Meiss, Millard. "Light as Form and Symbol in Some Fifteenth-Century Paintings." In his *The Painter's Choice: Problems in the Interpretation of Renaissance Art,* 3–18. New York: Harper & Row, 1976.

Miedema, Hessel. "The Term *Emblema* in Alciati." *Journal of the Warburg and Courtauld Institutes* 31 (1968): 234–50.

Mirollo, James V. *Mannerism and Renaissance Poetry.* New Haven: Yale University Press, 1984.

———. *The Poet of the Marvelous: Giambattista Marino.* New York: Columbia University Press, 1963.

Modzalevskii, V. L. *Malorossiiskii rodoslovnik,* 3 vols. Kiev, 1908–12.

Morozov, A. A. "Izvechnaia konstanta ili istoricheskii stil'?" *Russkaia literatura* 3 (1979): 81–89.

———. "Lomonosov i barokko." *Russkaia literatura* 2 (1965): 70–96.

———. "Problema barokko v russkoi literature XVII—nachala XVIII veka (Sostoianie voprosa i zadachi izucheniia)." *Russkaia literatura* 3 (1962): 3–38.

Morozov, P. O. *Istoriia russkogo teatra do poloviny XVIII stoletiia.* St. Petersburg, 1889.

Motto, Anna Lydia. *Guide to the Thought of Lucius Annaeus Seneca.* Amsterdam: Hakkert, 1970.

Nekrylova, A. F. *Russkie narodnye gorodskie prazdniki, uveseleniia i zrelishcha. Konets XVIII–nachalo XX veka.* Leningrad: Iskusstvo, 1988.

Nietzsche, Friedrich. *Human, All Too Human.* Trans. R. J. Hollingdale. Cambridge: Cambridge University Press, 1986.

Nikol'skii, A. S. *Osnovaniia rossiiskoi slovesnosti.* 2 vols. St. Petersburg, 1809.

Nisbet, R.G.M., and Margaret Hubbard. *A Commentary on Horace: Odes, Book 1.* Oxford: Clarendon Press, 1970.

Nykrog, Per. "The Literary Cousins of the Stock Market: On Mystification and Demystification in the Baroque Age." *Stanford French Review* 7 (1983): 57–71.

O'Connor, Sister Mary Catharine. *The Art of Dying Well.* New York: Columbia University Press, 1942.

Ors, Eugenio, d'. "La querelle du baroque." In his *Du baroque,* 161–73. Paris: Gallimard, 1935.

Ovsiannikov, Iurii. *The Lubok. 17th–18th Century Russian Broadsides.* Moscow: Sovetskii khudozhnik, 1968.

Panchenko, A. M. "Slovo i Znanie v éstetike Simeona Polotskogo (na materiale 'Vertograda mnogotsvetnogo')." *Trudy Otdela Drevnerusskoi Literatury* 25 (1970): 232–41.

Panofsky, Erwin. *Problems in Titian, Mostly Iconographic.* New York: New York University Press, 1969.

Parker, Alexander A. " 'Concept' and 'Conceit': An Aspect of Comparative Literary History." *The Modern Language Review* 77 (1982): xxi–xxxv.

Pavlutskii, G. G. "Barokko Ukrainy." In *Istoriia russkogo iskusstva,* 6 vols., ed. Igor' Grabar', 2:337–416. Moscow: Knebel', 1910–14.

Peretts, V. N. "Kukol'nyi teatr na Rusi." In *Ezhegodnik Imperatorskikh teatrov 1894–1895 gg.,* supplement, book 1, 85–185. St. Petersburg, 1895.

Petrov, N. I. *Ocherki istorii ukrainskoi literatury XIX stoletiia.* Kiev, 1884.

————. *Ocherki iz istorii ukrainskoi literatury XVII i XVIII vekov: Kievskaia iskusstvennaia literatura XVII–XVIII vv., preimushchestvenno dramaticheskaia.* Kiev, 1911.

————. *Ocherki iz istorii ukrainskoi literatury XVIII veka.* Kiev, 1880.

Pignatti, Terisio. *Titian.* 2 vols. New York: Rizzoli, 1981.

Pohlenz, Max. *Philosophie und Erlebnis in Senecas Dialogen.* Gottingen: Vandenhoeck & Ruprecht, 1941.

Popov, P. M. *Ksylohrafichni doshky lavrs'koho muzeiu.* Kiev: 1927.

Popova, O. S. "Russkaia knizhnaia miniatiura XI–XV vv." In *Drevnerusskoe iskusstvo. Rukopisnaia kniga,* 3 vols., ed. O. I. Podobedova, 3:9–74. Moscow: Nauka, 1972–83.

Praz, Mario. *Studies in Seventeenth-Century Imagery.* Rome: Storia e letteratura, 1964.

Preminger, Alex, ed. *Encyclopedia of Poetry and Poetics.* Princeton: Princeton University Press, 1965.

Propp, V. Ia. *Problemy komizma i smekha.* Moscow: Iskusstvo, 1976.

Pushkarev, L. N. "Povest' o Eruslane Lazareviche v russkoi lubochnoi kartinke XIX–nachala XX veka." In *Russkaia literatura na rubezhe dvukh épokh (XVII–nachalo XVIII v.),* ed. A. N. Robinson, 351–70. Moscow: Nauka, 1971.

Robinson, A. N., ed. *Razvitie barokko i zarozhdenie klassitsizma v Rossii XVII–nachala XVIII vv..* Moscow: Nauka, 1989.

Rovinskii, D. A. *Russkie narodnye kartinki.* 5 vols. St. Petersburg, 1881–93.

————. *Russkie narodnye kartinki.* 2 vols. Moscow: Golike, 1900.

Rudolf, Rainer. *Ars moriendi.* Cologne: Böhlau, 1957.

Ruthven, K. K. *The Conceit.* London: Methuen, 1969.

Ryl's'kyi, M. T., ed. *Ukraïns'kyi dramatychnyi teatr.* 2 vols. Kiev: Naukova dumka, 1967.

Ryndin, V. F., ed. *Russkii kostium 1750–1917.* 5 vols. Moscow: VTO, 1960–72.

Sakovich, A. G. "Russkii nastennyi lubochnyi teatr XVIII–XIX v.v." In *Teatral'noe prostranstvo,* ed. I. E. Danilova, 351–76. Moscow: Sovetskii khudozhnik, 1979.

Samaras, Zoe. *The Comic Element of Montaigne's Style.* Paris: Nizet, 1970.

Schilling, Michael. *Imagines Mundi. Metaphorische Darstellungen der Welt in der Emblematik.* Frankfurt am Main: Peter Lang, 1979.

Schwarz, Heinrich. "The Mirror in Art." *The Art Quarterly* 15 (1952): 97–118.

Serman, Ilya Z. *Mikhail Lomonosov.* Jerusalem: Hebrew University of Jerusalem, 1988.

Seymour, Barbara Jean. "A Radiant Trail: The Extension of the Conceit Through Eighteenth-Century English Poetry." Ph.D. diss., University of Oregon, 1985.

Shearman, John. "Leonardo's Colour and Chiaroscuro." *Zeitschrift für Kunstgeschichte* 25 (1962): 13–47.

Shcherbakivs'kyi, Vadym. "Materialy do istorii ukraïns'koho mystetstva (Ikonostas tserkvy het'mana Danyla Apostola v s. Sorochintsiakh." *Pratsy ukraïns'koho istorychno-filolohichnoho tovarystva v Prazi* 5 (1944): 47–70.

Sherotskii, K. V. 'Zhivopisnoe ubranstvo ukrainskogo doma v ego proshlom i nastoiashchem." *Iskusstvo v Iuzhnoi Rossii* 6 (1913): 261–70, and 9–10 (1913): 415–25.

Shoaf, R. A. "The Play of Puns in Late Middle English Poetry: Concerning Juxtology." In *On Puns,* ed. Jonathan Culler, 44–61. New York: Blackwell, 1988.

Sidorov, A. A. *Russkaia knizhnaia graviura.* Moscow: Akademiia Nauk SSSR, 1951.

Skrine, Peter N. *The Baroque: Literature and Culture in Seventeenth-Century Europe.* New York: Holmes & Meier, 1978.

Snapper, Johan P. "The Seventeenth-Century Dutch Farce: Social Refractions of a Guilded Age." In *Barocker Lust-Spiegel. Studien zur Literatur des Barock. Festschrift für Blake Lee Spahr,* ed. Martin Bircher, Jörg-Ulrich Fechner, and Gerd Hillen, 55–74. Amsterdam: Rodopi, 1984.

Sofronova, L. A. *Poétika slavianskogo teatra.* Moscow: Nauka, 1981.

Somov, Andrei. "Lubochnye kartinki." *Éntsiklopedicheskii slovar',* 86 vols., 35:57–58. St. Petersburg: F. A. Brokgauz and I. A. Efron, 1890–1907.

Spear, Richard E. *Caravaggio and His Followers.* New York: Harper & Row, 1975.

Stackelberg, Jürgen, von. "Das Bienengleichnis." *Romanische Forschungen* 68 (1956): 271–93.

"Strashnyi Sud." In *Éntsiklopedicheskii slovar',* 86 vols., 62:789–91. St. Petersburg: F. A. Brokgauz and I. A. Efron, 1890–1907.

Svientsits'ka, V. I. "Ukraïns'ka hraviura XVII st." *Narodna tvorchist' ta etnohrafiia* 4 (1970): 37–40.

———. "Ukraïns'ka narodna hraviura XVII–XVIII st." *Narodna tvorchist' ta etnohrafiia* 5 (1965): 47–50.

Svientsits'kyi, Ilarion. *Pochatky knyhopechatania na zemliakh Ukraïny.* Lvov: Zhovkva, 1924.

Sydorenko, Alexander. *The Kievan Academy in the Seventeenth Century.* Ottawa: University of Ottawa Press, 1977.

Sytova, Alla. *The Lubok. Russian Folk Pictures 17th to 19th Century.* Leningrad: Aurora Art Publishers, 1984.

Syvachenko, M. Ie. "Pro humoresku S. Rudans'koho 'Hospod' dav' ta ïi nimets'ku i italiis'ku literaturni paraleli." *Radians'ke literaturoznavstvo* 1 (1984): 44–55.

Tapié, Victor-L. *The Age of Grandeur: Baroque Art and Architecture.* New York: Praeger, 1966.

Terterian, I. A. "Barokko i romantizm: k izucheniiu motivnoi struktury." In *Iberica: Kal'deron i mirovaia kul'tura,* ed. G. V. Stepanov, 163–78. Leningrad: Nauka, 1986.

Teteriatnikova, Natal'ia. "O znachenii izobrazhenii sv. Nikity, b'iushchego besa." *Transactions of the Association of Russian-American Scholars in the U.S.A.* 15 (1982): 3–33.

Thompson, Elbert N. S. "Emblem Books." In his *Literary Bypaths of the Renaissance,* 29–67. New Haven: Yale University Press, 1924.

Tigay, Jeffrey H. *The Evolution of the Gilgamesh Epic.* Philadelphia: University of Pennsylvania Press, 1982.

Titunik, I. R. "Baroque, the Russian." In *Handbook of Russian Literature,* ed. Victor Terras, 40–42. New Haven: Yale University Press, 1985.

Tolmachev, Iakov. *Pravila slovesnosti.* 4 vols. St. Petersburg, 1815–22.

Toporov, V. N. "Eine Seite aus der Geschichte des russischen barocken Concettismus: Petr Buslaevs *Umozritel'stvo Duševnoe.*" In *Slavische Barockliteratur II (Forum Slavicum* 54), ed. Renate Lachmann, 57–86. Munich: Fink, 1983.

Tristram, Philippa. *Figures of Life and Death in Medieval English Literature.* New York: New York University Press, 1976.

Troyer, Nancy Jane Gray. "The *Macchiaioli:* Effects of Modern Color Theory, Photography, and Japanese Prints on a Group of Italian Painters, 1855–1900." Ph.D. diss., Northwestern University, 1978.

Uspenskii, B. A. *Filologicheskie razyskaniia v oblasti slavianskikh drevnostei.* Moscow: Izdatel'stvo MGU, 1982.

Van Hook, J. W. " 'Concupiscence of Witt': The Metaphysical Conceit in Baroque Poetics." *Modern Philology* 84 (1986): 24–38.

Vertkov, K. A., G. I. Blagodatov, and E. E. Iazovitskaia. *Atlas muzykal'nykh instrumentov narodov SSSR.* Moscow: Muzyka, 1975.

Vinogradov, Nikolai. "Velikorusskii vertep." *Izvestiia otdeleniia russkogo iazyka i slovesnosti Imperatorskoi Akademii Nauk* 10 (1905): 360–82.

Vozniak, Mykhailo. *Pochatky ukraïns'koï komedii (1619–1819).* Lvov, 1920.

Warner, Elizabeth A. *The Russian Folk Theatre.* The Hague: Mouton, 1977.

Warnke, Frank J. *Versions of Baroque.* New Haven: Yale University Press, 1972.

Weisbach, Werner. *Die Kunst des Barock in Italien, Frankreich, Deutschland und Spanien.* Berlin: Propyläen, 1924.

Wellek, René. *Concepts of Criticism.* New Haven: Yale University Press, 1973.

Wellington, James Ellis. "An Analysis of the *Carpe Diem* Theme in Seventeenth-Century English Poetry (1590–1700)." Ph.D. diss., Florida State University, 1956.

Wesselschmidt, Quentin F. "Stoicism in the Odes of Horace." Ph.D. diss., University of Iowa, 1979.

Wethey, Harold E. *The Paintings of Titian.* 3 vols. London: Phaidon, 1969–75.

Wiener, Philip P., ed. *Dictionary of the History of Ideas.* 4 vols. New York: Scribner, 1973.

Williams, Gerhild Scholz. *The Vision of Death: A Study of the "Memento Mori" Expressions in Some Latin, German, and French Didactic Texts of the 11th and 12th Centuries.* Goppingen: Kümmerle, 1976.

Wilson, John A. "Egypt." In *Before Philosophy: The Intellectual Adventure of Ancient Man,* ed. Henri Frankfort and Henrietta A. Frankfort, 39–133. Baltimore: Penguin, 1949.

Wittkower, Rudolf. *Art and Architecture in Italy 1600–1750.* Baltimore: Penguin, 1965.

Index

Abbas-Mirza, crown prince of Persia, 70n. 87
Adrian, patriarch, 175
Aksakov, Konstantin, 1n. 2, 124–25, 222–23
Aksakov, Sergei, 20, 34–35
Alciati, Andrea, 26, 106, 116n. 165
Alexander I, emperor of Russia, 172, 230
Alexis, tsar of Russia, 19
Anacreon, 151, 153n. 55
Apostol, Daniil, hetman, 11
Arguijo, Juan de, 215
Aristotle, 129, 194, 197, 199, 205, 224
Arndt, Johann, 125–26
Augustine, Saint, 131, 205, 214

Bagration, Petr, 72, 75
Bakhtin, Mikhail, 28n. 6, 87, 203n. 52
Balabin, Viktor, 22
Balabina, Mariia, 22–23, 223
Baranovich, Lazar', 15–16, 224
Bebel, Heinrich, 39
Belinskii, Vissarion, 1n. 1
Belobotskii, Andrei, 178
Belyi, Andrei, 3, 204, 210, 229n. 137
Bengel, Johann Albrecht, 172
Bernini, Gianlorenzo, 22
Berynda, Pamva, 58
Bezushko, Volodymyr, 13
Bibikhin, V. V., 161n. 72
Bobelina, 72–73
Boccaccio, Giovanni, 55n. 68, 203
Boissard, Jean-Jacques, 132
Borja, Juan de, 146
Borromini, Francesco, 22
Bossi, Giuseppe, 209
Bossuet, Jacques Bénigne, 13–14, 16, 155–
56, 162
Bourdaloue, Louis, 13

Bracciolini, Francesco, 149–50, 165
Bracciolini, Poggio, 25, 28, 29n. 10, 39, 55n.
68, 84n. 104
Briullov, Karl, 209
Browne, Sir Thomas, 174
Brückner, Aleksander, 28
Buzhinskii, Gavriil, 15, 18
Bylinin, V. K., 161n. 72

Caesar, Gaius Julius, 194
Calderón de la Barca, Pedro, 15, 131n. 7, 140
Calvi, Girolamo Luigi, 209
Caravaggio, 206, 212
Carracci family, 22
Casti, Giovanni Battista, 23n. 35
Catherine II (the Great), empress of Russia,
43n. 38
Cervantes, Miguel de, 2, 7, 15, 123
Chassignet, Jean-Baptiste, 163
Chicherin, Aleksei, 4n. 8
Chizhevskii, Dmitrii, 3–4, 113n. 157, 161n.
72, 199n. 38, 217n. 99
Chudakov, G. I., 7n. 12
Cicero, Marcus Tullius, 186, 194
Claude Lorrain, 22
Cortese, Giulio, 218
Cowley, Abraham, 15
Cox, Gary D., 203n. 50
Crashaw, Richard, 15, 200
Curtius, Ernst Robert, 129–30, 234

Danilevskii, Aleksandr, 125, 138n. 19, 147
Dante Alighieri, 1–2n. 2, 119–20n. 173, 184,
222
De Quincey, Thomas, 143
Debreczeny, Paul, 227
Denis, Ernest, 161n. 72

Derzhavin, Gavriil, 14, 17, 141, 147–48, 150,
    153n. 55, 166, 180n. 117, 195, 200–
    201, 216, 226–27
Derzhavina, Ol'ga, 30, 39
Dibich, Ivan, 70
Dmitrii of Rostov, Saint, 15–16, 18
Domenichino, 22
Donne, John, 15
Doroshenko, Mikhail, hetman, 12
Doroshenko, Petr, hetman, 12
Dostoevskii, Fedor, 4n. 8, 9n. 16
Dovgalevskii, Mitrofan, 56
Drayton, Michael, 15
Dryden, John, 15
Dürer, Albrecht, 58

Eckartshausen, Karl von, 231
Ehre, Milton, 47n. 48, 97
Éikhenbaum, Boris, 209–10
Elizabeth, empress of Russia, 189
Epicurus, 150, 155
Erasmus, 168n. 91
Erlich, Victor, 21

Falconet, Étienne Maurice, 21
Fanger, Donald, 179
Fénelon, François de Salignac de la Mothe,
    13
Fléchier, Esprit, 13–14
Fomichev, S. A., 203n. 50
Frederick II (the Great), king of Prussia, 141
Frederick III, duke of Schleswig-Holstein, 19
Furtenagel, Lucas, 161
Fusso, Susanne G., 38n. 23

Galiatowicz, Jakub, 79n. 100
Galiatovskii, Ioanikii, 15
Gardner, Helen, 221n. 110
Garzonio, Stefano, 220n. 108
Gibner, Johann, 53n. 62
Giorgione, 205–6
Gippius, Vasilii, 3, 30–31, 38–40, 201n. 47
Godyere, Sir Henry, 110
Goethe, Johann Wolfgang von, 130, 209, 234
Gogol, Mariia (Gogol's mother), 109, 167,
    178–79
Gogol, Nikolai, works of:
    "Bloody Bandura Player, A," 46–47
    *Book of Odds and Ends, or a Manual En-
        cyclopedia,* 12n. 4, 19

"Coach, The," 98, 106, 199, 235
"Christmas Eve," 55–57, 61, 64, 77, 134n.
    9
Dead Souls, 1n. 2, 2, 4, 23n. 35, 34n. 19,
    35–38, 40, 45, 45–46n. 43, 48–51, 55–
    57, 69, 71–73, 75–76, 80–81, 85, 98–
    104, 106, 109–11, 118n. 169, 119–26,
    133–34, 148–49, 155, 160–62, 165–
    66, 173–74, 179n. 112, 180–82, 189,
    192–93, 197–99, 203, 213–14, 217,
    221–23, 227–31, 234–35
"Denouement of *The Government Inspec-
    tor,* The," 38, 133
"Diary of a Madman," 2n. 3, 191–93
Evenings on a Farm near Dikanka, 31,
    32n. 15, 33, 34n. 20, 40, 56–57, 77,
    113, 115–16, 155, 192, 202, 204
"Fair at Sorochintsy, The," 39–40, 52, 55–
    56, 77, 79, 96n. 122, 116, 196, 199,
    202, 210, 235
Gamblers, The, 47–48
Government Inspector, The, 38, 40, 53,
    69–70, 79, 96, 101–2, 139, 173, 179,
    180nn. 114 and 115, 230
Hanz Kuechelgarten, 189, 191, 201–2
Hetman, The, 32–35, 40, 46, 48, 60, 196,
    210
"Ivan Fedorovich Shponka and His Aunt,"
    45n. 43, 57, 155
"Last Day of Pompeii, The," 209
"Leaving the Theater After a Performance
    of a New Comedy," 230
"Lost Letter, The," 12, 52, 202
"Maidens Chablov, The," 117, 228
Marriage, 21, 83n. 103, 87, 90–93, 96–98,
    106
"May Night, A," 60–61, 141–42, 192, 202
Meditations on Divine Liturgy, 217
Mirgorod, 45, 116, 155, 181, 203
"Nevsky Prospekt," 81, 84, 86–87, 103,
    134–35, 143–44, 160–61n. 70, 202
"Nights at the Villa," 150
"Nose, The," 38, 53–54, 56, 81, 84n. 104,
    87, 98, 101–2, 106, 135–37, 160–61,
    165, 217, 234
"Old-Fashioned Landowners," 2n. 3
"On Present-Day Architecture," 22, 201
"On Teaching Modern History," 19–20
"Overcoat, The," 34n. 19, 38, 50, 133–34,
    166, 217

"Petersburg Notes of 1836," 149
"Portrait, The," 21–22, 65, 70–71, 73, 76,
    85–86, 142, 160, 172–74, 197, 217, 229
"Rome," 22, 23n. 35, 52–53n. 61, 203–4,
    210
"Rule of Living in the World, The," 168–
    69, 190, 193
"St. John's Eve," 52, 202, 203n. 50
Selected Passages from Correspondence
    with Friends, 16–17, 20–21, 76n. 93,
    81, 118n. 169, 120n. 173, 161n. 72,
    169, 173–74, 178–79, 217, 220–21
"Sketches for a Play from Ukrainian His-
    tory," 149
"Songs of the Ukraine, The," 188–89
"Tale of How Ivan Ivanovich Quarreled
    with Ivan Nikiforovich, The," 42, 45–46,
    116, 181, 203, 227
Taras Bulba, 13, 22, 44–45, 47–51, 84,
    111–13, 137–38, 144, 148, 153–55,
    168, 170, 189–90, 203, 211–13, 217,
    220, 228–29, 235
"Terrible Vengeance, A," 34n. 19, 44, 50,
    69, 137–38, 179, 204
Textbook of Philology for Russian Youth,
    123
"Vii," 13, 42, 54–55, 59, 210–11, 227
Gogol, Ostap (Gogol's alleged ancestor), 12
Gogol, Vasilii (Gogol's father), 13, 39–40,
    56, 77n. 96, 79n. 100, 150, 196, 235
Gogol-Ianovskii, Afanasii (Gogol's grand-
    father), 12
Gogol-Ianovskii, Dem'ian (Gogol's great-
    grandfather), 12
Golokhvastov, Dmitrii, 228n. 134
Góngora y Argote, Luis de, 15, 146–47
Gorbachev, Mikhail, 37
Gracián, Baltasar, 18, 131, 218
Gryphius, Andreas, 157, 200
Guercino, 22
Günther, Johann Christian, 158, 160

Herrick, Robert, 151–52
Herzen, Aleksandr, 1n. 2
Hippisley, Anthony R., 108n. 146, 163
Hoffmann, Ernst Theodor Amadeus, 1n. 1,
    136, 143
Hofmannswaldau, Christian Hofmann von,
    184
Homer, 1–2n. 2, 123, 222–23

Honthorst, Gerrit van, 22, 206, 210, 212
Horace, 113, 150–51, 214

Iavorskii, Stefan, 4, 14, 16, 18, 160, 219, 224
Iazykov, Nikolai, 16, 20, 178–79, 193
Il'f, Il'ia, 230n. 138
Il'ia the Monk, 58
Ivan III (the Great), grand duke of Muscovy, 19
Ivanov, E. P., 102n. 136

Jakobson, Roman, 224n. 119
Jagodyński, Stanisław Serafin, 226
John Chrysostom, Saint, 131
John Climacus, Saint, 60
John of Salisbury, 131, 133n. 8
Jung-Stilling, Johann Heinrich, 172–73

Kachenovskii, Mikhail, 15, 18
Kadlubovskii, Arsenii, 3, 40, 56
Kanaris, Constantine, 72
Kapnist, Vasilii, 85
Karamzin, Nikolai, 18
Karpenko, Aleksei, 32n. 17
Kaukhchishvili, Nina, 45n. 43
Kent, Leonard J., 86n. 108, 190n. 19, 212n.
    78, 217n. 100, 228n. 133
Kheraskov, Mikhail, 18
Khmel'nitskii, Bogdan, hetman, 138
Khodasevich, Vladislav, 236
Khozrev-Mirza, prince of Persia, 70
Kochowski, Wespazjan, 15, 226
Kolokotronis, Theodore, 72
Komenský (Comenius), Jan Amos, 126, 161
Konisskii, Georgii, 13
Korobovskii, Aleksei, 113
Kotoshikhin, Grigorii, 20
Krivonos, Vladislav, 37n. 22
Krylov, Ivan, 85, 147
Kukol'nik, Nestor, 18
Kuz'mina, V. D., 52n. 61

La Feuille, Daniel de, 108
Leonardo da Vinci, 183, 205–6
Lermontov, Mikhail, 117, 121n. 175, 209
Lizogub, Semen (Efimovich), 12
Lizogub, Semen (Semenovich), 12
Logau, Friedrich von, 170
Lomonosov, Mikhail, 14–15, 17–18, 153n.
    55, 158, 160, 186, 188–89, 195, 201,
    216, 219

Louis XVI, king of France, 76
Lucretius, 113

Maderno, Carlo, 22
Maikov, Vasilii, 85
Maksim the Greek, 113
Maksimovich-Ambodik, Nestor, 18, 108–9,
    112–13
Mandel'shtam, Iosif, 196–97, 222–23
Mann, Iurii, 53n. 62, 179–80
Marino, Giambattista, 8, 15, 17–18, 23n. 35,
    207, 215, 218–20, 235
Markovskii, Mikhail, 121n. 176
Markovs'kyi, Ievhen, 42–43
Marucelli, Paolo, 22
Massillon, Jean-Baptiste, 13–14, 201
Matskin, Aleksandr, 48n. 49
Maturin, Charles Robert, 209
Mavrocordatos, Alexander, 72
Meierberg, Baron Augustin, 19
Merezhkovskii, Dmitrii, 57
Mérimée, Prosper, 209
Mersereau, John, 116n. 166
Miaoulis, Andreas Vokos, 72
Mickiewicz, Adam, 138n. 19
Milton, John, 13, 15
Mirollo, James V., 5n. 11, 207n. 68
Mochul'skii, Konstantin, 172
Molière, 85
Montaigne, Michel de, 145
Montanus, Martin, 28–29
Morozov, Aleksandr, 4, 157
Morsztyn, Hieronim, 153, 163, 187
Morsztyn, Jan Andrzej, 185, 195, 215, 219
Morsztyn, Zbigniew, 131, 133, 141, 143–44
Murav'ev, Mikhail, 18–19
Murner, Thomas, 28–29

Naborowski, Daniel, 110, 147, 157, 185, 200
Napoleon I, emperor of France, 72, 101, 234
Narezhnyi, Vasilii, 9n. 16
Nietzsche, Friedrich, 4n. 8
Nikol'skii, Aleksandr, 14, 108–9, 147n. 44,
    188, 195, 201
Nikol'skii, Parfenii, 18

Oldani, Robert, 123n. 180
Olearius, Adam, 19
Orlai, Ivan, 13–14
Ors, Eugenio d', 4n. 8

Osor'in, Kallistrat, 208
Ostranitsa, Stepan, 33n. 18

Parini, Giuseppe, 23n. 35
Paskevich, Ivan, 70–71
Passe, Crispin van de, the Elder, 152
Pauli, Johann, 39
Peace, Richard A., 179, 227
Peachem, Henry, 200
Pedrotti, Louis, 210
Pellegrino, Camillo, 218
Pereda, Antonio de, 140–41
Peregrini, Matteo, 218
Peretts, Vladimir, 3, 40, 54–55
Peter I (the Great), emperor of Russia, 21,
    64, 76, 108, 137, 139, 175, 221n. 109
Petrarch, 215
Petrov, Evgenii, 230n. 138
Petrov, Nikolai, 39–40
Petrov, Vasilii, 14–15, 17
Phaedrus, 85
Plato, 130, 137, 205
Pletnev, Petr, 127, 228n. 134
Plotinus, 130, 205
Poe, Edgar Allan, 143
Pogodin, Mikhail, 109n. 151
Polotskii, Simeon, 15, 107–8, 110, 126, 139,
    150, 157–58, 163, 166–67, 216
Ponzio, Flaminio, 22
Porta, Giacomo della, 22
Possevino, Antonio, 168
Potocki, Wacław, 126, 165–67
Praz, Mario, 113n. 157
Proffer, Carl R., 223
Prokopovich, Feofan, 14–15, 18
Prokopovich, Nikolai, 149
Przypkowski, Samuel, 170, 172
Pushkin, Aleksandr, 1n. 1, 2, 18, 121n. 175,
    142, 236

Quintilian, 184, 186, 193–94, 224

Rabelais, François, 28, 76
Radivilovskii, Antonii, 15
Rainaldi, Carlo, 22
Rastrelli, Bartolommeo Francesco, 21
Ravignan, Gustave François de, 16n. 20
Reavey, George, 72n. 89, 120n. 174, 189n.
    18, 193n. 23, 229n. 136
Reni, Guido, 22

Repnina, Vera, 142–43
Richter, Sigrid, 21
Ripa, Cesare, 107, 118
Rovinskii, Dmitrii, 65n. 81, 66n. 84, 72, 76, 102n. 136
Rozov, Vladimir, 3, 40, 49, 51

Sakovich, Antonina, 98, 99n. 128
Sarbiewski, Maciej Kazimierz, 218
Schopenhauer, Arthur, 209
Scott, Sir Walter, 1n. 1
Segel, Harold B., 147n. 41, 194, 216n. 95
Semenov, Ivan, 103n. 138
Senderovich, Savely, 135n. 11
Seneca, Lucius Annaeus, 113, 130, 145, 162
Setchkarev, Vsevolod, 40
Seymour, Barbara Jean, 221n. 110
Shakespeare, William, 2, 131, 139–40, 143, 225
Shevyrev, Stepan, 2–3, 147, 222–23
Siniavskii, Andrei, 3–4, 21–22
Skarga, Piotr, 168, 187
Skoropadskii, Ivan, hetman, 12
Skovoroda, Grigorii, 4, 7, 8n. 13, 107, 160, 166, 180n. 117, 200, 215–16
Smirnova, Aleksandra, 16, 22
Smirnova, Elena, 4, 121n. 176, 160n. 69, 179n. 112
Smith, John, 200
Snegirev, Ivan, 65n. 81
Socrates, 7
Soucek, Svat, 70n. 87
Sreznevskii, Iosif, 15, 17–18, 201, 216, 219–20
Sreznevskii, Izmail, 15n. 14
Stöber, Joseph, 18, 118–20
Strassburg, Gottfried von, 214
Stroev, Pavel, 20
Sumarokov, Aleksandr, 18, 85, 86n. 108
Suvorov, Aleksandr, 72n. 90
Sydorenko, Alexander, 12–13
Synesius, 131

Tallemant, Paul de, 18
Tanskii, Vasilii, 12–13
Tassoni, Alessandro, 23n. 35
Tesauro, Emanuele, 218
Thomas Aquinas, Saint, 205
Titian, 206–7
Tolmachev, Iakov, 14, 196, 201, 216, 227
Tolstoi, Aleksandr, 81
Troshchinskii, Dmitrii, 7–8, 12, 17, 53n. 62, 108, 112, 118, 231n. 140
Tulloch, Alexander, 189n. 16
Turbin, Vladimir, 4
Turgenev, Ivan, 112–13
Twardowski, Kasper, 15n. 16
Twardowski, Samuel, 15, 138, 168, 207–8

Ushakov, Simon, 191n. 21
Uvarov, Sergei, 19

Vasari, Giorgio, 205
Vega Carpio, Lope Félix de, 15, 194, 197
Velichkovskii, Ivan, 141, 165–66, 172, 178, 208, 226
Veselovskii, Aleksei, 2n. 3
Viel'gorskii, Iosif, 150
Vignola, Giacomo da, 22
Vinogradov, Viktor, 87, 222–23, 227
Virgil, 184
Vishenskii, Ivan, 185–87, 195
Vondel, Joost van den, 131, 166
Vos, Marten de, 152

Warnke, Frank J., 170
Wethey, Harold E., 207n. 67
Weisbach, Werner, 4n. 8
Woodward, James B., 49

Zavitnevich, Vladimir, 175
Zemka, Leontii, 58
Zhukovskii, Vasilii, 127, 142, 221
Zimorowic, Józef Bartłomiej, 59
Zinov'ev, Klimentii, 153, 172